D0214695

Well-weighed syllables

Well-weighed syllables

Elizabethan verse in classical metres

DEREK ATTRIDGE

Lecturer in the Department of English
Southampton University

CAMBRIDGE UNIVERSITY PRESS

Published by the Syndics of the Cambridge University Press
Bentley House, 200 Euston Road, London NW1 2DB
American Branch: 32 East 57th Street, New York, N.Y. 10022

Library of Congress Catalogue Card Number: 74–80362

ISBN: 0 521 20530 1

First published 1974

Made and printed in Great Britain by
William Clowes & Sons, Limited, London, Beccles and Colchester

CONTENTS

CONTENTS

PREFACE

I should like to thank the many friends, teachers, and colleagues who have been of assistance in manifold ways during the successive stages of my work on this subject, and to express in particular my indebtedness to Sidney Allen, John Rathmell, Peter Parsons, and Anna Attridge, without whose generous efforts this book would not even exist, and to all those – especially Jeremy Prynne, John Stevens, Catherine Ing, Jean Robertson, and Frank Prince – whose comments on earlier versions have ensured that however many faults I have failed to eradicate, they are less numerous and serious than they might have been. The book has greatly benefited, too, from the careful editorial attention it has received from Cambridge University Press. I am also grateful to those who made it financially possible to undertake this research: the Senate of the University of Natal, the General Board of the Faculties of Cambridge University, the Master and Fellows of Clare College, Cambridge, and the Governing Body of Christ Church, Oxford.

The system of references I have used is as follows: full details of works mentioned are not given in the text, but sufficient information (usually the author's name and the date of publication) is provided to enable the reader to refer to the alphabetically-arranged bibliography. References to Elizabethan writings on poetry are, whenever possible, to G. Gregory Smith's *Elizabethan Critical Essays* (London, 1904), cited throughout as 'Smith'. Passages in Latin are translated in footnotes, but, as the lack of clarity in the original is sometimes the point being demonstrated, the translations do not constitute a completely satisfactory substitute. Quotations from sixteenth-

and seventeenth-century sources follow the original spelling, except that abbreviated forms have been expanded, the use of *u* and *v*, *i* and *j* has been regularised, and a few obvious printing errors have been corrected.

D.A.

Southampton, 1974.

Introduction

Now, of versifying there are two sorts, the one Auncient, the other Moderne: the Auncient marked the quantitie of each silable, and according to that framed his verse; the Moderne observing onely number (with some regarde of the accent), the chiefe life of it standeth in that lyke sounding of the words, which wee call Ryme. Whether of these be the most excellent, would beare many speeches. The Auncient (no doubt) more fit for Musick, both words and tune observing quantity, and more fit lively to expresse divers passions, by the low and lofty sounde of the well-weyed silable. The latter likewise, with hys Ryme, striketh a certaine musick to the eare: and, in fine, sith it dooth delight, though by another way, it obtaines the same purpose: there beeing in eyther sweetnes, and wanting in neither majestie. Truely the English, before any other vulgar language I know, is fit for both sorts. (Smith, I, 204–5)

Sidney's scrupulous apportionment, in his *Apologie for Poetrie*, of equal praise to the traditional English manner of writing verse and to the imitation of classical metres in English, strikes the modern reader – as it must have struck most readers from a decade after its publication in 1595 to the present – as astonishingly over-generous to the latter species of verse. Sidney himself played a far from minor role in the advance to maturity and greatness of English verse in the native metrical tradition during the last quarter of the sixteenth century, and none of the experiments in classical metres of the period, from his or any other pen, provides the slightest challenge to that achievement. This judgement of Sidney's is, however, only one of the puzzling manifestations of a literary movement which, in the many accounts of it in commentaries on Elizabethan poetry and in separate studies, is characteristically discussed in a tone of perplexed bafflement, often coupled with a sense of modern superiority to such folly. Why should so many writers, among them poets of such distinction as Sidney, Spenser and Campion, have devoted so much time and effort to an enterprise which held out such slender hopes of success? And even more puzzling, why should the results of their experiments have been presented with such evident satisfaction, and received with approbation in so many quarters, when, in contrast to the verse they and others were producing in traditional accentual metres, it is so patently weak? Why, too, should so much of the Elizabethan theoretical and critical writing on literary topics (as a glance at Gregory Smith's collection of critical essays will indicate) revolve around the question of quantitative versifying?

To find the solutions to these and other problems posed by the quantitative movement it is necessary to consider in some detail the background to the whole enterprise, for it is impossible to tell from the experiments alone, or from the discussions that surround them, exactly what these men – and at least one woman – thought they were doing. We need to know just what an educated Elizabethan took to be the metre of a Latin poem, and this means we need to know how he pronounced the individual words, how he delivered the lines of verse, and how he had been taught Latin, and in particular Latin prosody, at school. It will also be useful to know what he would have learned from the prominent classical scholars of his day if he consulted their works. Part One deals with this background, after a brief consideration of the present state of our knowledge about Latin metre. The argument in Part Two is based on the conclusions reached in Part One, and takes the discussion into the realm of English poetry. I have tried to show why the prospect of English verse in classical metres held such temptations for the sixteenth-century poet, and why the results seemed far more successful to many among his immediate audience than they have to later generations; and I have given an account of the frequently misunderstood theoretical writings, concentrating particularly on those features which commentators have found hard to explain. This part also includes a chronological survey of the English experiments, largely to give an idea of the hold which the movement gained in the Elizabethan literary world. In Part Three the individual contributors are discussed, the more important figures separately, and the others grouped roughly into four schools, according to their approach to the problem of naturalising classical metres. Although the book as a whole is not organised chronologically, I have attempted in the final chapter and the epilogue to give some idea of the changing intellectual climate at the end of the century which resulted in the virtual abandonment of quantitative experimentation.

Although I have made some value-judgements on the verse under consideration, this has never been my prime objective; most of the verse is, by present standards, unquestionably bad – but it is for this reason that I believe a study of it has wider repercussions on our understanding of Elizabethan literature, and of late sixteenth-century aesthetic tendencies in general, than may at first sight seem to be the case. The obstacles to the full appreciation of the art of an earlier age are often most clearly evident – and hence most available for confrontation and, if possible, sympathetic consideration – in the works which to us seem the least successful of that age. I hope to show that an examination of these experiments and the theoretical writings which surround them reveals an understanding of metre which is the direct result of Renaissance humanism, and in particular its educational programme, and which provides an exceptionally clear example of some of the tendencies of sixteenth-century aesthetic thought most foreign to modern taste.

This conception of metre is also worth studying as a factor in the development of English versification from the stiff jog-trot of poulter's measure and fourteeners in the work of Googe and Turbervile to the fluid grace of the late Elizabethan lyrics, from the end-stopped regularity of the pentameters in the *Mirror for Magistrates* to the beautiful variety of Spenser, Daniel and Drayton and the expressive forcefulness of Donne, and from blank verse as a blunt instrument wielded by Sackville and Norton to a superb tool capable of almost any effect in Shakespeare's hands. Its part in this achievement was a negative one, for it was an attitude which existed as an obstacle to the flowering of the Elizabethan poetic genius, and it was only when it had been supplanted that English poetry could reach full maturity; but it is no accident that both the chief architects of the new mode of writing – Sidney and Spenser – should have faced in their own experiments the shortcomings of quantitative verse, and the conception of metre which lay behind it, before going ahead with their successful attempt to base English verse on the phonetic properties of the living language around them – thus taking up a tradition descended from Chaucer, but largely lost sight of since Wyatt, and laying new foundations for a way of writing poetry which has only recently been challenged.

PART ONE

The Elizabethan understanding of
Latin metre

1

Problems of Latin prosody

Since we shall find in the succeeding chapters that the average educated Elizabethan had a very peculiar notion of what Latin metre was, it will be prudent to begin our investigation with a brief look at present ideas on the subject, if for no other reason than to forestall, by showing how many problems remain to be solved, any unwarranted feeling of superiority on the part of the twentieth-century reader. It will also be useful to give at the outset a sketch of what *is* known about Latin prosody, and to establish the senses in which some technical terms are to be used.

The nature of quantity

Classical Latin verse is based on an initial categorisation of all syllables into two groups. These two types of syllable are arranged in predetermined patterns to makes lines of verse. The classification of syllables is not according to stress, or accent,[1] as in most English verse, but according to quantity, and one of the central questions around which much discussion has revolved and still revolves is simply, 'What *is* quantity?' To those not accustomed to close examination of metrical and phonological matters – and this includes the Romans and many twentieth-century readers of Latin as well as the Elizabethans –

[1] Because the English accent is, and the classical Latin accent in all probability was, a stress accent, I have tended to use these two terms interchangeably, except when it has been necessary to distinguish between the prominence of one syllable over others (accent) and that particular method of achieving this prominence used in languages like English and German (stress). (Fortunately, the further problems posed by the nature of stress itself need not concern us, though it should perhaps be noted that pitch, duration and intensity all play a part, probably in that order of importance – see Lehiste, 1970, ch. 4, for a survey of recent work on the subject.)

the traditional definition explains everything in a very simple fashion: 'quantity' refers to the duration of syllables, a long syllable taking twice the time of a short syllable, or thereabouts, in pronunciation, so that lines of verse can be constructed with patterns (or temporal rhythms) of longs and shorts. Thus Edwards, in his introduction to *The Eton Latin Grammar* of 1826, states:

By QUANTITY, then, we are to understand the time *actually* and *practically* devoted, in the act of speaking, to the enunciation of a syllable: thus, a syllable uttered *quickly*, as to time, is said to be short – but a syllable, uttered *slowly*, is said to be *long*.   (p. viii)

Every sixteenth-century Latin grammar contained a similar definition, though without so much emphasis on what 'actually' and 'practically' occurred (a significant omission, as we shall see), and modern textbooks also often assume that quantity is simply a matter of duration.

The origins of this explanation of quantity are, of course, Greek and Roman; Zirin (1970) gives a useful survey of the statements by ancient grammarians and discusses the two ways of looking at quantity that developed side by side: that of the *metrici*, who were concerned only with two kinds of syllable, short and long; and that of the *rhythmici*, who, by assigning time-values to the constituents of syllables, found a whole scale of durational values (pp. 42–54). These two attitudes could never be reconciled, since the arbitrariness of dividing the continuous durational scale into two could not be accounted for, and, in fact, by adding up time-units, some 'short' syllables emerge as longer than some 'long' syllables. Though this contradiction in the durational theory suggests that 'long' and 'short' syllables are distinguished by some other criterion, none of the ancient grammarians went further than pointing out the contradiction; and the Renaissance inherited the idea of quantity as something concerned purely with time.

To appreciate the unsatisfactoriness of this theory, it will be necessary to look first at the rules for determining the quantity of a syllable. These rules rely on a classification of every vowel as either long or short; however, since the difference between the two forms of a Latin vowel was one of quality as well as duration (see Allen, 1965, pp. 47–9), and this is clearly also the case with the so-called 'long' and 'short' forms of English vowels, I have preferred to use the terms 'tense' and 'lax' when referring to the phonetic properties of vowels in either language.[1] This will have the advantage of leaving 'long' and 'short' free to be used of the classification of vowels for prosodic purposes even when this classification bears no relation to the actual pronunciation of vowels as either tense or lax. Similarly, I shall use the terms 'heavy' and 'light' (following Allen, 1965, pp. 91–2) to refer to the two kinds of syllabic quantity that actually existed as a phonetic property in classical Latin, and 'long' and 'short' to refer to the two types of syllable distinguished on a theoretical level according to the rules of prosody (in both Latin verse and English imitations), whether or not there is a phonetic distinction in the pronunciation of the syllables.

The traditional account of quantity in Latin verse, which is still taught today (see Raven, 1965, pp. 23–5, for a detailed exposition), is, in outline, as follows (in the examples, only long vowels have been marked):

(i) a syllable containing a long vowel or diphthong is long (*mōs, vae*);

(ii) a syllable containing a short vowel followed by a 'double consonant' (*x* or *z*) or by two consonants (in the same or different words), *h* being discounted, is long (*nox*, first syllable of *culpa*, first syllable of *et dōna*); *unless* the consonants consist of a plosive (*b, c, d, g, p, t*) followed in the same word, or, in compound words, in the same part of a word, by a liquid (*l* or *r*), in which case the syllable is short *or* long (first syllable of *patrius*, second syllable of *adlacrimō* – but the first syllable is long since it constitutes one part of a compound word);

(iii) all other syllables are short.

Syllables of type (i) are traditionally described as being 'long

---

[1] A full description of the phonetic differences between tense and lax vowels is given by Chomsky and Halle (1968, pp. 68–9, 324–6), but for present purposes it will be sufficient merely to give some examples: the vowels in *bean, bane, balm, pawn, bone, boon* are tense and the vowels in *bin, Ben, bat, bun, pot, put* are lax. I have followed Chomsky and Halle in regarding diphthongs phonologically as tense vowels (an equivalence implicit in the bracketing of 'long vowels or diphthongs' in traditional accounts of Latin quantity and accent).

by nature'; those of type (ii) as 'long by position'. It will be obvious that the theory of quantity as duration stems from these rules, especially if consonants are thought of as adding arithmetically to the time taken for the pronunciation of a syllable. But further consideration reveals problems. Though the common assumption is that two consonants take about the same time to pronounce as the vowel they follow, and therefore double the duration of the syllable, whereas a single consonant is not sufficient to increase the length significantly (an assumption improbable in itself), it is difficult to explain why a long vowel or diphthong followed by two or more consonants (such as *mēns*) is no longer than a long vowel or diphthong alone (such as *mē*). Moreover, how is one to explain the fact that consonants at the beginning of a syllable play no part in determining its quantity, while consonants at the end are of crucial importance? Attempts have been made to explain quantity in terms of duration from syllable-peak to syllable-peak, and not from syllable-boundary to syllable-boundary, none of which, however, has succeeded in accounting for the details of the rules of Latin versification (see the discussion by Zirin, 1970, pp. 58–61).

It seems likely, therefore, that the distinction between 'long' and 'short' syllables in Latin was not simply a question of duration, but that a qualitative difference of some kind was also involved. The rules for ascertaining quantity are now often given in a form which relates more closely to the phonetic character of the two kinds of syllable, and makes the inadequacy of the theory of quantity as duration even more apparent (see, for instance, Allen, 1965, pp. 89–90). The rules in this form depend on an initial procedure of syllable-division (corresponding, presumably, to the division of syllables in classical Latin speech – see Hale, 1896), on the following principles: of two or more consonants at least the first goes with the preceding vowel (*fal-sus, flam-ma*), except in the case of a plosive plus liquid within a word, when *either* the first consonant goes with the preceding vowel, *or* both consonants go with the following vowel (*at-rox* or *a-trox*). Using the phonetic terms instead of the traditional ones, and referring to a syllable that ends in a vowel as an 'open' syllable and one which ends in a consonant as a 'closed' syllable, the definition of quantity can be stated as follows: a closed syllable or an open syllable with a tense vowel is heavy, while an open syllable with a lax vowel is light.

Various theories of quantity have been proposed which attempt to find an alternative to duration as the most important difference between light and heavy syllables. Jakobson (1960), for instance, has suggested that it is a matter of 'simpler and less prominent syllables opposed to those that are more complex and prominent' (p. 360). The notion of 'prominence' as the distinguishing characteristic is a more useful one than duration, but 'complexity' does not seem sufficient to account for it. Marouzeau (1954, 1955) has elaborated a theory which proposes as a basis for the distinction between heavy and light syllables the 'suspension' which occurs when consonants succeed one another, and although he does not solve all the problems (see Zirin, 1970, pp. 61–4), he at least does not feel obliged to prove that heavy syllables are markedly longer than light ones.

Writers on the classical languages tend to emphasise that habits of English speech can only obstruct our understanding of quantity, since it is a phenomenon foreign to the nature of English. However, Chomsky and Halle (1968), in their analysis of the rules governing stress-placement in English, arrive at some conclusions which suggest a close connection between the phonology of English and that of Latin. They refer to a lax vowel followed by one or no consonants as a 'weak cluster', and contrast this with a 'strong cluster', consisting of a tense vowel followed by one or no consonants, or of a vowel (tense or lax) followed by two or more consonants. They can then state their first approximation to a stress rule for verbs as follows: 'Primary stress is placed on the penultimate syllable if the final syllable terminates in a weak cluster; and...a final strong cluster receives primary stress' (p. 70). The structure of strong and weak clusters corresponds exactly to the structure of heavy and light syllables (Chomsky and Halle's definitions do not, of course, apply to syllables after syllable-division, but to strings of phonological elements within a word, so theirs is closer to the older account of quantity in Latin); and the role of these strong and weak clusters in determining stress placement in English is very close to that of heavy and light syllables in determining the position of the accent in Latin, where the accent occurs on the antepenultimate if the penultimate is light (*dóminus* – a proparoxytone word), but on the penultimate itself if it is heavy (*honéstus* – a paroxytone word). When Chomsky and Halle refine their definition of a weak cluster (p. 83), the parallel becomes even more exact, since they allow an optional *r*, *y*, *w*, and sometimes *l* after the consonant (if any).[1]

It seems justifiable to conclude that what is traditionally called 'quantity' is not so much a matter of syllable duration as of syllable structure – though it is a conclusion which has yet to be widely accepted – and that the differences of structure according to which syllables are classified into two groups are not arbitrarily chosen features or variations in complexity, but are fundamental differences, often closely linked with the operation of stress, and found in languages which appear to have very little in common. The most valuable discussions of accent and quantity in Latin in these terms are those of Allen (1964; 1965, pp. 89–92; 1969; 1973, ch. 4); and Zirin (1970) also concludes that

quantity in general then was a more complicated matter than the ancient grammarians realized. It is not based upon a system of time values at all, but rather upon a distinction of two syllable types, and a ratio of equivalence between them which, though it appeared to be basically durational, is only secondarily so, and finds its real basis in the relation between syllable and accent in the deeper morphophonemic structure of the language.   (p. 79)

Such an account of quantity, though it avoids many of the common errors, by no means solves the problem of its use as a basis for verse: we do not know how the difference between heavy and light syllables was actually perceived. That it was referred to in terms of syllable-length need not have any sig-

---

[1] For an interesting analysis of the physiological mechanisms involved in stress which has close affinities with this phonological account, see Stetson (1945, pp. 48–59; 1951).

nificance; untrained users of a language are notoriously in-accurate in describing its phonetic detail, and the Roman use of 'long' and 'short' may be no more accurate a reflection of the true nature of their language than their use of tonal terms to describe their accent seems to have been. Presumably, heavy syllables were somehow felt to be more prominent than light; but whether this was because they received more stress, especially when in important positions in verse, or whether their difference in structure itself was somehow perceived, is a question which has not as yet been satisfactorily answered.

The reading of Latin verse

The second major problem, closely associated with the first, is that of the actual reading aloud of quantitative verse. The structural basis of the lines is, as we have seen, the patterned arrangement of heavy and light syllables; but the crucial question is whether this pattern emerges naturally from a reading of the lines as if they were prose, or whether a special mode of delivery is necessary to bring out what is only latent. I shall take as an example the dactylic hexameter, since this was the verse-form which was most discussed and imitated by the Elizabethan experimenters in quantitative verse. The dactylic hexameter is made up of six feet, of which the first four are either dactyls ($-\smile\smile$) or spondees ($--$), the fifth is generally a dactyl, and the last is a spondee (although, as in most types of line, the quantity of the final syllable – which I mark throughout as long – can in fact vary). Thus the line most often quoted in Renaissance discussions of Latin metre, the first line of the *Aeneid*, is scanned as follows:

$$- \smile \smile | - \smile \smile | - \; - | - \; - | - \smile \smile | - \; -$$
arma virumque cano Troiae qui primus ab oris.

The technical term for the metrical beat (enunciated or imagined) on the first heavy syllable of each foot in quantitative verse is *ictus*, and one way of pronouncing this line is to give it what is often called a 'stressed-ictus' reading – in other words, to ignore the normal placing of the word-stresses,[1] and to stress

---

[1] I am assuming that the Latin accent was a stress accent, though even this is a matter of dispute, some authorities holding that it was a pitch accent (e.g. Beare, 1957, pp. 54–5). We have already noted that pitch plays an important

instead the first syllable of each foot, as follows (I mark stressed syllables ∕ and unstressed syllables ×):

> ∕　×　×∣∕　　×　×∣∕　×∣∕　　×∣　∕　×　×　∣∕×
> arma virumque cano Troiae qui primus ab oris.

This gives a very definite rhythm, especially to ears accustomed to stress-based metres like those of English, and this is a method which has long been common in schools. Some scholars have attempted a defence of this method not merely as a pedagogic device but as the correct way of reading Latin verse; among the more recent arguments in favour of some kind of stressed-ictus reading have been those of Herescu (1960), Allen (1964) (but see Allen, 1973, for a reconsideration of this theory), and Kollmann (1968).

The more common, and convincing, argument, however, is that the normal prose accentuation should be used when reading a line of Latin verse, thus:

> ∕　×　×∣∕　　×　∕∣×　　∕∣×　　×∣　∕　×　×　∣∕　×
> arma virumque cano Troiae qui primus ab oris.

The rules of Latin verse prevent the complete coincidence of accent and ictus in the great majority of lines, rules such as those which govern the placing of caesuras (a caesura is a break between words occurring *within* a foot). In the hexameter, for example, a caesura must occur in the third foot, either after the first syllable (a 'strong' caesura), or, less commonly, after the second syllable of a dactyl (a 'weak' caesura), in which case it is usually accompanied by strong caesuras in the second and fourth feet. Furthermore, word-division seldom occurs at the end of the second foot unless it contains a caesura. The effect of these rules, given the fact that no Latin polysyllable is stressed on the final syllable, is to prevent the coincidence of stress and ictus in the centre of the line; thus in the line already quoted the strong caesura after *cano* ensures that the stress does not fall on the first syllable of the third foot. At the end of the line, however, the tendency of the classical hexameter to end in words of two or three syllables (and to avoid an ending of two

part in stress, so the two kinds of accent are perhaps not as distinct as is often thought.

disyllables unless they are preceded by a monosyllable) has the opposite effect of preventing a clash of stress and ictus, for a stress will always fall on the first syllable of both final feet, and only very rarely on the other syllables of these feet.[1] Proponents of this method of reading assume that, given the correct pronunciation of Latin, the quantitative pattern (by which is often meant a durational pattern, thus encouraging at times a rendering with strict time-values which our discussion of quantity has shown to be unnecessary) will emerge in spite of the fact that the stresses do not fall in a corresponding pattern. The argument is usually taken further, and the changing relationship between accent and quantity is seen as a deliberate device whereby the expressive possibilities are greatly increased. It is held that the reader perceives the quantitative patterning and the occurrence of stresses simultaneously, and that the poet is able to use this interplay for poetic effects, while the basic rhythmic structure is asserted by the coincidence at the end of every line.

This view of the hexameter was fully elaborated by Jackson Knight in 1939, and is further exemplified in Wilkinson (1963, pp. 89–134), where it is called the Pulse–Accent theory. Wilkinson quotes several instances of the expressive use of coincidence and clash in classical Latin hexameters, three of which will serve to illustrate the theory. The complete absence of clashing feet is sometimes obtained by a weak third-foot caesura without the accompanying strong caesuras; thus the metre contributes to the sense of ease in the following line from the *Aeneid* (IV. 486) (I have expanded Wilkinson's notation of stress and ictus to a more complete indication of the scansion):

spargens umida mella soporiferumque papaver
sprinkling liquid honey and soporific poppy-seed.

(p. 125)

---

[1] Another popular metrical form in the Elizabethan imitations was the elegiac couplet, which also shows in its fully-developed classical form restrictions on word-length which determine the metrical character of its ending: the first line of the couplet is a regular hexameter, and the second is a pentameter of the form — ‿‿ | — ‿‿ | — | — ‿‿ | — ‿‿ | —. The pentameter ends regularly with a disyllable, which ensures that, although the final syllable cannot receive a stress, the initial syllables of the two previous dactyls in most cases do.

The disruptive effect of even a strong third-foot caesura can be minimised, as in the following line (*Aeneid* VI. 523), where the momentary tension on *quies* is released in the smooth dactyls that follow:

$$\text{/ }\times\text{ }\times\text{ | / }\times\quad\text{/| }\times\quad\times\text{ }\times\text{ | / }\quad\times\text{ }\times\text{ | / }\times\text{ }\times\text{ | / }\times$$
$$\bar{\ }\;\smile\smile\;\bar{\ }\;\smile\quad\bar{\ }\smile\quad\smile\smile\;\bar{\ }\quad\smile\smile\;\bar{\ }\;\bar{\ }\;\bar{\ }$$

dulcis et alta quies placidaeque simillima mortis
pleasant and deep repose most like to peaceful death.

(p. 125)

When the desired effect is one of harshness, however, the first part of the line can be made to be a succession of clashes, as in the description of shipwrecked men in *Aeneid* I. 118:

$$\times\quad\text{/| }\times\quad\text{/| }\times\quad\text{/ | }\times\text{ }\times\text{ | }\quad\text{/ }\times\text{ }\times\text{ | / }\quad\times$$
$$\bar{\ }\quad\bar{\ }\;\bar{\ }\quad\bar{\ }\;\bar{\ }\quad\bar{\ }\;\bar{\ }\quad\bar{\ }\;\smile\smile\;\smile\quad\bar{\ }$$

apparent rari nantes in gurgite summo
here and there appear men swimming on the surface of the deep.

(p. 126)

It is a neat and attractive theory, but as it stands it is not entirely satisfactory. The possibility of holding in the mind two such different patterns, and experiencing their clash or coincidence as an expressive aspect of the verse, has not been demonstrated (a comparison has been drawn with English, but there is really no parallel, since the commonly held view that part of the expressiveness of English verse comes from the relationship between the regular metre and the actual rhythm of the words relies on the fact that the actual rhythm departs from the metrical base only in very limited ways; moreover, one's sense of the metrical base springs directly from one's awareness of the rhythm, and is not derived from a pattern in a different medium). It is not surprising that text-books generally omit discussion of the problem, or gloss over the difficulties involved; for example, Raven (1965) states that 'the thorny question of *ictus*...has, for better or for worse, been disregarded throughout this work' (p. 23, n. 1), and Cooper (1952) at first insists that the ictus is manifested by stress (p. 36) but later says that the hexameter must be read with normal word-accents (p. 65).

The existence of so much disagreement and uncertainty in present-day discussions should encourage some leniency in our judgement of the attempts made by the Elizabethans to understand Latin metre, and the prevalence of false and unexamined views on the subject even today should make it easier for us to accept the apparently unthinking way in which educated Elizabethans accepted, and passed on, a conception of metre founded on inconsistencies and errors. Perhaps we assume too readily that the Romans themselves possessed the key to their verse, simply because they produced systematised rules as an aid to its creation. After all, we are still a long way from understanding the operation of traditional English metre; is it more likely that the Roman or Greeks understood theirs? Add to this the fact that quantitative Latin verse was the result of an attempt to impose upon one language a metrical system natural to another, and very different, language, Greek, while the natural Latin system of stress-based verse apparently remained in existence in the popular tradition, and one sees that Roman accounts of their metre must be treated with caution.[1] In view of the praise lavished for centuries upon Latin poetry and its beautiful rhythms by readers whose pronunciation of the language could have given them no aural appreciation of the quantitative metre intended by the poets,[2] is it not possible that the Romans, imitating the Greeks in their poetry as in their sculpture and architecture, should have exaggerated the importance of the quantitative aspect of the new metres? Waltz (1948), in considering the history of the word *rhythmos*, concludes that whereas for the Greeks the idea of rhythm suggested movement, for the Romans, 'moins artistes que calculateurs', it conveyed the sense of measure and number (p. 119). The Romans no doubt admired and took pleasure in

---

[1] An interesting example of the difficulty experienced by classical Latin poets when a natural property of Latin contradicted a rule inherited from the Greeks can be seen in the treatment of a final lax vowel followed by initial s+consonant: Greek rules made the syllable heavy, but Latin syllabification left it light, and the result of this conflict was, for the most part, the avoidance of this combination (see Hoenigswald, 1949).

[2] For instance, Westaway (1913), in discussing the reformed Latin pronunciation, states: 'Professor Saintsbury tells *The Times* that he "plumps" for the old pronunciation "because it is more likely to bring home to an English boy the beauty of Latin literature."...There are probably not a few scholars whose keen appreciation of the music of their Horace and their Virgil is so intimately associated with the pronunciation of a life-time that they cannot bring themselves to make a change' (p. vii).

the precision and attention to detail of quantitative metres, as later generations have done,[1] and it was to this aspect that they devoted their theoretical attention; it nevertheless seems possible that, as far as rhythmic organisation of sound is concerned, they actually responded to the stress patterns when reading and listening to verse.[2] (Notice that in the examples of the expressive use of metre quoted above, the effects discussed are not destroyed if one focuses on the accentual rhythm, since the contrast between the harshness of an irregular pattern of stresses and the smoothness of a dactylic or trochaic rhythm is still present.)

A metrical form which furnishes further evidence of the importance of the accentual pattern is the sapphic, and because of this, and its importance in the history of English prosody, it merits separate consideration. Horace made extensive use of the sapphic stanza, which was of course Greek in origin, and in doing so introduced certain restrictions on the metre which had the effect of giving it a distinct accentual character. The longer lines of the stanza have the following quantitative pattern:

$$- \cup - \underline{\cup} - \cup \cup - \cup - -$$

Horace, however, does not allow the fourth syllable to be light, and introduces a caesura after the fifth syllable, and these two restrictions combine to limit greatly the number of accentual patterns possible. Whether or not he made these changes for this reason is not of importance here (Wilkinson, 1940, and 1963, pp. 106–10, argues that nothing was further from his thoughts, and that his increasing use of a caesura after the sixth rather than the fifth syllable in his later sapphics is the result of the realisation that his audience was paying attention to an irrelevant accentual rhythm); the fact remains that a large number

---

[1] This attitude, which we shall consider in the Elizabethan context later, has not disappeared. Kuryłowicz (1966) states that 'Greek and Latin poetry, though represented by many works of prominent rank in world-literature, impresses us not only by its artistic, but also, *sit venia verbo*, by its *artificial* character', and ascribes this impression in part to the 'multiple, rigorous and intricate rules of versification' (p. 163).

[2] For an account of the Latin hexameter which discusses evidence suggesting that the unsophisticated hearer, at least, perceived the accentual pattern in the final two feet while remaining oblivious to the quantitative pattern of the line, see the appendix to Allen (1973).

of his sapphics have this rhythm, which can best be indicated by quoting one of the Odes with the accents marked (secondary stress is indicated by a grave accent; I also give the scansion of the first stanza):

     /   / ‖ / \ /
    – ᴜ – – – ᴜᴜ – ᴜ – –
Persicos odi, puer, apparatus,
    / ᴜ – / ‖ /   /
    – ᴜ – – – ᴜᴜ – ᴜ – –
displicent nexae philyra coronae;
    / ᴜ /‖/   /
    – ᴜ – – – ᴜᴜ – ᴜ – –
mitte sectari, rosa quo locorum
       / ᴜ /
      – ᴜ ᴜ – –
      sera moretur.

    /   / / \ /
simplici myrto nihil allabores
    /   /   / \ /
sedulus curo: neque te ministrum
    /   / / \ /
dedecet myrtus neque me sub arta
     /   /
    vite bibentem.

                   (1. 38)

As is clear from these lines, the pattern is one of stresses on the first, fourth, sixth, and tenth syllables, and sometimes on the eighth. The short line also has a distinctive rhythm. It is difficult to imagine that Horace's public read these lines without noticing, and responding to, the accentual rhythm, and as we shall see when discussing the Elizabethan imitations of the sapphic in Chapter 14 it was this aspect of the sapphic which was seized on by readers from medieval times onward.[1] If the accentual pattern of Latin verse did play an important part in the response of its readers, it would mean that in spite of the alterations in the pronunciation of Latin since classical times (some of which we shall be considering in the following chapter), one feature of Latin poetry remained relatively constant (except for those who preferred a stressed-ictus reading), since accent-placement changed little during the succeeding ages. But the weight of theoretical attention has always fallen on the quantitative structures, and we shall see that the Renaissance was no exception.

[1] The history of the sapphic is traced by Needler (1941, pp. 7–47), as part of his study of the background to the 'Canadian Boat-Song'.

As we move on to consider the Elizabethans, then, we must bear in mind that the problems with which they grappled (even though they seem sometimes to have been unaware of their existence) have to a large extent still not been solved, and may even have been a puzzle to the Romans; and that where we have added to our knowledge (and the few apparent certainties will be a useful background to our study of the Elizabethan understanding of quantitative metre), we have exposed centuries of careless and self-contradictory thinking.

2

The Elizabethan pronunciation of Latin

To understand the Elizabethan conception of Latin metre, we must know with some degree of certainty how Latin was normally pronounced in England at this time; only then can we begin to consider what a line of Latin verse would have sounded like in the mouth of an Elizabethan, and what models the venturesome poet held in his aural imagination when he set about writing English verse in classical metres. Of particular importance is the extent to which vowels retained the tenseness or laxness which they had had in the classical pronunciation of Latin, for, as we have seen, the quantity of an open syllable depends on whether its vowel is tense or lax; and it is on this question that we shall concentrate our attention (the problem of changes in the quantity of closed syllables as a result of a differing pronunciation of consonants is a much slighter one, and will be ignored).

Historical developments

By the fifth century A.D. a change had taken place in the pronunciation of Latin which altered radically the distribution of tense and lax vowels: while the position of the accent had remained fixed, all stressed vowels had become (or remained) tense in open syllables, and lax in closed syllables (for further details of the change see M. K. Pope, 1952, pp. 72–3, and Vossler, 1954, pp. 87–9). This meant, of course, that the quantities on which Latin verse was based ceased to be a property of the spoken language and had to be learned for the purpose of scanning and writing poetry in classical metres; thus St Augustine, writing early in the fifth century, notes that the

21

grammarian's insistence that the first syllable of *cano* is short is based not on its pronunciation, but on the fact that it was used as short in surviving classical Latin verse (*De Musica*, Migne, *Patrologia Latina*, XXXII, cols. 1099–100). The Latin which was taught by Pope Gregory's missionaries in England in the seventh century manifested this characteristic (this and some further features are mentioned by Bradley, 1920, p. 3), and loan-words from Latin in Old English reflect a similar pronunciation in Late Latin (thus Classical Latin *sānctus* becomes Old English *sănct*, and Classical Latin *sŏnus* becomes Old English *sōn*) (see Luick, 1914–40, part I, pp. 200–1 and Serjeant-son, 1935, p. 291). Aelfric, in his grammar of about the year 1000, makes a clear distinction between the pronunciation of *pater* and *malus* in normal speech with long initial syllables, and their use in verse with short initial syllables – and he castigates those who assume that one's pronunciation should make manifest the quantities that words have in verse (ed. Zupitza, 1880, p. 2).

A further characteristic of the Old English pronunciation of Latin for which Luick and Serjeantson find evidence is a tendency for vowels in open stressed antepenultimate syllables to become lax, and this became a firm feature of the traditional English pronunciation of Latin, as may be seen seen from John Walker's clear description of it in his *Key to the Classical Pronunciation of Greek and Latin Proper Names* of 1798:

Every accented antepenultimate vowel but *u*, even when followed by one consonant only, is, in our pronunciation of Latin, as well as in English, short; thus *tabula, separo, diligo, nobilis, cucumis*, have the first vowels pronounced as in the English words, *capital, celebrate, simony, solitude, luculent*, in direct opposition to the Latin quantity, which makes every antepenultimate vowel in all these words but the last long; and this *we* pronounce long, though short in Latin.

(p. xxix)

As Walker implies, it is a deeply-rooted phonological rule of English itself, which no doubt carried over to the pronunciation of Latin. Chomsky and Halle (1968) give a rule for Late Middle English, which is basically the same (p. 253, Rule 3*b*); it may be put into words as follows: 'a vowel which occurs before a single consonant followed by an unstressed vowel and at least one further syllable is *lax*'. They find evidence for the existence of this rule before 1100.

The other characteristics of this pronunciation of Latin that we have discussed are also mentioned by Chomsky and Halle as long-standing features of the pronunciation of English: the laxing of vowels before two consonants, provided that the second is not *r*, *l*, *y*, or *w* (p. 253, Rule 3*a*), is found about the year 1000, and tensing in open syllables is 'a phenomenon well attested in English since at least the thirteenth century' (p. 253). (These processes, they remark, are still operative in contemporary English.) One of the most notable features of the traditional English pronunciation of Latin, then, was, from a very early period, its similarity to the pronunciation of English; and this remained true right up until the reforms of this century.[1]

When the Great Vowel Shift occurred in English in the fifteenth and sixteenth centuries, the altered vowel-qualities were mirrored in the pronunciation of Latin, which became even less like continental pronunciations – themselves far from uniform – than it had been. The differences were noted by a number of writers at the time,[2] and many stories exist about the incomprehensibility of English Latin to continental listeners. Drummond quotes Jonson as saying, 'Scaliger writtes ane Epistle to Casawbone wher he scorns the Englishe speak of Latine for He thought he had speken English to him' (Jonson, *Works*, I, 146–7).[3] Some scholars preferred to cultivate a pronunciation of Latin in an Italian manner, this being regarded

---

[1] This traditional English pronunciation of Latin is described and discussed by Bradley (1920), Sargeaunt (1920), Moore Smith (1930), Allen (1965, pp. 102–10), and Wilkinson (1963, pp. 3–6). The one period during which English speech-habits may not have predominated was when, after the Conquest, Latin was taught through the medium of French (see Ellis, 1869–89, I, 246; III, 803–4, n.; and Dobson, 1968, II, 929).

[2] Among those who commented on the idiosyncracies of the English pronunciation of Latin were Geofry Tory in 1529 (see Newdigate, 1939, p. 245), John Hart in 1569 (ed. Danielsson, 1955, p. 190), Justus Lipsius in 1586 (p. 33), and Thomas Coryate in 1611 (II, 59–60). The vowel-sounds used by the English seemed strange even to Welsh and Scottish ears – see Salesbury (1550, sig. CI*r–v*), and Hume (ca. 1617, pp. 8–9).

[3] The reference is in fact to a letter from J. J. Scaliger to Stephanus Ubertus, published in the former's *Opuscula* (1610, p. 454).

by many, not surprisingly, as the 'purest' of continental pronunciations. Dobson (1968) comments that the sixteenth-century orthoepist Hart 'seems to take Italian as a standard for Latin pronunciation, and indeed he does not always appear clearly to distinguish between the two languages' (I, 65), while Palsgrave in 1530 describes the pronunciation of the French *a* as 'lyke as the Italians sounde a or they with us that pronounce the latine tonge aryght' (fol. 1), and makes the same statement about the French *e, i,* and *o* (fols. 1v, 2v–3). However, there is no reason to believe that the Italian pronunciation came any nearer to achieving correct quantities;[1] nor is there much evidence to suggest that this pronunciation was at all widespread.

The smooth change in Latin pronunciation, parallel to the changes in English pronunciation, was threatened in the sixteenth century by what could have proved a great obstacle. With the rejection of medieval scholarship and literature that accompanied the rise of humanism during the Renaissance, and the return to classical models, it is not surprising that some prominent humanists sought to erase the medieval inheritance in their pronunciation of Latin and Greek, and to attempt a reconstruction and reintroduction of the classical pronunciation. Erasmus took the task upon himself in his dialogue *De Recta Latini Graecique sermonis pronuntiatione* (1528), and the Cambridge humanists John Cheke and Thomas Smith attempted to introduce the reformed pronunciation, at least of Greek, into England in about 1534 or 1535.[2] The outcome can be traced in detail in the letters exchanged by Cheke and the Chancellor of Cambridge University, Stephen Gardiner, which were published by Cheke in 1555 under the title *De Pronuntiatione Graecae potissimum linguae disputationes*, and in the letter

---

[1] Coryate's admiration of the Italian pronunciation of *fides* as 'feedes' (1611, II, 59–60) reveals his unawareness of the fact that although the Italian *i* is closer to the classical pronunciation than the English *i*, both substitute a tense vowel for a lax one. In Chapter 6 we shall discuss comments by Dutch, French and Italian scholars of the time on the lack of an audible correlate of quantity in Renaissance Latin pronunciations.

[2] For accounts of the movement for reform see Brittain (1955, pp. 44–8); Allen (1965, pp. 103–5); Dobson (1968, I, 38–40); and Gabel's edition of Caius (1574, pp. 1–4).

from Smith to Gardiner published in 1568 as part of the former's *De recta & emendata Linguae Graecae Pronuntiatione*. Gardiner did his best to crush the movement, and John Caius, in *De Pronunciatione Graecae et Latinae Linguae* (written in 1569 or 1570) joined in, defending the traditional pronunciation against the inroads of both Italianate and classical reforms.[1] In spite of this hostility, the movement for reform was eventually successful with regard to Greek; but very little change occurred in the much more deeply ingrained pronunciation of Latin, and it seems likely that the efforts in this direction were in any case relatively slight. John Robotham, in his preface 'To the Reader' in Horn's translation of Comenius' *Janua Linguarum Reserata* (1640), attacks the English pronunciation of Latin, which he regards not as something natural to English speakers, but as much more difficult to learn because less amenable to analysis into rules. But all is not lost:

Nor is the cure of this error to be despaired, if our University-professors and some of the eminent learned would *dare* to begin. In *vulgar* tongues, the grosse of the mixt multitude must bear sway: but in the *learned* languages, which are exempted from popular use, the *learned*, if they will, may *command*. Some forreine nations do at this day exactly retaine the right sound; and who knows not, that the *Greek* pronunciation was far more and more generally corrupted; which yet by the endevours and courage of some undaunted spirits, is now, even in despite of the great opposers, generally reformed?

(sig. A5*v*–6)

Robotham reckoned without the force of the intuitively-held rules of English pronunciation, and underestimated the influence of the 'mixt multitude'.

---

[1] Some idea of the unscholarliness of Caius' reasoning can be gained from the following argument against the reforms: 'Eadem pronunciatione honestissima verba turpissimè sonent, ut *ascitum* & *asciscunt* apud nostros. Etenim in harum vocum prima, si c. proferas ut ch. & in secunda utrumque c. ut k. more novo, utrumque vocabulum tanta turpitudine proferetur, quanta non sinit verecundia mea explicare' (p. 15). ('Pronounced in this way, the most respectable words sound most foul, as is the case with *ascitum* and *asciscunt* among us. For if in the first of these words you pronounce *c* as *ch*, and in the second *c* as *k*, according to the new fashion, both words will be spoken with so much filthiness that I may not in my modesty explain.')

Tense and lax vowels in the Elizabethan pronunciation

Though no extended study of the Elizabethan pronunciation of Latin has been made, the work that has been carried out is sufficient to give a clear picture of the essential features. The most useful source of evidence is a 22-line poem in Latin transcribed by Robert Robinson into his invented phonetic script and published in his *Art of Pronuntiation* (1617) as an illustration of his symbols. (Although the treatise dates from a short time after Elizabeth's death, the pronunciation described in it can be assumed to be very similar to that of the latter half of the sixteenth century, and as far as the distribution of tense and lax vowels is concerned, it is highly unlikely that any changes would have occurred in the intervening period.) Transliterations of the poem into a more readable phonetic script are given by both Fiedler (1936) and Dobson (1957), and the latter does the same for Robinson's phonetic transcription of *Lady Pecunia*, a long poem in English by Richard Barnfield containing many classical names, and for a fragment of another poem prefaced by a Latin sentence (MS Ashmole 826). Further, though slighter, evidence, supporting that furnished by Robinson, occurs in *A briefe and a playne introduction teachyng how to pronounce the letters in the British tong* by William Salesbury (1550), *An Orthographie* by John Hart (1569), William Bullokar's *Booke at large, for the Amendment of Orthographie for English speech* (1580), *Coryats Crudities* by Thomas Coryate (1611), *Of the Orthographie and Congruitie of the Britan Tongue* by Alexander Hume (written in 1617 or thereabouts), and Alexander Gil's *Logonomia Anglica* (1619).

What is important, for our purposes, about the pronunciation revealed by these writers is, in Dobson's words, that 'the vowel-quantities...bear no necessary relation to the original Classical quantities, but are nevertheless determined by ascertainable rules' (1957, p. xix). These rules are basically the same as those which we have seen at work in the earlier English pronunciation of Latin, and which were to remain a feature of the traditional pronunciation until the recent reforms: stressed vowels in closed syllables and in open antepenultimate syllables are lax; stressed vowels in open penultimate syllables are tense.

An exception is *u*, which is always tense in open and lax in closed syllables; and *a*, *e*, *o* in stressed antepenultimate syllables are tense if the following two syllables have adjacent vowels (as occurs also in English words like *alien, deviate, podium*). Vowels with secondary stress seem to behave like those in stressed antepenultimate syllables; unstressed vowels are less regular, and were probably often reduced in speech to something like the obscure vowel that is so common in modern English (as in the final syllables of *father* and *gallop*).[1]

The best way of indicating what Latin verse sounded like to an Elizabethan will be to give Robinson's poem from *The Art of Pronuntiation* in Dobson's transliteration of the special phonetic symbols in which it appears,[2] followed, as in the treatise, by the same poem in normal spelling:

[1] For further details of these rules, see the discussions of Robinson by Fiedler (1936, pp. 15–18) and Dobson (1957, pp. xviii–xxi), and the comments of Luick (1914–40, part II, p. 749), Brittain (1955, pp. 51–2), and Dobson (1968, II, 493–7).

[2] The phonetic values of the vowels in Dobson's transliteration of Robinson's symbols are approximately as follows:

a...[a] as in Germ. *Mann* or [ae] as in Eng. *bat*
ā...[ae:] as in Eng. *bad* or [ɛ:] as in Fr. *père*
e...[e] as in Eng. *bet*
ē...[ɛ:] as in Fr. *père* or [e:] as in Germ. *See*
i ...[ɪ] as in Eng. *bit*
o...[ɒ] as in Eng. *hot*
ō...[o:] as in Germ. *Sohn*
u...[ʊ] as in Eng. *pull* or [ʌ] as in Eng. *but*
eī ..[ɔi] similar to the diphthong in Eng. *bite*, but beginning with the reduced vowel as in the second syllable of Eng. *father*.

The consonants for the most part have their modern values, but the following special symbols should be noted:

š...[ʃ] as in Eng. *shop*
ž...[ʒ] as in Eng. *measure*
ŋ...[ŋ] as in Eng. *ring*
ṛ...the unvoiced equivalent of [r]; and similarly with ṇ and ŋ̣.

Robinson's use of accent-marks (which is not consistent with his account of the accents and their symbols given immediately before the poem) is, in its essentials, as follows: acute and grave accents indicate stressed and unstressed syllables respectively, but only certain syllables are so marked. In disyllables, the final syllable is marked (it is always unstressed in Latin, of course); in trisyllables the middle syllable is marked (if it is unstressed, the stress falls on the initial syllable); in quadrisyllables, the second and fourth syllables are marked – either both are stressed, in which case the main stress falls on the second syllable, or both unstressed, in which case the main stress falls on the third syllable. There appear to be a few misprints in the accent-marks.

Breve de voce poema Latinum in novo ordine literarum ante edocto, iuxta Anglicanam nostram pronuntiationem conscriptum.[1]

parvà leīsèt, tenyìwiskwi leīset, meīhì magnà pōtéstas,
    per teràm viktrìks, per mārì sum domìna,
kwem kālòr et freīgùs siŋgùnt meīhì subdžǎset āer
    ēkwì ut pa̧rtísipém, sik dēùs instítyiwít:
non meīhì magnà kōhòrs, mēà seī kwādrǎta katùrva,
    kwiŋkwi teībì sōlùm, prestàt iwbeíkwi lātùs,
kwōs seī duks sapyìens nektàt seīmùl ordìni rektǒ,
    sunt fasìlēzkwì bōneì, sunt ridžìdeīkwì bōneì:
hōs diwsìt seī kwan[d]ǒ ekspèrs rāšǒni rimíseī,
    barbàreī et insulseī, terìbilézkwi fǒrent:
kwālìs ēgǒ ta̧ntè keī veīrèz? nomìna ku̧ŋtìs
    impózyiweí, nōmèn voks kwōkwì fingǒ meīhì;
mentis ēgǒ intȩ́rprēz, artìs ku̧ŋtékwi madžístra,
    ekspózitríks vēlòks diskríminís vāryìeī
doktreīnē rādìks, sēlǒs et ta̧rtàra rāmeì
    ta̧ŋgùnt, et fruktùs, mors mōdù, veītà mōdù;
mē fāmàm lāšìumkwì sāgáks mē grēšìa doktà,
    mē tenyìwit preīmùm sa̧ŋtà džiwdéa dēkùz,
et (džōvì prōpíšiǒ) mē magnà britányiá rōmàm
    konkúsit tētràm, pan[d]ít et insíšiám:
hok ta̧ntùm, relìkwis, lišìat meīhì disìri, misìs:
    non meīhì sit rektòr, kweì seī seībì non domìnus.

                    (Dobson, 1957, p. 27)

Parva licet, tenuisque licet, mihi magna potestas:
    Per terram victrix per mare sum domina,
Quem calor & frigus cingunt, mihi subiacet aer,
    Aequè ut participem, sic Deus instituit.
Non mihi magna cohors, mea si quadrata caterva,
    Quinque tibi solùm praestat ubique latus,
Quos si dux sapiens nectat simùl ordine recto.
    Sunt facilesque boni, sunt rigidique boni:
Hos ducit si quandò expers ratione, remissi.
    Barbari, & insulsi terribilesque forent:
Qualis ego, tantae cui vires? nomina cunctis
    Imposui, nomen vox quoque fingo mihi;
Mentis ego interpres, artis cunctaeque Magistra,
    Expositrix velox discriminis varii.
Doctrinae radix caelos & tartara rami

---

[1] 'A short Latin poem on the voice, using the new set of letters already explained, written out in accordance with our English pronunciation.'

Tangunt & fructus mors modo, vita modo;
Me famam Latiumque sagax, me Graecia docta,
    Me tenuit primum, sancta Iudaea decus.
Et (Iove propitio) me magna Britannia Romam
    Concussit tetram, pandit & inscitiam:
Hoc tantum reliquis, liceat mihi dicere missis:
    Non mihi sit rector, qui sibi non dominus.

(Dobson, 1957, p. 28)

When someone like Spenser or Campion read their favourite Latin poets, and admired the metre so much that they wished to re-create it in English, it was verse which sounded like this that constituted their model and their goal.

3

The Elizabethan reading of Latin verse

Just as the way in which a modern scholar reads aloud a Latin hexameter reveals a great deal about the theory of Latin metre he holds, consciously or unconsciously, so any conclusions we can come to about the way the Elizabethans read Latin verse will help us understand what Latin metre meant to them. We cannot hope to understand the quantitative experiments unless we understand how the Latin verse they were meant to imitate was read; and the light in which metre in general was regarded must have been partly determined by whatever method of reading was used. As we have seen, the central problems of quantitative metres – questions about quantity and ictus – are closely connected with the actual reading of the lines. However, it is not sufficient to look at the definitions and explanations of these concepts in the accepted text-books on prosody of the time, since such definitions and explanations were arrived at by following authority, as in so many other fields of Elizabethan 'scholarship', not by any kind of examination of the verse itself and the way its metre worked. We need to find comments made about the actual reading itself, out of the context of the traditional grammar. In the fairly extensive body of work on the quantitative experiments, and the few treatments of the neo-Latin verse of the period, very little evidence has been produced on this crucial question,[1] though varying opinions have

---

[1] The evidence cited by Hendrickson (1949) on this subject (pp. 258–60) has no direct relevance to sixteenth-century England; he quotes a passage from Beza's work on the pronunciation of Greek (to be considered with other continental discussions in Chapter 6), which he misattributes to Mekerchus, 'long resident in England', to whose *De Veteri et Recta Pronuntiatione* of 1565 it formed an appendix, and his other evidence dates from the seventeenth century (*De Poematum Cantu*

occasionally been expressed by those who have realised its importance. Vivian, in his edition of Campion's works (1909, p. lx), and Liddell (1926, p. 118) assert that the Elizabethans read Latin verse with a stress on the ictus of each foot; Hendrickson (1949, p. 243) and Kabell (1960, ch. 3, 'Wie die Verse Gelesen Wurden') believe that they read it with normal prose stresses; and McKerrow (1901) states that the former method of reading was the common one, but that the 'group of scholars' who attempted English hexameters adhered to the latter one, though with long syllables pronounced more slowly than short ones (p. 177). The correctness or incorrectness of the Elizabethan mode of reading is not important here (as we have seen, it is a matter which even today has not been settled with any finality); we simply need to know what sort of aural pattern, if any, the Elizabethans took to be the metre of the Latin poetry they read.

The possible alternatives in reading a line of Latin verse have been discussed in Chapter 1 (I shall use hexameter verse for most of my examples, since it is the verse-form which was the most discussed and imitated by the Elizabethans, and probably the most important in shaping their ideas about metre). Firstly, one can assume that the quantitative pattern is something present in the words as they exist in normal speech, and therefore pronounce the verse simply as if it were prose, though perhaps more carefully and deliberately. Or one can assume that the quantities of syllables are only potentially present in normal pronunciation, or present to only a small degree, and therefore read the verse, still with prose stresses, but with an attempt to emphasise the quantities – which will nearly always mean an attempt to speak heavy syllables slowly and light syllables quickly. Or finally, one can assume that no pattern of quantities is or could be made perceptible, and that the ictus of each foot needs to receive a stress, whether or not that

et Viribus Rythmi, 1673, by Isaac Vossius) or later. Nevertheless, the works he mentions do testify to the existence outside sixteenth-century England, geographically and chronologically, of the same method of reading Latin verse that we shall find prevailed within it. Kabell (1960) also gives some useful evidence relating to the continental tradition of verse-reading (ch. 3), though he seems to be misinformed about English practice.

syllable is one normally accented in prose. Which of these was the accepted Elizabethan method?

The delivery of verse

The clearest statement that I have found is made by John Brinsley, master of the public school at Ashby-de-la-Zouch, in a chapter of his *Ludus Literarius; or, the Grammar Schoole* entitled, 'Of pronouncing naturally and sweetly without vain affectation', in the section on Latin verse (I give references to Campagnac's modern edition, based on the 1627 edition, but identical in these passages, as in most respects, with the 1612 edition): 'So in all Poetry, for the pronuntiation, it is to bee uttered as prose; observing distinctions [i.e. punctuation] and the nature of the matter' (p. 213). Robert Robinson's *Art of Pronuntiation* (1617), mentioned in Chapter 2, also gives direct evidence of the use of normal word-accents, since he has no hesitation in giving as the example of his phonetic script a Latin poem in elegiacs, and marking the words with their normal accents, something he would be unlikely to do if he thought his readers might stress the ictus.

One of the most interesting pieces of evidence I have encountered is a passage in a translation by Thomas Browne of Johann Sturm's *Nobilitas Literata* (1549), published in London in 1570 under the title *A ritch Storehouse or Treasurie for Nobilitye and Gentlemen*. We are not justified, of course, in taking this as direct evidence concerning Latin verse-reading in England; but Sturm's book was an influential one in England from its publication in 1549 (Edward VI probably possessed a copy, and its educational theory influenced Cheke and Ascham – see Baldwin, 1944, I, 241–2; II, 263), and the translation reflects, and must have increased, its influence. The passage is worth quoting in full, as it shows a remarkable anticipation of some modern writing on Latin metre (it follows a discussion of Virgil's variations of style and mood, illustrated by diagrams showing structures extending over several lines):

This practise bringeth this commoditie, that though thinges differ but a verie little, yet wherein they differ, we may plainely perceyve.

For these two Latine verses have like feete as Grammarians terme them.

> Tityre tu patulae recubans sub tegmine fagi,
> Protenus aeger ago, hanc etiam vix Tityre duco.

Which I put into English in this sort,

> O happie art thou Tityrus that under Beechen tree.
> I sicke doe drive my Gotes a farre, scant able this to leade.

Yet doe they differ both in the conjunction of the wordes and letters, and also in harmonie and tune. Whereof springeth the Poeticall number, and that may be understanded by this draught.

／   ／   ／   ／   ／
••• ••• ••• •• ••• ••

For the first foote and the last have semblable harmonie and time. For the sounde of the voyce is in the first sillable, that is to saye, in the thirde sillable from the ende: and the seconde and thirde foote have the sounde in the middest. But in this verse it is otherwise.

> Protenus aeger ago, hanc etiam vix Tityre duco.

For though it be measured with the lyke feete, yet doth it differ in the sound & placing of the letters, as appeareth in this draught.

／   ／／ ／／   ／ ／
••• ••• ••• •• ••• ••

For the first and seconde heroicall feete hath two sharpe soundes: and the thirde hath a contraction of vowels: and the two spondaicall feete are more sounding: so that this verse as it is in matter more dolefull than the first: so is it also graver in sounde. (fols. 28–9)

One puzzling feature of the translation, which suggests that Browne did not understand the subtleties of Sturm's argument, is that the references to both of the lines mention the wrong feet: for Sturm's 'primus pes & quintus' Browne has 'the first foote and the last', and for 'secundus & tertius numerus heroicus' he has 'the first and seconde heroicall feete' (see Sturm, 1586, pp. 328–9). With these corrections, the passage shows not only that normal word-accents were used in reading verse (and Sturm gives no indication that he expects this assumption to be questioned), but also that some people at least – though probably very few – regarded them as being an integral part of the poetic effect of Latin verse.

In spite of the unhelpfulness of their definitions of concepts like quantity and verse, the grammar-books provide some indirect evidence in support of our conclusion. When the subject of correct pronunciation is handled in the grammars, the list of faults does not include anything about false quantities or incorrect accents – which one would expect to be the most common kind of fault in a method of verse-reading that insisted on the quantitative pattern being made obvious. The anonymous *Certaine grammar questions for the exercise of young Schollers* (1602?) includes the following exchange:

Q. Nowe what thinges doe yee observe in reading:
R. These two thinges. 1 ⎰*Cleane sounding.*
                  2 ⎱*Dewe pawsing.*
Q. Wherein standeth *cleane sounding:*
R. In giving to every letter his just and full sounde. In breaking or dividing every worde duely into his severall syllables, so that every syllable may bee hearde by himselfe and none drownd, nor slubbered by ill favouredly.   (sig. B1)

What seems called for is a clear, deliberate reading of the words; but there is no question of getting quantities right. The list of vices which is given immediately afterwards is the one which occurs in most grammars (with names like 'Iotacismus', 'Ischnotes', 'Traulismus', and 'Plateasmus') – a list which, like much of the 'Prosodia' section, probably reflects tradition more than English practice (much the same list is given by Quintilian in his *Institutiones Oratoriae*, 1.5.32). It is difficult to resist the conclusion that some schoolmasters regarded their task of teaching pronunciation as complete when the boys could give the correct answers, with the correct Latin names of the vices, to his questions, though a few examples of the 'Abusing of letters' are given which may be peculiarly English (like the pronunciation of *facio* as *fasho*). 'Due pausing' is explained as the 'right observation' of punctuation-marks; and that is the end of the discussion of reading – one of the most extended in the grammatical works of the period.

If, then, Latin verse was read with normal word-accents, what are we to make of the comments on 'arsis' and 'thesis' which occur in the more detailed treatises on prosody? For instance, Gualtherus' *De Syllabarum et Carminum Ratione* (1573) includes the following passage:

Ἄρσις & θέσις est in pede, qua in initio una aut plures syllabae elevantur, in fine verò una aut plures deprimuntur, ut in Iambo ᵕ— prior brevis attollitur, posterior longa deprimitur: in Dactylo —ᵕᵕ attollitur prima longa, deprimuntur duae posteriores breves: …& sic in reliquis. Unde & hoc notandum est, quòd una syllaba longa licet sit, & binis constet temporibus, pedem efficere non potest: omnis enim pes cum & ἄρσιν & θέσιν habeat, etiam duos (ut Terentianus ait) ictus requirit.[1]　　　　　　　　　(fol. 51)

Fabricius' *De Re Poetica Libri Septem* (1575), also a very detailed study of Latin versification, and, like Gualtherus' manual, used in Britain (the British Museum has William Drummond's copy), contains a similar, and even briefer, definition: 'Arsis & Thesis, quibus attolluntur vel deprimuntur in pedibus syllabae. Arsis…est in initio pedis, unius pluriumve syllabarum elatio. Thesis…est in fine pedis, unius pluriumve syllabarum depressio'[2] (fol. 307). The fact that the subject is so summarily treated, even in works which discuss Latin versification in the minutest detail, and is ignored in briefer studies, suggests that it was yet another piece of the traditional apparatus, inherited from the Romans, and therefore possessing the truth of authority (often a weightier truth than mere observation, we must remember), but probably having no direct connection with the actual reading aloud of Latin verse. The most important point about arsis and thesis (and ictus) for Gualtherus seems to be the corollary about the length of the foot; a theoretical stepping-stone, but probably little more.

It seems certain, then, that the accepted practice in England (and elsewhere) was to read Latin verse with normal word-accents. Was an attempt made in such a reading to bring out the quantitative pattern by pronouncing light syllables quickly

[1] 'Arsis and thesis exist in a foot when at the beginning one or more syllables are raised, whereas at the end one or more are lowered; thus for example in the iambus, ᵕ—, the initial short syllable is lifted up, and the final long syllable is lowered; in the dactyl, —ᵕᵕ, the initial long syllable is lifted up, and the two final short syllables are lowered;…and similarly with the rest. Hence this too is to be observed: a single syllable, though it may be long and consist of two units of time, cannot make a foot; for every foot, since it has both arsis and thesis, also requires (as Terentianus says) two beats.'

[2] 'By virtue of arsis and thesis, syllables in feet are lifted up or lowered. Arsis…is the rising of one or more syllables at the beginning of a foot. Thesis…is the falling of one or more syllables at the end of the foot.'

35

and heavy syllables slowly? The complaints by Beza and other continental scholars, some of whom we shall consider in Chapter 6, that the quantitative pattern cannot be heard in verse suggest that, although they would wish quantities to be made audible, the common practice was to pronounce verse simply as prose (and therefore, of course, to make stressed syllables the only prominent ones); and we have seen that the faults of pronunciation in the grammars do not include incorrect quantities. But all the grammars give the traditional definition of quantity in terms of duration (see Chapter 1 above), and sometimes the notion of 'time' was further defined in terms of speed of utterance. Thus Fabricius (1575) states, 'Tempus, est syllabae...momentum, id est, vel tarditas vel brevitas'[1] (fol. 307v), and Granger defines 'Time' in his *Syntagma Grammaticum* (1616) as 'the holding out of a Syllable in the pronunciation thereof' (sig. C4v). So we might expect an Elizabethan who took these definitions seriously to attempt to put them into practice. Let us take as an example the first line, a hexameter, of Robinson's poem, and imagine him setting out to read this line, keeping his normal word-accents and vowel-qualities, but trying to give 'long' syllables twice as much time as 'short'. To achieve such a reading, he would have to exercise strict control over the duration of vowel-sounds, since most of the intervening consonants do not allow of much variation. The result would be an attempt to impose upon the natural pattern of tense and lax vowels an artificial, and very different, pattern of long and short vowels. I give here the line, marking above it the tenseness of the vowels in the normal pronunciation as shown by Robinson's transcription; above that the quantitative pattern (referring here to the actual duration of vowel-sound, and possibly consonant-sound in some cases, but not necessarily to tenseness) which the reader would have to make audible, and above that, the stresses:

Parva licet, tenuisque licet, mihi magna potestas.

Even with the classical pronunciation the achievement of an

---

[1] 'Time is the motion of syllables, that is, either slowness or shortness.'

actual durational pattern without disturbing the accents is extremely difficult (and, as we saw in Chapter 1, probably not necessary); with the pronunciation of Latin as it was in Elizabethan times it would have been virtually impossible. The problem is not simply one of new pronunciations which have to be learned; it is often one of contradicting firmly-established speech-habits. For instance, both occurrences of the word *licet* in this line would, in a 'durational' reading, require the first syllable (containing a diphthong in Robinson's pronunciation) to be pronounced short, while keeping the stress, and the second long but unstressed. Thus a deliberate effort would have to be made to go against the normal tendency to lengthen a stressed syllable (particularly one with a tense vowel) and to shorten an unstressed one. This kind of difficulty would be constantly recurring in an attempted reading of this sort, so it seems likely that even if some Elizabethans attempted to square their theory with their practice in this way (and we have no evidence that anyone did), they would soon have given up.

The scansion of verse

This examination of the difficulty of a durational pronunciation may seem unnecessary in view of the other evidence we have showing that the normal pronunciation was as prose. However, it is important to consider it carefully, because there can be no doubt that besides the normal method of reading there existed a method of 'scanning aloud', and a durational reading is one of the possibilities. Our plainest evidence is again Brinsley's *Ludus Literarius*; the passage quoted above is not the whole of his account of reading verse. I quote the whole paragraph (which has the marginal note: 'Poetry to bee pronounced as prose, except in scanning'):

So in all Poetry, for the pronuntiation, it is to bee uttered as prose; observing distinctions and the nature of the matter; not to be tuned foolishly or childishly after the manner of scanning a Verse as the use of some is. Onely to tune it so in scanning, or getting it without booke, unlesse you would have them to pronounce some speciall booke, for getting authorities for quantities; or others, onely to that same purpose.   (p. 213)

Brinsley also refers to this mode of verse-reading in an earlier chapter on 'How to make Schollers perfect in the Grammar':

In getting withoute booke, when they can read it perfectly, they may be much helped thus, in all things which they learn in verse; to reade them over in a kinde of singing voice, and after the manner of the running of the verse; oft tuning over one verse untill they can say that, then another; and so forward: which they will doe presently, if the Master do but reade them so before them.

Also, to say these rules at parts sometimes, after the same manner of scanning, or running as a verse, shall make them both more easily kept, and be a good help for right pronunciation of quantities,[1] and to prepare them the more easily to make a verse, for authorities and the like. (p. 73)

What Brinsley is advocating, then, is a manner of reading which makes the metrical pattern perfectly clear, so that when a boy wishes to ascertain the syllable-quantities of a word before him, and the rules for deciding quantities (which we shall discuss later) do not help, he can mentally refer to lines he has learned by heart in this manner in the hope of finding an instance of the word in question. It also seems to be a strongly rhythmical form of reading, since it is easier to learn the lines by heart when read this way. We have seen the difficulties involved in bringing out the quantities by duration without altering the stress, as we know that such a reading is not very rhythmical, at least to ears accustomed to a stress-rhythm, so it seems very likely that what Brinsley is referring to is the reading of Latin verse with stress not where word-accent dictates, but on the ictus. Once this is done, it becomes easy to chant the lines in such a way as to give heavy syllables greater duration than light: all the stresses fall on syllables which the metre demands should be long, so the kind of clash we saw in the first syllable of *licet* would not occur. Moreover, when someone with English speech-habits reads – or chants – a line with regularly occurring stresses he finds it completely natural to adjust the duration of the syllables (something fundamental to English

---

[1] If Brinsley did not state so clearly that verse was to be read as prose, and omit any suggestion that quantities should be made audible, this remark would seem to indicate some kind of 'quantitative' reading. Perhaps he means boys will more easily state the quantity of any syllable when doing the kind of scanning exercise to be discussed in this and the following chapter.

metre – see Abercrombie, 1964), so that he has no difficulty in, for instance, equating two light syllables with one heavy syllable in the unstressed sections of the feet of a hexameter.

Brinsley's scorn of those who 'foolishly or childishly' believe that this is the correct way of reading verse, and not just a method to be used for special purposes, suggests that it was perhaps not an uncommon way of reading. As it succeeds in turning Latin verse into something similar to English verse, this is not surprising, even in a period when English metre tended to be regarded with much less favour; we know that it was a method common in the last century, and perhaps it is still used in some schools today. Bentley provides evidence that early in the eighteenth century the situation was much the same as a hundred years earlier, when, in the introduction to his edition of Terence (1726), he attacks the method of reading with stressed ictus 'ut pueri in Scholis' ('like boys at school') (p. xvii). It also seems likely that the two different ways of reading Latin verse had existed since at least the third century A.D. – a 'scanning' reading would, of course, begin to be a particularly useful aid when the changes in quantity, mentioned in Chapter 2, started to manifest themselves (though it may have existed in classical times as well – see Allen, 1973, Appendix: 'The Latin Hexameter'). Norberg (1965) mentions the evidence for this:

Godefroid de Vinsauf dit par exemple que la syllabe est à accentuer de la même manière dans la poésie et dans la prose et que les règles d'accentuation sont toujours à observer.

Mais, peut-on objecter, pourquoi mettre en garde contre une prononciation artificielle si elle n'existait pas. Un autre grammairien du moyen âge, Aiméric, s'exprime d'une manière plus précise quand il prescrit que le vers soit à réciter *non scandendo sed enuntiando*...Et nous pouvons très bien comprendre qu'à cette époque la scansion des vers est devenue nécessaire dans l'enseignement...Un des grammairiens, Sacerdos, a observé que les accents des pieds se trouvent parfois en désaccord avec les accents des mots. 'Nous devons savoir', dit-il, 'que les accents que nous employons en scandant les vers ne sont pas les mêmes que quand nous prononçons chaque mot'. (pp. 506–7)

So it seems likely that there existed a strong tradition of verse-reading of this kind, though it is improbable that anyone in

Elizabethan England who took a serious interest in metre considered this to be the correct method.[1] Even Daniel, who finds the unrhythmicality of the normal reading of Latin verse unsatisfactory, does not appear to regard a stressed-ictus reading as correct, for he says in the *Defence*, referring to the words in Latin verse, 'Sometimes, unlesse the kind reader out of his owne good nature wil stay them up by their measure, they will fall downe into flatte prose, and sometimes are no other indeede in their naturall sound' (Smith, II, 364). This appears to mean that it is entirely up to the reader to impart rhythmicality if he wishes, presumably by stressing the ictus – a view which, like many of the views expressed in the *Defence*, would no doubt have met with the disapproval of the humanists of an earlier generation.

We may conclude that the best-educated men in England at the end of the sixteenth century would have held that the correct way of reading Latin verse was with prose stresses, but that even they would be accustomed to using the stressed-ictus method for learning by heart or for scanning. Those who did not give much thought to the matter may well have assumed that the stressed-ictus method was correct; but there is no evidence to suggest that such a method had any acceptance among the higher cultural and academic circles as anything but a useful tool for specific purposes.

[1] It is possible that the Scottish tradition of verse-reading differed from the English, just as the pronunciation of Latin differed. Jonson informed Drummond that 'he said to the King his master M. G. Buchanan, had corrupted his [King James's] eare when young & learned him to sing Verses, when he sould have read them' (*Works*, I, 148). (Brinsley, we remember, described the scanning manner of reading as using 'a kinde of singing voice'.) Perhaps this is what Hume is referring to when, in his *Grammatica Nova* of 1612 (an important Scottish grammar), he says, 'Quia vulgus accentum a quantitate non distinguit: de hoc discrimine imprimis videndum. In hoc errore ipse fateor me natum, educatum, & maximam vitae partem vixisse non inficior' ('Schola Grammatica', p. 4). ('Because the common people do not distinguish accent from quantity, particular attention must be paid to this distinction. I confess that I was born and brought up in this error, and do not deny that I have lived the greater part of my life in it.')

4

Latin prosody in the Elizabethan grammar school

It is quite clear that the quantities in the normal Elizabethan pronunciation of Latin were far removed from those of antiquity, and that this normal pronunciation was used in the reading of Latin verse. How, then, are we to account for the Elizabethan admiration of quantitative metre, and its importance in Elizabethan education, when there is no sign that they could have appreciated it as an audible quality of the verse which, to them, manifested it in its most perfect form? The answer to this question is central to an understanding not only of the Elizabethan attitude to Latin metre and its direct expression in the quantitative experiments, but also of the sixteenth-century conception of metre itself.

The teaching of Latin prosody

We must not think of Latin prosody as something with which only a few specialists had any familiarity; studies of Elizabethan education have brought out clearly just how important and how thoroughly instilled it was (see, for instance, Watson, 1908, and Baldwin, 1944). 'Prosodia' was one of the four divisions of grammar in the traditional arrangement, and as such formed part of the book that served as the basis for school education, the authorised Latin grammar, known to generations of school-goers as 'Lily'. More detailed collections of prosodic rules supplemented the general text-book – we know, for instance, that Sidney used Gaultherus' *De Syllabarum et Carminum Ratione* at Shrewsbury School (see Baldwin, ii, 392).

Some indication of how deeply ingrained the rules – and practice – of Latin metre would have been in the mind of an educated Elizabethan can be gained from Brinsley's remarks on the subject in *Ludus Literarius*:

I finde this a most easie and pleasant way to enter them; that for all the first books of Poetry which they learn in the beginning, they use to reade them dayly out of the Grammaticall translations: first resolving every verse into the Grammaticall order, like as it is in the translation: after into the Poeticall, turning it into verse, as the words are in the Poet...A little triall will soone shew you, that very children will doe it as fast almost as into prose: and by the use of it, continually turning prose into verse, they will be in a good way towards the making a Verse, before they have learned any rules thereof.

Then when you would have them to go in hand with making a verse; that they be made very cunning in the rules of versifying, so as to be able to give you readily each rule, and the meaning thereof.

That they be expert in scanning a verse, and in providing every quantity, according to their rules, and so use to practise in their Lectures daily. (p. 192)

To increase the pupils' skill, he advises the teacher to read English translations of Latin verse to them, and have them copy down the English, translate it into grammatical Latin, convert it into Latin verse, and finally read the original Latin, 'that they may see that themselves have made the very same; or wherein they missed' (p. 193). He continues:

After that they have practised this for a little time; if for speedinesse, and for saving paper (because they may soone runne over much) you do use but onely to reade the English Grammatically, and appoint some one of them to deliver it in Latine; then all to trie which of them can soonest turne them into a verse: you shall see them come on apace, and an earnest strife to be wrought amongst them. (p. 193)

He goes on to describe other exercises: varying Latin verses, contracting 'seven or eight verses into foure or five' (p. 194), and versifying *ex tempore* on a theme given by the master, an exercise which they are to be given twice daily, 'or of a sodaine ever before they are to play' (p. 195). Finally, he adds that he holds 'daily practice and diligence (following the best patternes) to be the surest and speediest guide' (p. 197). We must remember, too, that the pronunciation of Latin at the time was such that learning a word did not automatically mean learning its quantities – these had to be drummed in by constant practice in scanning and by learning the immensely detailed rules governing quantities.

Most of the evidence for the conception of Latin metre held at this time comes from teaching manuals like Brinsley's and from the school textbooks themselves, for in England the question was hardly discussed at all in its own right (some continental discussions will be considered later). Though the works of this period on English metre rely heavily on the conception of Latin metre held by their authors, it is partly as an approach to such works that I am investigating this conception, so, to avoid circularity, I shall not use the writings specifically concerned with English as evidence here. We shall see later that such writings are greatly illuminated by the conclusions reached here, thereby providing additional support for the conclusions themselves.

I shall, therefore, attempt to reconstruct the stages through which an Elizabethan schoolboy would have progressed in his training in Latin, examining the ideas about metre that would have been likely to arise as he did so. This study will revolve around the authorised grammar, a book which gradually took shape during the sixteenth century, various sections and revisions being contributed by, among others, Colet, Lily, Erasmus and Wolsey (though for convenience I shall refer to it as if it were by Lily). It reached its final form in about 1540, and remained substantially unchanged until the eighteenth century, its influence on school grammars lasting well into the nineteenth. Its importance in the education of the time stems from the uniformity with which it was used throughout the country, as a result of the proclamation first made by Henry VIII, and repeated by Edward VI and Elizabeth, and printed at the beginning of the book. I am using the 1567 edition as this is available in a modern facsimile, and the date is an appropriate one if we are considering the education of those who were to become the great Elizabethan poets (though later editions brought very few changes). Flynn contributes a useful introduction summarising the history of the grammar; and fuller details are given by Watson (1908, pp. 243–75). I shall also take into consideration the translations and extensions of Lily which might have been used in schools, as well as other handbooks and rival grammars, where these throw added light on the questions under discussion (though for the most part there is great uniformity among the various works). Although the seventeenth century saw an increased questioning of the traditional attitudes to Latin prosody, the same preconceptions remained the basis for the treatment of the subject in the schools, and I have drawn freely on text-books up to the Restoration, especially where these expand or comment upon the traditional rules and definitions.

The age at which most of the schoolboys were taught Latin must be borne in mind: Brinsley recommends seven or eight as the best age for entering the grammar school (by which time the boy had to be able to read and write English – and some schools expected a little Latin as well), and the statutes prescribe ages between six and nine (see Brown, 1933, pp. 44–7). By the age of fifteen or sixteen a boy should be ready for university. The understanding of Latin metre instilled by the grammar schools, then, would have taken root at an age at which concepts are not examined thoroughly, but are likely to take a firm hold, and prove effective in conditioning a lifetime's responses, simply because they are embedded too deeply to be brought out and questioned at a later age. Schools differed greatly in numbers of forms, but the general pattern of work in most was the same and the East Retford curriculum in the mid-sixteenth century, summarised and quoted in part by Stowe (1908), will serve as a typical example:

FIRST FORM

A. B. C.

Inflection of Nouns and Verbs.

Acquisition of small Latin vocabulary.

SECOND FORM

'Usual repetition of the inflection of Nouns and Verbs, which is attained in the first form.'

'A more full explication of the Eight Parts of reason, with the

Syntaxis or Construction.'

'*Colloquia Erasmi*, and some harder Epistles of Tully.'

Translation of English into Latin.

Old and New Testaments.

Salust, Salern, and Justinian's Institutes.

THIRD FORM

'King's Majesty's Latin Grammar.'

'*Virgil, Ovid*, and *Tully's Epistles*.'

'*Copia Erasmi verborum et rerum*, or so many of the said Authors as the said Schoolmaster shall think convenient for the capacity and profit of his Scholars.'

Daily translation of English into Latin.

Constant review of the Eight Parts of Speech.

FOURTH FORM

'The Breves and longs.'

'Verses.'

Latin Epistles.

Greek and Hebrew Grammar, 'if the master were expert in the same.'

Greek authors, so far as the master's 'learning and convenient time will serve thereunto.' (pp. 112–13)

Some idea of the familiarity with Latin, spoken according to the traditional English pronunciation, which the boys were expected to achieve is given by the insistence on the use of Latin at all times, even among the boys themselves. Watson (1908) quotes the following from the Harrow rules for 1580, along with several other similar statutes:

None above the first form shall speak English in the School or when they are together in play, and for that and other faults also, there shall be two monitors appointed, who shall give up their rolls every Friday in the afternoon, and the Schoolmaster shall also appoint privately one other monitor, who shall mark and present the faults of the other two, and other faults which they either negligently omit, or willingly let slip. (pp. 317–18)

'*A Shorte Introduction of Grammar*'

Lily's *Grammar* mirrors the typical school curriculum. It is divided into two parts, and is designed to be worked through from beginning to end, as the schoolboy progresses to higher forms. The first part, *A Shorte Introduction of Grammar* (the title by which the whole work is commonly known), is in English, and the bulk of it is taken up with 'An Introduction of the Eyght Partes of Latine Speache', which would give our schoolboy the basic knowledge he would need to cope with the second part of the grammar, which is in Latin. Only two points in this first part need concern us. One is that on sig. A4, before the 'Introduction' proper, the letters of the Latin alphabet are given, with the traditional definitions of a vowel ('a letter whiche maketh a full and perfect sounde of himselfe'), a consonant ('a letter which needes must be sounded with a vowell'), a syllable ('the pronouncing of one letter or mo, with one breathe'), and a diphthong ('the sound of ii vowels in one Syllable'). However, there is no suggestion that vowels or syllables are of two kinds, long and short; it is obvious that the Latin words that the boy proceeded to learn would be spoken by the master, and repeated by the pupils, using the traditional English pronunciation which I have described, and that notions of vowel-length and quantity have no part to play in this section of the grammar. In fact, the principle of pronunciation with attention to syllable-quantity is explicitly contradicted on this page, with reference to the diphthongs: 'In steede of *ae* & *oe*, we commonly do pronounce E.' This treatment of *ae* and *oe* as if they were simply *e* was a regular feature of the traditional pronunciation, and meant that diphthongs were sometimes pronounced as lax vowels, as in Robinson's *prestat* for *praestat* (Dobson, 1957, p. 27). If we turn to what was probably the most important rival to Lily in Elizabethan times, the Latin grammar by Ramus,[1] we find a much longer section on the pronunciation of the vowels, with detailed descriptions of the manner of articulation (pp. 2–3), but even here there is no mention of long and short vowels, or even different pronunciations of any vowel.

The other point of interest in this part is that conjugations are distinguished as follows:

The Firste conjugation hath *â* longe before *Re* and *Ris*: as *Amâre, amâris*.

[1] Two editions of the same translation, *The Latine Grammar of P. Ramus Translated into English*, appeared in 1585; the original had been available since 1559 in

The Seconde conjugation hath *ê* longe before *Re* and *Ris*: as *Docêre, docêris*.

The Thirde conjugation hath *ĕ* shorte before *Re* and *Ris*: as *Legĕre, legĕris*.

The Fourthe conjugation hath *î* longe before *Re* and *Ris*: as *Audîre, audîris*. (sig. B3)

It seems likely that a child learning this would, without consciously formulating the association to himself, assume from his teacher's pronunciation that 'long' meant 'stressed' and 'short' meant 'unstressed', since this would be the obvious difference between the two kinds of syllable, and he would know of nothing which might contradict this assumption. The marks ∧ and ᴗ would be associated with stressed and unstressed syllables respectively; though he would later learn that the former was primarily an indication of accent and the latter of quantity.

The second section is entitled *Brevissima Institutio seu Ratio Grammatices cognoscendae* and it too has an initial page devoted to the alphabet, this time, however, the Greek alphabet, with a column called 'Pronuntiatio', where the equivalents in Roman letters are given. We might expect that in distinguishing between the two forms of the Greek equivalents of *e*, ε and η, and of *o*, o and ω, the role of duration might be made explicit. However, the equivalents in Latin of these letters are given as 'e tenue' ('thin, weak') and 'e longum vel densum' ('long or thick'); and 'o parvum' ('small') and 'o magnum' ('large') – an almost complete avoidance of the notion of duration, even though syllable-quantity is always referred to later in durational terms.

The main body of the *Grammar* is in four sections: 'Ortographia', 'Etymologia', 'Syntaxis', and 'Prosodia'. The first begins with a section 'De Literis' (sig. A2r–v) which not only repeats the vowel/consonant/diphthong classification, but gives such subdivisions as mutes, semivowels, liquids, and double consonants; there is, however, again no mention of vowel-length. Since the pronunciation of Latin was so close to the

several successive editions – see Ong, *Ramus and Talon Inventory* (1958, pp. 310–30). My references are to the translation published in Cambridge.

pronunciation of English, our schoolboy would have little difficulty in picking it up without the need for any conscious examination of what he was doing; and even the position of the accent, which he would have to learn for each word, was, as we have seen, governed by similar rules to those which governed and continue to govern English, so that he probably learned it from his master's pronunciation without ever having consciously to formulate the concept. In the section headed 'orthoepia' (sig. A3–4) the faults of pronunciation are dealt with in some detail; and we have already seen that the list is in part traditional, and nowhere touches on errors concerned with vowel-length or syllable-quantity. Most of the faults mentioned, in fact, would be faults in any language: the schoolmaster must take care lest 'ad singulas quasque voces longa interspiratione consilescant, ructu, risu, singultu, screatu, vel tussi, sermonis tenorem inepte dirimentes'[1] (sig. A3).

The second major division of the grammar, 'Etymologia', is an expanded version of the *Shorte Introduction*, though it is, of course, in Latin. After a brief introductory passage comes a table of the eight parts of speech, which are then dealt with in turn. The first is the noun, and of interest to us is the subsection on ascertaining the genders of nouns, which comes soon after the beginning of the section, and occupies some nine quarto pages (sigs. A6–B2*v*) (which gives an idea of the tendency of Renaissance grammarians to reduce everything to sets of rules, however complicated – partly owing, no doubt, to the lack of generally available reference books). The rules were written by Lily in hexameters, and are known by their opening phrase, 'Propria quae maribus'. It is difficult to tell what kind of reading these hexameters would have been given; Brinsley's remarks on scanning quoted above (p. 38) suggest that a stressed-ictus reading would have been fairly common for the purpose of learning the rules by heart, but at the same time we must remember that the boys were totally unfamiliar with the metrical structure of the lines, and that to make them learn by

---

[1] 'they should fall silent with a long breath drawn between separate words, foolishly interrupting the flow of their speech by belching, laughing, sobbing, hawking or coughing'.

heart not only the rules but also their rhythmical pattern would have increased the difficulty of the teacher's task, especially if, like Brinsley, he wished it to remain clear that the normal and correct method of reading Latin verse was as prose. In view of the widespread assumption that Latin poetry, even though read as prose, embodied a pattern of quantities which contributed to the beauty and memorability of the words, it is quite possible that Lily assumed that rules in hexameter form, read in the normal manner, were easier to learn than rules in prose. Charles Hoole, in his *New Discovery of the old Art of Teaching Schoole* (1660), makes no explicit distinction between the two methods of reading, so it seems reasonable to suppose that he has the normal method in mind when in the second part of the book (entitled *The Usher's Duty, or A Plat-Forme of Teaching Lilies Grammar*) he advises the learning by heart of lines from Mantuan's *Eclogues*, and continues,

The reason why I desire children (especially those) of more prompt wits, and better memories, may repeat what they read in Poets by heart...is, partly because the memory thrives best by being often exercised...and partly because the roundness of the verses helpeth much to the remembrance of them, wherein boyes at once gain the quantity of syllables, and abundance of matter for phansie.

(p. 67)

In the section on teaching in the higher forms, *The Masters Method*, he recommends that boys should take six to eight lines from Ovid's *De Tristibus*,

which they should first repeat *memoriter* as perfectly as they can possibly, because the very repetition of the verses, and much more the having of them by heart, will imprint a lively pattern of Hexameters and Pentameters in their minds, and furnish them with many good *Authorities*. (p. 157)

And later he advises that

the Master indeed should cause his Scholars to recite a piece of *Ovid* or *Virgil*, in his hearing now and then, that the very tune of these pleasant verses may be imprinted in their mindes, so that when ever they are put to compose a verse, they make it glide as even as those in their Authors. (pp. 187–8)

Though Hoole may be ignoring completely what his contemporaries believed to be the correct manner of reading Latin
verse, and referring throughout to a 'scanning' reading, it is
equally likely that he is assuming that a prose reading has a
'lively pattern' and 'tune' of its own – the one created by the
author; and Lily may well have made the same assumption
about his versified grammar rules. In fact, of course, they made
the task more difficult – something which Robotham pointed
out in 1640:

To disguise the *principall rule* under the veil of poetry, is to teach
them to *dance*, who as yet cannot *goe*; and proves (as painting to
glasse) a means to darken the sense and overcast the clearer light
with a needlesse cloud.   (sig. A6)

We should perhaps, not be too quick to condemn readers of
Latin verse in the sixteenth and seventeenth centuries for
finding a rhythm of some kind in what they read, because, in
spite of their completely unclassical treatment of quantity, they
used the same stresses as the Romans had, and, as I suggested
in Chapter 1, this might have been a more important link than
if they had kept correct quantities and distorted the stress
patterns. Although the rules which bring about the particular
accentual patterns of some of the metres (see above, pp. 14-
15) are not prominent in Renaissance works on Latin verse,
they do sometimes occur; Fabricius, for instance, states in his
discussion of elegiac couplets, 'Versus longus malè definit in
dictionem unius syllabae, aut quatuor syllabarum'[1] (1575,
p. 267), and Farnaby follows a similar comment with the
instruction, 'Pentameter claudatur dictione dissyllabâ'[2](1641,
p. 94). Elizabethan hexameters in Latin and, as we shall see, in
English show an awareness of the importance of coincidence of
stress and ictus in the final two feet; though how conscious the
writers were that they were doing this rather than simply
trusting their ear to tell them when a hexameter sounded like
the ones in Virgil and Ovid is difficult to tell – Sturm, in the
passage quoted above (pp. 32–3), comes closest to formulating
anything precise about the role of stress. It seems certain, at

[1] 'The long line should not end in a word of one syllable, or of four syllables.'
[2] 'The pentameter should end in a disyllabic word.'

any rate, that the vast majority of those who had been through a grammar-school education would have no hesitation in describing Latin verses purely in terms of quantitative patterns, as their text-books did; but that some, through close acquaintance with Latin poetry, would have unconsciously developed an ear for some of the accentual characteristics of the verse-types. Much the same sort of thing can be seen in the history of theories about English metre: it was not until well into the eighteenth century that the accentual basis of English verse was widely recognised (see Fussell, 1954), though poets had been writing and readers responding with unerring ears for centuries.

It is in the course of the 'Propria quae maribus' that the other point of interest in the 'Etymologia' section occurs. One of the special rules runs

> Nomen crescentis, penultima si genitivi
> Syllaba acuta sonat, velut haec pietas pietátis,
> Virtus virtûtis monstrant, genus est muliebre.[1]
>
> (sig. A7v)

This is the first mention of accent, but our schoolboy would probably not have any difficulty with the rule, once the function of the accent-marks as indicators of the stressed syllable was pointed out to him (the practice of using both circumflex and acute marks for this purpose is another of the many features inherited from the Romans, who in turn were following the Greeks – for whom, of course, the distinction had meaning). It would probably seem to him that this was the same kind of distinction as that which he had been taught existed among the conjugations (as indeed it is); and what was there called a 'long' syllable is here called an 'acute' one. (William Haine translates 'acuta' in this passage as 'long' in *Lilies Rules construed*, 1638, sig. A5). The use of the same mark (the circumflex) over the accented syllable as was there used over the long syllable would strengthen his sense of interchangeability of the two terms, especially with reference to the penultimate syllable. The acute accent at this stage would probably be regarded as

---

[1] 'A noun which increases in the genitive is feminine if the penultimate syllable of the genitive is sounded as acute, as illustrated by *pietas/pietatis, virtus/virtutis.*'

51

an alternative to the circumflex, since there would be nothing to distinguish between the two in pronunciation – if, that is, our schoolboy bothered to think that clearly.

He might be more puzzled by a reference to this matter on the following page: one of a list of noun-classes runs, 'In Er, longum, quae Graecis ηρ scribuntur: ut Crater, Character, Stater, Soter. êris.'[1] Not knowing Greek, he would not be helped by the origin of the words, and would probably not attach the 'longum' to any feature of the spoken word, at least in the nominative form (the inclusion of the Greek spelling, where the length of the vowel is indicated graphically, is itself suggestive of the non-auditory nature of the distinction being made). There would be no difficulty, however, in distinguishing between the genitives of, say, *agger* and *crater*, since the first is stressed *ággeris*, and the second *cratéris*; and here our schoolboy might again wonder if there was any difference between an accented penultimate and a long one. The possibility of confusion would be increased by the choice of symbol to indicate an unstressed penultimate: among words ending in *o*, those like 'Lectio, ônis' are distinguished from those like 'Macedo, ŏnis' (sig. A8), and this use of the mark for a short vowel (or syllable), which had been used as such in the account of the conjugations, is consistently used in the rules which follow to indicate an unstressed penultimate. It is, of course, quite correct; but it would hardly be surprising if a boy who had not been introduced to the concept of quantity, nor to the rules for stress-placement, assumed that it referred to the opposite of the feature indicated by the acute and circumflex accent marks.

We now pass over the rest of the 'Etymologia' section, and the whole of the 'Syntaxis' – in other words, to the end of the treatment of grammar proper – to the 'Prosodia' section. By the time he reached this section, our schoolboy would have mastered written and spoken Latin, and would have met nothing, at least in books (and probably not in his master's teaching either, which was unlikely to have been any clearer than the teaching handbooks), to contradict the vague ideas

[1] 'Those ending in long -*er*, which is written in Greek ηρ; such as *crater, character, stater, soter, -eris*.'

about accent and quantity he might have picked up from the statements we have discussed. He would have read and heard Latin verses, but would probably have assumed that he could not properly appreciate their metrical qualities until he had completed the fourth part of the grammar. He could hardly have associated the metre that was said to underlie Latin verse, and with which he was still to grapple, with the obvious rhythm of the English verse he would have come across, or the beat of the ballads he heard sung (and the regular iambic thump of most of the English verse written in the fifteen-sixties and seventies must have made Latin lines, with their lack of immediately apprehensible rhythm, seem particularly alien). He was going to be introduced to something that raised language to a higher pitch of perfection than any device he had so far encountered.

'*Prosodia*': accent

The section begins as follows:

Prosodia, est quae rectam vocum pronuntiationem tradit, Latinè accentus dicitur.

Dividitur autem Prosodia in $\begin{cases} \text{Tonum,} \\ \text{Spiritum,} \\ \text{Tempus.} \end{cases}$

Tonus est lex vel nota, qua syllaba in dictione elevatur, vel dep[r]imitur.

Est autem tonus triplex, $\begin{cases} \text{Acutus,} \\ \text{Gravis,} \\ \text{Circumflexus.} \end{cases}$

Tonus acutus, est virgula obliqua, ascendens in dexteram, sic ╱.

Gravis, est virgula obliqua, descendens in dexteram, ad hunc modum ╲.

Circumflexus, est quiddam ex utrisque conflatum, hac figura ∧.[1]

(sig. G4*v*)

---

[1] 'Prosody is that which teaches the correct pronunciation of words; in Latin it is called *accentus*. Prosody is divided into Tone [i.e. accent], Breathing, and Time [i.e. quantity]. The tone is the rule or mark by which a syllable in a word is raised or lowered. There are three tones, acute, grave, circumflex. The acute tone is an oblique stroke rising to the right, thus ╱. The grave is an oblique stroke falling to the right, in this way ╲. The circumflex is something which combines the other two, and looks like this ∧.'

There are several points of interest here. We may note once more the way in which definitions and classifications originally developed by Greek grammarians, and subsequently adopted, with less validity, by Roman grammarians, are repeated without question. This is the explanation for the subdivision of prosody into 'Tonus', 'Spiritus', and 'Tempus'. 'Spiritus', however, is disposed of in three lines, and 'Tonus' in two pages; while 'Tempus', and its function in verse, is the subject of twelve of the fifteen pages on 'Prosodia'.

Also worthy of notice in this passage is the emphasis on the written rather than the spoken word, in spite of the definition given of 'Prosodia'. This is clear in the distinction made between the acute and circumflex accents, which has no equivalent in the spoken language (it had been an important distinction in Greek, but was applied with no justification by Latin grammarians to their own language – see Allen, 1965, p. 84), and is suggested also by the idea that the accent-mark alters the pronunciation rather than being a visual indication of an aural phenomenon. The present-day linguist's assumption that the written language is merely a representation of, and therefore secondary to, the spoken language would have puzzled an Elizabethan grammarian, not so much because he felt that the reverse was true, but because he did not make any clear distinction. But in matters of Latin grammar, and particularly prosody, he unconsciously tended to think in terms of the written language.[1] When a feature of the language appeared to exist in its written form only, he was concerned, but not unduly so, as appears from the following 'appendix' to the rules governing accents: 'Quia hodie propter hominum imperitiam

---

[1] Ong (1962, pp. 164–76) stresses that it is only recently that the written form has ceased to be regarded as more basic to a language than the spoken form. The assumption held by James Harris in the mid-eighteenth century that 'oral speech is the effect of reading, reading the effect of writing, and writing the effect of grammar', as Ong puts it, can be paralleled 'in a thousand places in the world around him, and not only in the eighteenth century world but all the way back through antiquity as far as we can go' (p. 166). Even when a distinction between the *figura* (the graphic sign) and *potestas* (the sound) of a letter is made, the latter is not seen as existing in its own right, but as a derivative of the former (p. 167). This was, of course, especially true of Latin – see p. 76 below. Foucault (1966) gives an interesting account of the 'privilège absolu de l'écriture' (p. 53) during the Renaissance.

circumflexus ab acuto vix prolatione discernitur, grammatici circumflexum cum acuto confuderunt'[1] (sig. G5). However, this was no excuse for not making our schoolboy learn when a syllable was acute and when circumflex, a distinction which he could make no use of, even in writing. Thus he had to learn, for instance, the rule (derived originally from Greek) that 'in dissyllaba dictione, si prior longa fuerit natura, posterior brevis, prior circumflectitur: ut *Lûna, Mûsa*. In caeteris acuitur: ut *Sítus, Látus, sólers*'[2] (sig. G4*v*).

The ease with which the thoughts of an Elizabethan slipped from the spoken to the written language is strikingly illustrated by the account of the five things which disturb the rules governing accents. These are for the most part concerned with the spoken language, but the first of them is 'differentia':

Differentia, tonum transponit: ut Uná adverbium, ultimam acuit, ne videatur esse nomen. Sic eó, alió, aliquó...& id genus alia... Haec igitur omnia sicut graeca acutisona: in fine quidem sententiarum acuuntur, in consequentia veró gravantur.[3] (sig. G5)

As Gilbert (1939) points out, the function of these 'mock accents', as he calls them, which were used until the eighteenth century, and sometimes later, was 'merely that of distinguishing words identical in spelling, or with identical endings, that might otherwise be confused' (p. 608). Whereas the real accents were never indicated in the written language (except for special illustrative purposes), these accents were regularly given, though they had no counterpart in spoken Latin. To us it seems obvious that the same word is being used with quite different meanings, but there is no sense of this in the sixteenth- and seventeenth-

---

[1] 'Because nowadays, as a result of men's ignorance, the circumflex is scarcely distinguished from the acute by prolongation, grammarians have confused the circumflex and the acute.'

[2] 'in a disyllabic word, if the first syllable is long by nature and the second short, the first syllable has a circumflex, as in *lûna, Mûsa*. In all other cases it is acute, as in *sítus, látus, sólers*.'

[3] 'Differentiation causes the tone to shift: thus *uná* as an adverb has the last syllable acute, to show that it is not a noun. Similarly with *eó, alió, aliquó*...and other such words...So all these words have acute accents as in Greek: that is, they have an acute at the end of a sentence, but a grave when they come within one.' Some Latin grammarians claimed that such 'differentiative' accents existed in Latin – see Allen, 1965, p. 87, n. 2.

century grammars. Though he continued to stress the first syllable of *una* when used adverbially, our schoolboy learned that the second syllable received an acute accent at the end of a sentence, or otherwise a grave accent, and so he wrote it. The point I wish to emphasise, however, is that he may even have thought of it as something which occurred in his speech as well (we are still conditioned in our thinking about the spoken language by its written form – thus, for instance, we tend to associate very different sounds simply because they are represented by the same letter).[1] Barnabas Hampton's translation of Lily in his *Prosodia Construed*, which first appeared in 1639, seems to suggest that he thought so (I omit without indication the Latin original which is interspersed among the words of the translation):

An adverb makes the last syllable acute (or lifts it up) that it may not seem to be a noun...Therefore all these...are sounded acute (or are lifted up) in the end of sentences, but among words following (them) they are (sounded or) made grave tones (or pressed down).

(sig. A3*v*)

Even the Ramist grammar, usually more aware of the aural realities of the language than the traditional grammar, seems to regard these accents as equally evident in written and spoken Latin. Thus Ramus, in the words of his translator, says that accent is 'likewise a note to distinguish: as in *uná*, *verò*, and in other doubtfull wordes, in pronouncing and writing whereof this shalbe the distinction' (p. 12). Hoole, however, thinks of accent almost entirely in graphic terms, in spite of his use of the word 'speech':

There are three *Tones, a Grave*, which is seldome or never made, but in the last syllable of such words as ought to have had an Acute in the last syllable, & that in the contexture of words in this manner; *Nè si forte sopor nos occupet. an Acute*, which is often used to difference some words from others, as uná, together, seduló, diligently, remain

---

[1] The story of the developing skill of the orthoepists in the sixteenth and seventeenth centuries is partly a story of the increasing ability to distinguish between written and spoken forms of the language. For example, Dobson says of Bullokar, 'He has only the rudest notion of the study of sounds apart from symbols; thus he draws a distinction between the sounds of *c* and *s* when they are both pronounced [s] which is based on the difference of the names of the letters' (1968, i, 101).

acuted at the end of a Speech, and in continuation of speech have their acute accents turned into a Grave to make them differ from una, one, and sedulo, diligent. *A Circumflex* which is often marked to denote a lost syllable, as amârunt, for amaverunt.

(1660, pp. 74–5)

But Hoole himself, although his treatment of the accent avoids some of the confusions of the earlier grammarians, like them makes no clear distinction between the two modes of the language: he would probably have tended to think of words as having an existence independent of their appearance in print or speech, and of the accent as residing in the word itself. It is important to grasp this attitude to spoken and written accents if we are to appreciate the Elizabethan idea of quantity, which relies on a similar failure to make distinctions where they seem obvious to us.

Before considering this question, however, it will be useful to devote a little more attention to the vocal qualities ascribed by the grammarians to accents. The theory inherited by the Elizabethans was a simple one: that accent was simply a matter of pitch, as the word 'tone' suggests. But the different words used to describe the accents and their operation indicates a certain amount of understandable confusion surrounding the concept. Perhaps the most common are the words used in the passage from Lily quoted above (p. 53): 'Tonus est lex vel nota, qua syllaba in dictione elevatur, vel deprimitur.' Lily goes into no further detail, except about the accent-marks themselves, but the description of the circumflex suggests that the sound mirrors the symbol, both being combinations of the other two accents. Granger, in his *Syntagma Grammaticum* (1616), sticks closely to the musical definition: 'Tone, is the tuninge, or accenting of a Syllable...The sharpe is accented with a rising voyce...The flat is accented with a falling voice' (sig. C7*v*). Hampton translates Lily literally in talking of syllables 'lifted up' and 'pressed down' (sig. A2); and the translator of Ramus' grammar uses similar terms, while betraying further uncertainty about the terms 'sharp' and 'flat' (the latter being a translation of 'hebes' – see Ramus, 1584, p. 13):

An *accent* is that, wherby the word is as it were tuned: and there is but one *accent* in a word, although there be many syllables: & it is *sharpe, or flat.* By the *sharpe accent* a syllable is lifted up. The *flat accent* is either *grave* or *bended*: by the *grave accent* the syllable is depressed: by the *bended* it is both lifted up and also depressed.

(1585, p. 11)

This confusion, which was carried over into discussions of accentual English metre, is understandable if one considers the difficulties which faced someone trying to explain, to himself or to others, the nature of accents. He had the traditional definition safeguarded by the authority of the ancients, and could not contradict it. Yet if he thought about it, his usage did contradict it; he did not speak in a series of tones like a singer, and even if he was persuaded that he did, he certainly did not use three clearly defined accents. He could ignore the actual practice of his time, regarding it as a sad decline from the pronunciation of the ancients, and expound the theory alone, or he could try to effect some sort of compromise. Erasmus (1528) does the former, giving a purely musical account, and even trying to distinguish between acute and circumflex in terms of pitch: for instance, the difference between *vídi* and *vîdit* is explained as being equivalent to the difference between the musical sequences *fa re* and *fa mi* (p. 127). Ramus seems to have recognised not only that the acute/circumflex distinction no longer existed, but also that the definition in terms of pitch was not appropriate to the usage of his time: the statement from the translation of his grammar quoted above is followed by: 'The *sharpe accent* onely hath beene of long tyme used, or rather a certaine *pause* for every accent, which *pause* maye be called an *accent*' (p. 11). Another Ramistic work, Charles Butler's *Rhetoricae Libri Duo* (based on the *Rhetorica* of Talaeus, in which Ramus had a large hand) has a chapter in the 1629 edition entitled 'De Tono, Sono, & Prosodia', which makes an unusually clear distinction between pitch ('ut in notis Musicis') and loudness ('unde faciliùs vel difficiliùs audiatur')[1] (sig. O1*v*), and lays the foundations for a more accurate description of accent than had

---

[1] 'as in the notes of music...by which it is heard with greater ease or greater difficulty'.

hitherto been produced. However, he seems to see accent as a third variable in speech: 'Prosodia (seu Accentus) est quâ aliqua Dictionis syllaba prae caeteris accinitur. Accentus, qui Graecis triplex est...Latinis unicus est, Acutus'[1] (sig. O1*v*). Nor is the note on the first sentence of this definition any clearer: 'clariùs, & apertiùs, cum majori mora, effertur'[2] (sig. O2). Nevertheless, the passage shows a sharpness of perception usually lacking from discussion of Latin pronunciation at this time,[3] as does his note on the statement that Latin has only one accent:

Gravis enim nihil aliud est, quàm Acuti absentia seu privatio. Notatur quidem alicubi, sed in alium usum: ad Pronunciationem nihil confert. Circumflexus etiam notatur; & in duplicem usum: sed in voce, vel, tanquam gravis, nullam habet vim, ut in *Musâ*; vel eam quam Acutus, ut in *gustâram*. Neque enim *Musâ* ablat. secus effertur, quàm *Musa* nominat. quia omnia disyllaba prioremacuunt; neque *a* in *gustâram*, aliter quàm in *gustare*; cum utrobique penultima longa similiter acuenda sit.[4]   (sig. O2*r–v*)

The recognition of the purely graphic function of the circumflex is highly unusual, as is the clear identification of acute with stressed and grave with unstressed: in the grammars the grave accent is usually seen, like the other two, as a specific accent for specific purposes. What is most important for us is the uncommonness of Butler's clarity of mind on these matters (though the passage is a useful reassurance that the statements of the traditional grammarians do reflect a failure to distinguish between written and spoken accents, and not a pronunciation of Latin otherwise unrecorded). Neither the first version of the

---

[1] 'Prosody (or accent) is that by which one or other syllable of a word is made to stand out from the others by its enunciation. Accent, which in Greek is of three kinds, is of only one kind in Latin, the Acute.'

[2] 'pronounced more clearly and more openly, with a longer pause'.

[3] Butler's account of the position of the Latin accent also shows a clearer understanding of the difference between the accent-mark and the speech stress; for instance, one of the things that 'disturb the accent' in Butler's account, but not Lily's, is one of the few occasions where the natural word-accent *is* shifted to a different syllable, namely, when similar words are contrasted, as in Butler's example, 'non *emissus*...sed *immissus*' (1629, sig. 02).

[4] 'For the grave is no more than the absence or the removal of the acute. It is indeed written in some places, but for a different purpose; it makes no contribution to the pronunciation. The circumflex is also written, and for two purposes;

book, published in 1597 under the title *Rameae Rhetoricae Libri Duo* (no copy of a possible edition of 1593 survives), nor the earlier editions of it under the new title (1600, 1618) contain this section (for a brief account of the book's history and importance see W. S. Howell, 1956, pp. 262–3). Its presence in the 1629 edition is probably a reflection of the growing awareness, partly due to the influence of Ramus, of the inadequacy of the old account, and must have been instrumental in fostering this awareness, since the book was a widely-read school text, and was recommended by both Brinsley and Hoole, and by John Bird, in his *Grounds of Grammer Penned and Published* (1639) (though Bird's own account of accent is on traditional lines). Butler was by no means a traditional grammarian, concerned with accepted theories; he wrote an important grammar of English (1634), and advocated an improved orthography, which he used in another work, his *Principles of Musik* (1636). Those whose concern was more with the physical realities of language, like Butler, broke free from the bonds of tradition much sooner than the grammarians; as Dobson's work on pronunciation (1968) shows, Robinson's *Art of Pronuntiation* is merely one of a series of examinations of language, and the English language in particular, which compensate for the unoriginality of the English grammarians. Robinson shows a sharp awareness of the difference between pitch and stress (though his treatment of the latter is less accurate than it might have been, owing to the influence of the grammarians: having identified it with the grammarians' 'tone', he tries to find three degrees of it to correspond to the three accents – see Dobson, 1957, pp. 25–6). However, the influence of such works as Robinson's on the Elizabethan understanding of phenomena like accent would have been very much less than that of the standard grammars.

Those who did not bother with the theory of accents, like our

but either, like the grave, it has no effect on the sound, as in *musâ*; or it has the same effect as the acute, as in *gustâram*. For *musâ* in the ablative is pronounced no differently from *musa* in the nominative, since all disyllables receive an acute accent on the first syllable; nor is the *a* in *gustâram* pronounced differently from that in *gustare*, since in both places the penultimate is long and must receive an acute accent in the same way.'

schoolboy, probably did not have too much trouble with them. As far as the actual pronunciation of Latin was concerned, he had been learning and using words with the correct accent long before he reached the theory; and as far as written Latin was concerned, the rules for placement of the accent-marks could be learned quite quickly, and must have been already familiar to him from the texts he had read. The only point where the two kinds of accent met was in the rules for the ascribing of an acute or a circumflex to the stressed syllable, and these had very little practical bearing, and were probably not studied much. John Danes, in his preface to *A Light to Lilie* (1637), gives as his reason for not considering the accent rules that 'they are of small, if any use to children' (sig. A8*v*).

'*Prosodia*': *quantity*

In going through the accent-placement rules for the first time, schoolboys could hardly have had a very clear understanding of them, since not only do they bring up the concept of long and short syllables again, but they include the first mention of the two ways in which a syllable can be long, by nature or by position. However, the section on quantity soon follows, and is the one to which most attention would have been devoted. It begins with a reiteration of the threefold division of 'Prosodia', and gives the traditional definitions:

Hactenus de Tonis & Spiritibus, deinceps de syllabarum tempore & carminis ratione pauca adiiciemus.
    Tempus, est syllabae pronuntiandae mensura.
    Syllaba brevis, unius est temporis, Longa verò duorum.
    Tempus breve sic notatur, ᵛ. *vel sic*, ᵛ. Longum autem sic. —, *vel sic* ^: ut, –ᵛ, Terra.[1]   (sig. G5*v*–6)

If we turn to the other grammars and handbooks that a schoolboy (or his teacher) might have looked at, we find great consistency, early and late, in these definitions – there is none of the variation and groping for the correct word as there is with

---

[1] 'Thus far we have discussed tones and breathing; next we shall add a little about the times of syllables and the nature of verse. Time is the length of the syllable to be pronounced. A short syllable contains one time, and a long syllable two. A short time is indicated thus: ᵛ or ᵛ; a long time thus: — or ^; as in —ᵛ, *terra*.'

regard to accent: '*A short syllable* is that, which doth consist of one time...*A long syllable* is that which doth consist of two times' (*The Latine Grammar of P. Ramus*, 1585, p. 9); 'Time, is the holding out of a Syllable in the pronunciation thereof' (Granger, 1616, sig. C4*v*); '*Time* or *Quantitie* is the measure of pronouncing a Syllable, or the space of tuning a Vowel, whereby wee measure how long it is in pronouncing' and a syllable is '*Short*, which hath one time, or which is quickly pronounced' (Hoole, *The Latine Grammar Fitted for the Use of Schools*, 1651, p. 276).

As in the case of accent, then, we have a definition, inherited from the ancients, which does not fit the language as pronounced by the Elizabethans. But unlike accent, there would be nothing in the Latin he spoke with which our schoolboy could identify quantity. In a way, this made matters simpler, since there was nothing like the clash between theoretical and actual accents; once he was told about quantity, and told that it existed in the language, he could simply accept that it was there in his speech. All the grammar-books agreed on its nature, and none of them suggested that quantity had been lost in spoken Latin, whereas even Lily admitted that there was some confusion in the use of accents. But when he came to learn which syllables were long and which short, our schoolboy would have found himself faced with a much greater task than in the case of accent, because, although quantity was said to be in the Latin he spoke, it was not there in the same way as accent was, immediately accessible in such a way that if he pronounced a word with the wrong accent, it could be heard as wrong. Some who thought about it perhaps decided that quantity was not a property of pronunciation, but something in the word at a deeper level; or perhaps felt that the rules were arbitrary, having been decided upon by the Latin poets purely for the purpose of writing poetry; but such questions would have been unusual, for the grammars, though they nowhere ask for any effort to be made to bring out the quantities in pronunciation, firmly describe quantity in terms of pronunciation (much as they describe accent – even purely graphic accents – in similar terms). We can only assume that our schoolboy would accept that quantity existed in Latin, without asking whether it was in the written or in the spoken language, or why he could not hear it if it was so clearly defined as the time taken for syllables to be pronounced.

If the teacher followed Lily closely, he would go through the two sections 'De Carminum Ratione' and 'De Generibus Carminum' before reaching the rules of quantity. In this case, our schoolboy would find himself learning definitions like 'Est autem Pes, duarum syllabarum pluriúmve constitutio ex certa temporum observatione' and 'Est enim carmen oratio iusto atque legitimo pedum numero constricta'[1] (sig. G6) before he had any idea of what makes a syllable long or short. He would learn the twelve types of foot, what scansion was ('legitima carminis in singulos pedes commensuratio',[2] sig. G6), and the five 'accidentia' of scansion (the last of which is 'Caesura', of which he would learn the five types),[3] and would then move on to learning the quantitative patterns of six kinds of verse. The mechanical nature of the whole procedure must have contributed something to his idea of metre; it would have seemed primarily a question of rules, a highly abstract and intellectual game of arranging counters in predetermined patterns. Bird's English definitions keep the flavour of Lily's and show clearly the Elizabethan attraction to what is ordered

---

[1] 'A foot is composed of two or more syllables according to a fixed rule of times.' 'For a verse is an utterance held together by an appropriate and rule-governed number of feet.'

[2] 'the measuring of a verse into individual feet according to rule.'

[3] The most common definition of caesura in Latin grammars published in England is not the modern one, but refers specifically to the occasional lengthening of a short syllable when it ends a word but begins a foot. Bird's definition is a translation of Lily's: 'Caesura, is when afte[r] an absolute foot, a short syllable in the end of a word is made long' (1639, p. 184). The same definition occurs as late as 1826, in Edwards' Eton Latin Grammar, though with the following note: 'The definition of Caesura, here given, is certainly very vague, and incorrect. Caesura signifies "a cutting off", and is the name applied to any final syllable that remains after a perfect foot in poetry – without reference to the quantity of the syllable so remaining' (p. 200, n. 7). That Edwards, in spite of his strictures, feels it necessary to repeat the traditional definition is an interesting example of the force of Lily's authority, for the more correct definition had long been used in other countries. Fabricius, for example, in De Re Poetica (1575), defines it as 'apta & conveniens pedum divulsio, & vocis interspiratio' (fol. 306v) ('an appropriate and harmonious dividing of feet and drawing of breath in utterance'). G. J. Vossius' definition in his Grammatica Latina (1644–5) is similar to Edwards':

and lawful, rather than to what is individualistic or expressive, in art:

> A Foot is the setting together of two syllables or more, according to the observation of the quantity thereof...Feete being placed together in a just number and order doe make a Verse. A Verse is a speech made of a just and lawfull number of feet.... Scanning is the lawfull measuring of a Verse, into his severall feete.
>
> (1639, p. 181)

Finally, the seal is set upon the conception of verse as abstract and mechanical by the final section of the grammar: the rules for ascertaining syllable-quantity, which we shall find taking up much of the discussion of quantitative verse in English.

In Lily, this section is divided into three: 'De Quantitate Primarum syllabarum', 'De Mediis Syllabis', and 'De Ultimis Syllabis'. The first division (sigs. G7*v*–H1) gives eight rules for ascertaining the quantity of initial syllables, the first of these (and the most important in all treatments of the subject) being the rule of 'position'. It is the usual statement about the lengthening of a syllable when followed by two consonants, in the same or different words, and with the usual exception of a combination of a 'mute' plus a liquid. The other rules are 'vowel before vowel' (the first of two successive vowels being short), 'diphthong' (always long), 'derivation' (a derivative has the same quantities as the word from which it is derived), 'preposition' (common prepositions are listed with their quantities), one simply called 'Regula' (which consists of two rules governing the quantity of initial syllables in preterites and supines), and 'authority'. The last is the closest approach made to the modern method of learning quantity at the same time as the words (though of course there is no sense that one's *pronunciation* of a word would indicate its quantities): 'Quarum verò syllabarum quantitas sub praedictas rationes non cadit, à

'Caesura est, cum post pedem superest syllaba, quae finit dictionem' (p. 308) ('Caesura occurs when, after the end of a foot, a syllable remains, which completes the word'), though he indicates the origin of Lily's definition in going on to state, 'Ob caesuram saepe syllaba naturâ brevis producitur' (p. 310) ('Because of the caesura a syllable short by nature is often lengthened'). We shall see that these different definitions are reflected in differences in the practice of the quantitative poets, though the interpretation of caesura as a pause is the most common one.

poëtarum usu, exemplo atque autoritate petenda est, certissima omnium regula'[1] (sig. H1). The section on middle syllables (sig. H1*r–v*) is the shortest; it refers back to the rules for initial syllables, to the section on nouns that increase in the genitive in the 'Etymologia' section (see above, p. 51), and to the description of the conjugations in the *Shorte Introduction* (see above, p. 46). The only rules it contains concern the regular endings of some verbs and adjectives, and it also ends with an appeal to the usage of poets. The most detailed rules occur in the final section (sig. H1*v*–3*v*), where the inflected nature of Latin makes quantities most predictable. Final syllables which are of common occurrence in Latin are dealt with one by one, and the section occupies nearly four pages.

Other grammars and handbooks differ in arrangement and exhaustiveness, but not at all in the general approach to quantity. Bird sets out the rules as clearly as he can, beginning,

If thou desirest to know whether a Syllable be Long or Short, thou must consider what Syllable of the Foote it is. If thou desirest to know the reason why it is long or short, thou must observe what Syllable of the word it is. In which regard, a Syllable is said to be three fold, First, Middle, Last, and every syllable is said to be middle save the first and the last. Concerning which there are Generall rules, lesse generall, and particular. (pp. 171–2)

The general rules are those that apply to all syllables, the less general those that apply to the first and middle syllables only; and the particular apply to only one type of syllable. Bird's account of 'Authority' gives a vivid impression of how important it was:

Authority, being the testimony and warrant of the most approved Poets, which is the most profitable and surest way of all: for in words above two Syllables whenas the quantity of the last syllable save one, is known neither by the increase of the noune, nor by the analogy of the conjugation, nor the quantity of other middle syllables by derivation and composition, nor any other way, we presently fly unto authority, as our last, surest, and safest refuge. (p. 175)

---

[1] 'As regards syllables whose quantity does not fall under the above rules, their quantity is to be ascertained from the usage, example, and authority of the poets, the most reliable rule of all.'

The frequent claim in the writings on English quantitative metres that it was the prerogative of the first poets to decide on the quantities of the words they used, and the duty of later poets to follow them, is clearly linked to this attitude towards 'authorities' – though Bird seems to imply that quantities have a real existence of some kind, but that the 'most approved Poets' were much better judges of it than he and his contemporaries. The translation of Ramus' grammar shows the simplifying tendency of the Ramist method in its account of quantity, though the arrangement would probably be less useful to a schoolboy than those in Lily and Bird: it deals with short syllables, syllables long by nature, and syllables long by position each in turn, summarising the circumstances in which each occurs. For a much more detailed account of the ways of ascertaining quantities, boys could turn to handbooks like Gualtherus' *De Syllabarum et Carminum Ratione* (1573) or Henricus Smetius' *Prosodia...Promtissima* (1614). The former was, as I have mentioned, used by Sidney, and was basically a more detailed version of the 'Prosodia' section of the grammar; the latter was recommended by Brinsley and Bird, and was an extensive list of Latin words whose quantities are not obvious from the basic rules, with examples of occurrences in verse to serve as authorities. As an introduction it contains Fabricius' 'Methodus cognoscendarum syllabarum', which is another expansion of the usual rules.

The most important point to emerge is that quantity was not felt as something immediately apprehensible in the pronunciation of the word, and which could therefore be learned when the word was learned, but as a complex system which could be applied to words, in order to construct verses according to a further system of rules. Admittedly the theory of quantity, in so far as the grammars contained any theory, was different, and, if pressed, a schoolboy would no doubt have described quantity as a feature of pronunciation; but at the level of unformulated attitudes, the way in which the notion of quantity was learned, and the fact that it bore little relation to spoken Latin, could have had no other effect than that of making it seem something abstract and intellectual. The boy was not asked to read verse with correct quantities; he was asked to apply the rules he had learned by marking its syllables. Hoole describes the practice of scansion:

1. Let them write a verse out, and divide it into its just feet, giving a dash or stroke betwixt every one; and let them tell you what feet they are, and of what syllables they consist; and why they stand in such or such a place...
2. Let them set the mark of the Time or Quantity over every syllable in every foot, and give you the reason (according to the Rules) why it is there noted long, or short.   (1660, pp. 76–7)

Of course, this mechanical attitude to scansion, with its emphasis on the written, not the spoken, language, did not end in the seventeenth century; Ellis (1874) remembers the state of Latin pronunciation and verse-reading at Shrewsbury and Eton in the years 1826–33:

If the accent were placed right...the speaker was held to have made no 'false quantities'; and if in his verses he followed the laws of his 'gradus' which were at utter variance with the custom of his speech, he was also held to have made no 'false quantities'. That he did not pronounce a single vowel correctly by intention, that he did not understand the nature of long and short vowels or syllables, or the rhythm that they made in verse,...of this he had no conception whatever.   (p. viii)

But after the sixteenth century, such a misunderstanding would be confined to the field of classical verse; what is important about such ideas in Elizabethan times is that they were likely to colour the thoughts of those who were beginning to consider English poetry as deserving the same kind of attention as that of the ancients.

Robotham in 1640 is ahead of his time in his attitude to the learning of quantity, as he is in his criticism of grammar rules written in verse, though he somewhat naïvely supposes that an English child would find it easier to learn Latin with a classical pronunciation than in accordance with English speech-habits. He sees clearly that if quantity were really something inherent in the pronunciation of Latin, the mere knowledge of a word would mean a knowledge of its quantities:

To begin with our very *spelling* and teaching to read, what checks and chidings (if not blowes and strokes) must a child endure, to make him mis-pronounce? what accurate diligence is used, to wean him from the true, ancient, *genuine* sound (which were *soonest attainable*) and enure him to a new, barbarous, *gothish* pronunciation, which yet is far *more intricate* and difficult? for, not to speak of the confusion of *vowels*, whose quantity (long or short) every cobler might better discerne *once* by the bare uttering of the word, then we can *now* with all our rules of *prosody*...   (sig. A5*r–v*)

But Robotham went unheeded; in 1816 we find J. P. Smith in his *Manual of Latin Grammar* recommending, with very few exceptions, that one should 'pronounce all Latin words according to the powers of the letters in English' (p. 1), and Edwards is conscious of doing something new in writing a grammar in 1826 in which syllable-quantities are marked 'to the end that, boys learning Latin, might, from their very entrance upon that language, become familiar with Accentuation, and Quantity' (p. v).

That theory and practice in matters of accent and quantity should have been so inconsistent, and yet so little questioned, is not surprising in an age when authority and analogy were important ways of discovering truth, and induction and experimental method relatively unregarded. An interesting parallel can be found in the history of music, where, as Hollander has described in *The Untuning of the Sky* (1961), 'speculative' and 'practical' music grew further and further apart, until the former, the conglomerated inheritance of musical theory from classical and medieval times, became trivialised in the seventeenth century. Latin grammar clung to its theory longer, though the greater attention to the audible features of the language in the seventeenth century brought about some changes, and encouraged the rise of grammars of English which sometimes escaped being merely versions of Lily.

5

Vowel-length, quantity and accent

Vowel-length and quantity

I should like to consider in more detail two aspects of the Elizabethan conception of quantity which will be of particular importance in the discussion of the quantitative experiments: the relationship between vowel-length and quantity,[1] and the relationship between quantity and accent. We have seen how all the discussions of the vowels themselves omit the concept of vowel-length, so important in modern grammars, and whatever the schoolboy may have observed about the way vowels differed in pronunciation, their division into long and short was not part of the theory he had to learn. The most obvious reason for this is that the disparity between the theory and the actual pronunciation of the vowels would probably have been too great, even for an Elizabethan schoolboy. But there is perhaps another reason why even at a theoretical level the idea of two varieties of sound represented by a single letter was hard to accept: the difficulty, already discussed, which the Elizabethans had in making a distinction between the written and the spoken symbol. Whereas it is easy to accept long and short equivalents if these are represented by different symbols, as occurs to a certain extent in Greek, a single symbol could not, for the Elizabethans, really represent two different things – simply because it was not a symbol to them, but an entity in itself.[2] This is connected with the common Renaissance view

---

[1] By 'vowel-length' I mean, of course, the traditional classification of the vowels of Latin words into long and short (i.e. tense and lax in the classical pronunciation), which, as we have seen, bore little relation to the actual tenseness of the vowels in the Elizabethan pronunciation.

[2] For a good account of the Renaissance tendency to regard letters, syllables, and

of the 'power of the letter' (see Sledd, 1946) – that each letter manifests itself naturally in pronunciation as a single sound. Only a few moved from this theory to question a pronunciation which did not bear it out; most people accepted both the theory and the pronunciation without examination, with the result that the ability to make clear distinctions between different sounds represented by the same letter was curtailed, and the English pronunciation of Latin was accepted more easily.[1] Robotham (1640) saw more clearly than most just how varied the pronunciations of a single letter were, but his attack reveals the same assumptions about the single nature, ideally at least, of the sound and its symbol: 'None, I think, would plead for the continuance of this corruption, but some Jesuiticall patron of *equivocation*: for a letter *double-toned* is like a man *double-tongued*, a *deceiver*' (sig. A5*v*).

Like most of the conceptions we are discussing, this idea of the singleness of the Latin vowel would not have been a conscious doctrine for many, and there are numerous examples of the same kind of confusion between vowel-length and syllable-quantity that occurs, as we saw in Chapter 1, in the ancient grammarians; for instance, Lily gives the rule of position as 'Vocalis ante duas consonantes, aut duplicam in eadum dictione, ubique positura longa est'[2] (sig. G7*v*), and most statements of the rule imply in a similar way that it is the *vowel* that is lengthened, the most explicit being William Wyatt's 'If a vowell come before two consonants...it is long by position: as, [*e*] in *sentis*' (*A new and easie Institution of Grammar*, 1647, p. 99).

words as things with intrinsic properties, see Foucault (1966), especially the section entitled 'L'Écriture des choses' (pp. 49–57).

[1] With the increasing importance attached to experiment and observation in the seventeenth century, the gap between written and spoken English (and Latin) began to have a different effect; as Abercrombie says, 'A new, speculative, approach to the problems of pronunciation was forced on us because of the inadequacy of the traditional approach, derived from the classical grammarians, in the face of these discrepancies' (1948, p. 18). See also Abercrombie (1949) for an interesting study of the use of the word 'letter' to refer to the sound, the name, and the character, from the sixteenth until the nineteenth century (though a clear distinction among these three would have been rare in the sixteenth century).

[2] 'A vowel before two consonants, or before a double consonant in the same word, is everywhere long by position.'

Confusion between the two notions might also have been encouraged by the marking of syllable-quantity above the vowel; and Hoole seems to make no distinction between the two in his definition of quantity, in which he talks of 'the measure of pronouncing a Syllable, or the space of tuning a Vowel' (1651, p. 276). It would be wrong to assume that most people made a conscious distinction between vowel-length and quantity of syllables – the evidence we have suggests that any thinking on the matter was imprecise, and that Hoole's sense of the interchangeability of the two terms would have been widespread, precisely because there was no phonetic feature with which quantity could be identified, either in the vowel or in the syllable. However, it is more commonly described as a property of the syllable than of the vowel, and it would probably have been in these terms that our schoolboy would have tended to think as he worked through the rules governing initial, middle and final *syllables*. The Ramist grammar reveals a clearer awareness than most of the contradiction implicit in the usual definition of length by position, and states '*A long syllable by position* is when two consonants doe followe the vowel of a syllable in the same word' (p. 10). Smetius' *Prosodia* deals only with syllable-quantity; and Thomas Thomas' *Dictionarium Linguae Latinae et Anglicanae* (1587) marks the quantity of syllables only where this is not obvious from the most common rules – in other words, vowels in syllables long by position are not marked, and hence, as in the grammars, there is no conception of the possibility of 'hidden quantity' (that is, of a long vowel in a syllable long by position). This omission reflects both the tendency to think in terms of the syllable rather than the vowel, and the unimportance of such a distinction to the Elizabethans; it is not so much that they would have assumed that all vowels in syllables long by position were long, according to the literal wording of Lily's rule, but that if one knew that the syllable was long, one had no further interest in the vowel (one's pronunciation, of course, at no point entered into consideration). And if anyone thought in terms of the *vowel* being long by position, he did not need to take the additional step and say, 'therefore the syllable is long' – quantity was a single feature, and no purpose could be served by applying it twice in the same syllable.

If they did talk about a vowel as being long or short (as they had to, for instance, in giving the 'mute plus liquid' rule, since only a short vowel can be made common), it was usually with the implication that it had been made so by authority, derivation, or some other rule. Whereas for modern readers of Latin verse the primary rule in ascertaining quantities is that a syllable containing a long vowel is long, for the Elizabethans the primary rule was that of position. The modern rule occurs nowhere, and would not have made sense to an Elizabethan if it had: he would want to know by what rule you ascertained the vowel to be long, and would not understand why you then thought it necessary to make a further rule about the quantity of the syllable. If our schoolboy were asked to scan and prove a verse, as he was continually being asked to do (see Hoole's description, above, p. 67), and gave as the reason for the quantity of a particular syllable that it contained a short or a long vowel, he would not be deemed to have said anything at all. Even less acceptable, of course, would be to reply that the syllable contained a vowel which could be *heard* to be long (that is, a tense vowel) – the use of such criteria would have made the whole art of Latin prosody impossible. It should be clear now why a modern reader who sets out to scan a line of Elizabethan quantitative verse in English usually concludes that the writer had only a confused notion of what he was doing, where an Elizabethan reader, setting about the task in a different manner, would have been quite satisfied that the Latin metre had been accurately imitated.

Quantity and accent

The other point to which I wish to give some special attention has already been touched on in describing the earlier parts of the grammar. We have seen how our schoolboy, when he was learning to distinguish between the conjugations, and again when he was learning how to ascertain the gender of nouns, might have been led into identifying quantity with stress. Is there any possibility that he might have continued to make this identification, especially as there was nothing else in his speech which corresponded in any way to quantity?

To examine this question, we need to look at one of the most useful ways of ascertaining quantity, which nevertheless does not occur in its complete form among Lily's rules. This is the position of the accent in words of three or more syllables: to ascertain the quantity of the penultimate syllable of such a word one simply needs to know if it is stressed (and hence long) or unstressed (and hence short). In theory, of course, the schoolboy could only ascertain the position of the accent if he knew the quantity of the penultimate, and this is perhaps why the rule does not occur in Lily; but he would actually have known the accent placement of a large number of words before he even reached the stage of learning about quantity. In books more expressly concerned with the practicalities of scansion, the rule has a place. Thus we find the following in Clajus' *Prosodiae...libri tres* (1576):

Quomodo cognoscitur quantitas syllabarum ex accentu?

Si accentus est in penultima, longam illam esse necesse est: Et contrà: Si accentus est in antepenultima, sequitur penultimam brevem esse.[1] (p. 11)

It also occurs as one of the two rules pertaining to middle syllables in Fabricius' 'Methodus cognoscendarum syllabarum' (included in Smetius' *Prosodia*, 1614, sig. ¶¶ 8*v*), and is clearly stated by G. J. Vossius in his grammar (1644–5, p. 294) and by Butler in his rhetoric (1629, sig. H3). In some treatments of quantity, this rule is given only with reference to nouns which increase in the genitive, and it is in this form that it occurs in Lily. He is somewhat vague about it: 'De incrementis genitivi nominum polysyllabarum, supra in generibus nominum abundè dictum arbitramur'[2] (sig. H1); but Hoole (1651) spells it out:

The last syllable save one of Nouns increasing
  1. *Sharp*, is long.
  2. *Flat*, is short. (p. 286)

---

[1] 'How is the quantity of syllables ascertained from their accent? If the accent is on the penultimate syllable, that syllable must be long, and, conversely, if the accent is on the antepenultimate, it follows that the penultimate is short.'

[2] 'With regard to the increases of polysyllabic nouns in the genitive, we think that quite enough has been said in discussing the types of noun.'

73

What is interesting about the occurrence of the rule in its various forms is that it may have given rise to a confusion in some minds between stress and quantity – since a penultimate is either short and unstressed or long and stressed. In *The Rules of the Latin Grammar Construed* (1657), Edmund Reeve, in dealing with the same point, does not make a clear distinction; he writes of 'nouns which sharpen (or make long) the last syllable saving one of the genitive increasing' and those which 'contrariwise doe make flat (or shorten) the penult' (pp. 14, 17). Hoole (1651) in discussing the position of the accent talks of 'short' and 'long' when he really means unstressed and stressed: 'Those syllables which are common are pronounced short in Prose, i.e. where a mute and a liquid do follow a short vowel, as Célebris, Cáthedra; otherwise they are pronounced long, as, Uníus, illíus, ubíque' (p. 275). And in his *Vocabularium Parvum Anglo-Latinum* (1666), Hoole makes the pronunciation of words clear when necessary either by marking a stressed syllable with an acute, or marking an unstressed penultimate as short. Morley, in his *Plaine and Easie Introduction To Practicall Musicke* (1597), writes (in a passage derived from Zarlino, 1558, p. 340) of 'long' and 'short' syllables (p. 178), but as his examples all concern the penultimate syllable of Latin words, he is probably referring to stress – something which plays a much more important role in the setting of words than quantity.

It is obvious that when thinking of the properties of the penultimate, most people did not make a clear distinction between stress and quantity (and in Chapter 10 we shall see how important this was in the discussions of quantitative verse in English). However, they would probably have had no difficulty in keeping separate the functions of quantity as the determiner of accent, and as the medium of verse. In the former case, 'long' and 'short' meant 'stressed' and 'unstressed', and were more convenient terms than those which clustered in confusion around the notion of accent; in the latter, quantity was something quite different. The two touched in the rule of quantity by penultimate accent, but only touched. As usual, we must not expect this distinction to have been consciously formulated.

74

We must remember that there is evidence to suggest that some schoolmasters encouraged stressed-ictus readings of verse to imprint the quantities, and a boy could understandably think that what he was doing was bringing out the quantities more forcefully than in normal verse-reading. We might expect, then, that to some people the closest approximation to a Latin hexameter in English would have been an accentual hexameter, in which syllables in ictus position are replaced by stressed syllables, and others by unstressed syllables; and that even those who realised the incorrectness of this view (no doubt the majority of those with a serious interest) may at times have failed to distinguish between quantity and accent especially with regard to penultimate syllables. We shall find in examining the quantitative experiments that this was so.

In general, however, although quantity was in theory an attribute of the sound of syllables, and was occasionally identified with a particular feature of sound, it had in practice very little to do with the audible characteristics of Latin. Though this made it in effect a purely conventional attribute, it must not be supposed that this was how it was viewed; to the Elizabethans, even if the assignment of quantity was in part the work of the first poets, it was something actually present in the language – though this did not automatically mean present in the spoken manifestation of the language. Willcock (1934) gives a partial explanation of how it was possible for the Elizabethans to ignore the phonetic characteristics of syllables in ascertaining – and responding aesthetically to – quantitative patterns:

It seems strange that the intelligent should have found it difficult to think of the quantitative differentiation of vowels as a natural, that is physical, feature of language to be accepted as we accept long days in summer and short in winter. But Nature-in-itself was still too alien a concept for the humanist. Everything existed either for a purpose or by tradition, and language, as the basis of literature, could not in any of its aspects be thought of apart from purposive or arbitrary human agency. (pp. 9–10)

This perhaps exaggerates the awareness of how arbitrary the quantitative distinctions were – it would be possible for an

Elizabethan to feel that quantity was, because of the weight of the tradition, more important and, in a sense, more real than a mere physical property – but it does illuminate one aspect of the intellectual setting which we have to reconstruct. We must remember that an Elizabethan would seldom have thought of the pronunciation of a passage of Latin in complete isolation from its written representation (to use a word which expresses our conception of the role of the written language, not theirs). Unlike English, which they had learned mainly as a spoken language, and the uncertain orthography of which would have made it difficult to think of in primarily written terms, Latin was a language which obeyed fixed rules of spelling and grammar (and hence a much more perfect language than English), and which they had started to learn by studying the letters, lower case and upper case, so that from the beginning it was something they saw as well as heard. And the knowledge of the written form could not have been far from the consciousness of someone speaking or hearing Latin: *ae* would be sensed as a diphthong, and as different from *oe* and *e*, though in speech they were all identical; the nominative and the ablative of the first declension were different because the final letter of the latter had a circumflex accent, though the voice made no distinction.[1] This, I think, helps us to understand how our Elizabethan schoolboy, at the end of his school training, could read a line of Latin verse, and respond to the metre. It was an intellectual apprehension, not an aural one; if he knew his rules and his authorities well enough, he could ascertain as he read the line that it was made up of the correct pattern of longs and shorts, and that, unlike a piece of prose, it was a highly skilled execution of a challenging task, the shaping of the unordered particles of language into an intricate and carefully proportioned artefact. He may well have thought that even if he did not consciously scan the line as he read it, the quantitative pattern ensured a certain harmoniousness of sound, and he

---

[1] Ong (1962) gives a good account of the inseparability of the written and spoken embodiments of Latin during the period when it was no longer in family use, but still widely spoken, emphasising that it was only through its written form that it served as a common language for the countries of Europe, and that 'there was no-one who could speak it who could not also write it' (pp. 208–9).

certainly would not have described his response in the way I
have done; but if there was anything in the sound of the verse
which played a part, it would in fact have been the few regu-
larities of stress – which would not have entered his theory at
all. He probably accepted in good faith that others with acuter
senses or finer minds than his had worked out which syllables
were long and which short, and what kinds of pattern were the
most challenging and the most satisfying; and perhaps he
believed, though he probably never tried to test the belief, that
the long syllables were really twice the length of the short ones.
But his prosodical training led him far away from any conception of metre as a rhythmic succession of sounds, akin to the
beat of the ballad-monger or the thumping of a drum, into a
world pervaded by a sense of subtle intelligence and high
civilisation, where words are anatomised and charted with a
precision and a certainty unknown in the crude vernacular.

6

Continental discussions of
Latin quantity

The understanding of quantitative metre I have been outlining
has had to be very largely deduced from school grammars
because the problems involved were not discussed by any
English writer; to most readers of Latin verse, of course, they
did not even constitute problems. However, several continental
scholars recognised and attempted to deal with the contradictions inherent in the views about quantity that were current in
Europe, and a few of these will be worth considering briefly,
both because they furnish direct evidence of the presence on the
continent of attitudes similar to those we have found by indirect
means in England, and because they were the obvious sources
of information for an English poet who wished to study the
theory of quantity in more detail in order to write quantitative
verse in English (and we shall see that one of the most influential of the experimenters, Sidney, was almost certainly familiar
with some of these discussions). They also provide abundant
evidence of a continental tradition of reading Latin verse with
normal prose stresses.

In his dialogue *De Recta Latini Graecique sermonis pronuntiatione*
(1528), Erasmus illustrates the correct pronunciation of Latin
by discussing the reading of some lines of verse. He quotes, for
instance, the following lines from Virgil's *Georgics*, marking the
accents and some of the vocalic quantities:

Óptimă quaêque díēs míserīs mŏrtálibus áevi
Prîma fŭgit, sŭbeūnt mŏrboi, trîstísque sĕnéctūs,
Et lábor, & dírae rápit inclēméntia mórtis.

(p. 185)

In the discussion of the pronunciation of these lines which follows, it becomes quite clear that there is no thought at all of
reading them with anything other than the normal word
stresses indicated by the accent marks. Erasmus also insists that
vowel-quantities be observed, even when the syllable is long by
position; thus the *o* in *mortalibus* is to be pronounced short
though the syllable is long (p. 187) – something our Elizabethan
schoolboy would have found difficult to understand. He com-
plains in another passage, as many scholarly writers were to do,
that in the reading of Latin verse by his contemporaries, the
only prominent syllables are the stressed ones, quantity being
completely obscured. The mispronunciation is slighter in Latin
than in Greek, he states,

sed tamen illic quoque tonus acutus ac inflexus obscurat caeterarum
sonum, ut in vidébimus, congruit accentus cum quantitate, at in
legebámus, sola penultima videtur esse producta, quum secunda sit
aeque longa: in amavérimus sola antepenultima, quum ea sit brevis,
secunda producta.[1]   (p. 115)

As we have seen, his solution is to appeal to the notion of 'tonus'
as enshrined in the Roman grammarians: accent is a matter of
pitch, and should be distinguished from quantity, which is a
matter of duration. So he continues:

In amāvérimus, sonantior esse deberet ma secunda, quàm a, prima, ut
in ama sit iambus, verimus tribrachus, nisi quod prima trium acuitur,
& ob hoc sonantior, quasi musicus per brevem longam & tres breves
sonet, re re fa re re, ămāvérĭmŭs. In hac dictione sonantiores
sunt secunda, quia producta, & proxima tono acuto, licet brevis.[2]

---

[1] 'but there too the acute and circumflex tones make other sounds indistinct; thus
in *vidébimus* accent coincides with quantity, but in *legebámus* only the penultimate
seems to be lengthened, when the second syllable is equally long, and in *amavérimus* only the antepenultimate seems long, when it is short, and the second
syllable is long.'

[2] 'In *amāvérimus*, the second syllable, *ma*, ought to be more sounding than the
first, *a*, so that there is an iambus in *ama*, and a tribrach in *verimus*, except that
the first of the three syllables has an acute accent, and because of this is more
sounding, just as a musician might sing a short, a long, and three shorts on the
notes *re re fa re re*, thus *ămāvérĭmŭs*. In this word the most sounding syllables are
the second, because it is long, and the following one, with an acute tone, even
though it is short.'

Erasmus marvels at the way in which, according to Cicero, the Roman populace was said to have reacted violently towards an actor who pronounced a syllable with the wrong quantity, and he bemoans the lack of any audible correlate of quantity in the reading of his day, for 'frequenter accentus ducit in errorem, dum facit videri longam quae brevis est, & contrà'[1] (pp. 110–11). Ramus was also struck by Cicero's remarks, and when in 1564 he published the first two books of his *Scholae Grammaticae* (1559) separately, with revisions, as *De Veris Sonis Literarum & syllabarum*, he added the following comments at the end of the second book (the passage was retained when the *Scholae Grammaticae* appeared as part of the monumental *Scholae in Liberales Artes* in 1569 – see cols. 65–6):

Sed quae de syllaba longa & brevi differuntur, ea feré sunt intelligentiae & mentis, non prolationis & linguae. A Romanis enim quantitas cuiusvis syllabae proferebatur. Varro de lingua cum docet pluit & luit praesenti & praeterito differre. In praeteritis (ait) u dicimus longum plūit, lūit: in praesenti breve, lŭit, plŭit. Ideoque in venditionis lege fundi ruta caesa ita dicimus, ut u producamus. Haec Varro. At istam differentiam vox nostra nullam facit. Quin Grammatici pluit & luit praeterita, quia vocalis est ante vocalem, prima corripiant: in quo tamen errare eos, non Varronem falsum scripsisse indico. Nero (ait Suetonius) Claudium morari inter homines desiisse, producta prima syllaba iocabatur. at ut nunc pronuntiamus, nihil iste iocus percipitur: cúm morari á moror, & morari ἀπὸ τοῦ μωράινειν deliré & fatué agendo, simili modo proferamus. Histrio (ait in paradoxis Cicero) si paulo se movit extra numerum, aut si versus pronunciatus est syllaba brevior aut longior, exibilatur & exploditur. Itaque rudis olim & imperita plebs longas & breves sentiebat & sonabat, quas nemo, vel eruditissimus, hodie sentit aut enuntiat.[2]   (fol. 53*v*)

---

[1] 'often the accent leads to error, by making a short syllable seem long and vice versa.'

[2] 'Distinctions made according to the length or shortness of a syllable belong generally to the sphere of the understanding and the mind, not that of enunciation and speech. For the quantity of every syllable was brought out in pronunciation by the Romans. When Varro, in *De Lingua*, states that *pluit* and *luit* as present tenses differ from *pluit* and *luit* as past, he says, "In the past tense we pronounce the *u* long, thus *plūit*, *lūit*; in the present tense we pronounce it short, thus *lŭit*, *plŭit*. Similarly, in a contract relating to the sale of an estate we say *ruta caesa* [minerals and timber] in such a way as to lengthen the *u*." So says Varro. But our mode of pronunciation does not make this distinction. Now

His view of quantity in his time as something of the mind rather than of the audible reality of the language is one of the most perceptive remarks on the subject that we find in the writings of the time, or indeed of much later times. Quantity and quantitative patterns must have been just this for countless readers of Latin verse, who perhaps thought they were responding to something they could hear, but who, given the pronunciation of the language, could only have been responding to something they *assumed* to be there, from the rules they had learned.

Ramus (1559) repeats the analysis of quantity handed down from the ancient grammarians (see Chapter 1 above):

Longae syllabae genera duo sunt, alterum natura, alterum positione: In longis natura vel positione...duo sunt tempora, ut dos, ars, duo & semis, quando post vocalem natura longam una sequitur consonans, ut sol, tria, quando post vocalem natura longam, duae consonantes sequuntur, vel una duplex, ut mons, rex: Tamen in metro necesse est unamquamque syllabam vel unius vel duorum accipi temporum.[1]   (p. 89)

As we have seen, this theory is far from satisfactory, but it does

indeed grammarians shorten the initial syllable of *pluit* and *luit* in the past tense, because it is a vowel before a vowel; but in that I maintain they are mistaken, not that Varro has written an untruth. Nero, says Suetonius, used to jest that Claudius had ceased to linger [*mŏrari*] among men, with a long initial syllable [*mōrari*, to be a fool]. But in our present pronunciation, this joke would never be understood, for we utter *morari* from *moror*, and *morari* from the Greek verb to behave foolishly and idiotically, in the same sort of way. Cicero says in the *Paradoxa* that an actor used to be hissed and clapped off the stage if he strayed a little from the metre, or if he pronounced a line with one syllable too few or too many. So there was a time when the coarse and uneducated populace recognised and pronounced long and short syllables, which nowadays not even the most learned recognise or enunciate.' Ramus appears to take the statement about the actor as referring to the length or shortness of an individual syllable, in which he may be following Erasmus, who actually misquotes the passage at this point as 'syllaba breviore aut longiore' to make it mean this (see Cicero, *Paradoxa Stoicorum*, III, 26).

[1] 'There are two kinds of long syllable, one long by nature and the other by position. In long syllables, whether by nature or by position...there are two times, as in *dos, ars*; or two-and-a-half, when a syllable long by nature is followed by a single consonant, as in *sol*; or three, when a syllable long by nature is followed by two consonants or by one double consonant, as in *mons, rex*. However, in metre it is necessary that every syllable should be taken as being of one or two times.'

go further in attempting to understand quantity than most schoolboys and their teachers would have done. It enforces a clear distinction between vowel-length and syllable-quantity, and emphasises the difference between a long vowel and a short vowel, even in cases of hidden quantity. Justus Lipsius, in *De Recta Pronunciatione Latinae Linguae* (1586), sees the disappearance of these distinctions as part of the misunderstanding and mispronunciation of Latin by his contemporaries:

Cùm enim Vocales omnes ancipites sint Latinis (de quantitate loquor) & modò longae eae, modò breves: curae inprimis habuerunt prisci, ut sono ipso distinguerent quantae illae in quâque dictione. Ex ipso inquam enunciatu colligebas, A, an I, longum in *Palus*, in *Sinus* dicerem: O, an U, in *Populus* in *Uter*: & *Legimus*, praeterito tempore efferrem an praesenti. Decorè, imò utiliter. nam hodiè quae confusio & turbela? Omnium pariter idem sonus, brevium longarumq́ue. adeóque Vocalem unam non discernimus, ut nec eam à Bivocali. Itaque iure ambiguitatibus scatet & sordet hic noster sermo, prae antiquo.[1]   (p.22)

Once the distinctions are made as clearly as this, the existence of hidden quantity becomes manifest, and Lipsius gives an account of it in a later chapter:

Agellius, inquis, verbum *Quiescit, perpetuâ linguae Latinae consuetudine ĕ littera correptâ pronunciatum* adfirmat. *Quiesco* igitur dixêre. Lipsi erras. Non enim haec doctissimi viri mens, & de litterâ se loqui non de sillabâ clamat clarè. ergo nec de Tenore, cui in sillabâ sedes. Quid igitur vult? an potest E littera illîc corripi, quam duae consonantes excipiunt? Non potest, fateor. sed ad meam illam Elementarem pronunciationem referenda istaec. quâ docui E litterae duplicem sonum; Tenuem sive Brevem, Pinguem sive Longum. Hoc igitur tunc quaesitum *Quiesco* E subtili & brevi, ut *Here* diceretur: an longâ, ut

[1] 'Since all vowels in Latin are common (as regards quantity, I mean), the same vowel sometimes long, sometimes short, the ancients took particular pains to make clear by the sound itself what quantity there was in any word. That is, you would infer from the pronunciation alone whether I was saying a long *a* or *i* in *palus* and *sinus*, or a long *o* or *u* in *populus* and *uter*, and whether I was uttering *legimus* in the past tense or the present. A pretty, and indeed a useful, practice! After all, what disorder and confusion nowadays! Everything sounds the same, long and short alike. So far are we from making the distinction where a single vowel is concerned, that we do not even distinguish a single vowel from a diphthong. So it is only just that this speech of ours swarms with and is degraded by ambiguities compared with its ancient form.'

Nescio, Calesco. Et abit illuc, ut in usu pronunciatum breviter velit, etsi longiter *Quies.*[1] (pp. 107–8)

Even though Lipsius is in error about the length of the *e* in *quiesco* and *nescio*, the incisive clarity of his discussion is worlds away from the vagueness of the Elizabethan grammars.

Another continental scholar, this time an Italian, who remarked on the distortion of Latin verse through mispronunciation was J. C. Scaliger, in his *Poetices libri septem* (1561), pp. 207–8. Scaliger interprets literally the standard theory of quantity and accent – the former as duration, the latter as pitch – and he illustrates it by a musical notation of the first line of the *Aeneid* (giving, incidentally, no indication of ictus or of arsis and thesis). The view that accent is a matter of pitch is also presented by Francesco Patrizio in his *Sostentamenti del Nuovo Verso Eroico* (1557), an extract from which is given by Carducci (1881, pp. 441–50). He illustrates the three accents by notating the opening line of the *Aeneid* as follows:

$$\text{Arma vir\'umque cano Tr\'oiae qui primus ab \'oris,}$$

and explaining that the syllables with a mark above them are read in a high-pitched voice, those with a mark beneath them in a voice of middle pitch, and the others in a bass voice (pp. 449–50.) Again, he clearly expects Latin verse to be read with accents in their normal places.

Someone who goes into the whole problem more thoroughly is Theodorus Beza (Théodore de Bèze), the Calvinist scholar and poet, whose treatise on the pronunciation of Greek was added to the *Alphabetum Graecum* published in 1554, and was included, under the title *De Germana Pronuntiatione Graecae*

---

[1] 'Well, you say, Agellius asserts that the word *quiescit* was pronounced according to the general usage of the Latin language with the letter *e* shortened. Therefore, they said *quiesco*. But you are mistaken, Lipsius. For this was not that learned man's meaning; he makes it clear that he is talking of the letter, not the syllable. So he is not concerned with the accent, which is situated in the syllable. What then does he mean? Can the letter *e* be shortened, when two consonants follow it? It is impossible, I agree. We must go back to my treatment of the pronunciation of letters. There I stated that the letter *e* has two sounds, thin or short, and thick or long. The question was then raised, whether *quiesco* was pronounced with a fine, short *e*, as in *here*, or a long one, as in *nescio, calesco*. And the conclusion was, that by usage it should be pronounced short, though it is long in *quies*.'

Linguae, in the collection of essays on Greek and Latin pronunciation published by Henricus Stephanus (Henri Estienne) in 1587, from which I quote. Beza's main concern was, of course, the pronunciation of Greek, but he was also very dissatisfied with the usual way of reading Latin verse:

Sic ergo pueri in ludis literariis hodie docentur pronuntiare, aut potius ineptissimè cantare,

– ⏑ ⏑– – ⏑ – ⏑⏑ ⏑ ⏑ ⏑ –
Arma virumque cano Troiae qui primus ab oris

⏑–⏑⏑ – ⏑ – ⏑ ⏑ ⏑ –⏑ ⏑ –
Italiam fato profugus, Lavinaque venit

Hac autem ineptissima pronuntiatione quis non sentiat gravissimos horum versuum numeros ita frangi, ut, si duos ultimos pedes excipias, versus videri non possint? Contrà verò, si ita ut par est pronuntiaris,

⏑ ⏑ ⏑ – ⏑ ⏑ – – – ⏑⏑ – ⏑ ⏑ –
arma virumque cano Troiae qui primus ab oris

– ⏑⏑– – – ⏑ ⏑ – – – ⏑ ⏑– ⏑
Italiam fato profugus Lavinaque venit[1]

si hoc, inquam, modo pronuntiaris, servata syllabarum quantitate, etiam ut versus non digeras in pedes, quis tamen ἄρσιν & θέσιν non audiat, & suavissima horum versuum, gravitate non capiatur? ... Iam verò in Iambicis versibus, praesertim Latinis, quis Iambum ullum percipiat? cuius tamen pedis repetitione tota eorum versuum venustas constat. Solent enim paedagogi vulgò ita suos erudire, ut in omnibus disyllabis penultimam producant. itaque sic recitant hunc Catulli versum,

⏑ – – – ⏑–⏑ – – – –
Quis hoc potest videre, quis potest pati?

Ego verò putidam istam pronuntiationem miror quenquam esse posse qui possit audire, qui possit pati.[2]   (pp. 51–2)

---

[1] Here Beza actually quotes the initial lines of the *Iliad* as well, with the same diacritics for both, illustrating his point about their near identity. This accounts for the incorrect dactyl in the fourth foot of the first line, though the mark giving the initial syllable of the line as short must be a misprint. The spacing of the words in the original is also rather erratic, but Beza's intention is clear.

[2] 'So children in grammar schools these days are taught to speak verse (or rather to utter it in a silly sing-song) as follows:...Now who would not feel that this silly way of speaking so destroys the stately metre of these lines that, apart from the last two feet, they might well not seem to be verse at all? On the other hand, if you speak them in the proper way,...if, I say, you speak them in this way, observing the quantity of the syllables even if you do not divide the lines into feet, who could fail to hear the arsis and thesis, and to be captivated by the most sweet solemnity of these lines?...Again, in iambic lines, especially in Latin, who could pick out any iambus by ear? Yet it is in the repetition of this foot that all the beauty of these verses consists. The reason is that teachers are generally

Though it is difficult to be certain what kind of reading Beza is recommending, it is clear that he objects to a tradition of reading verse with normal stresses which entirely masks the metrical pattern.[1]

An Elizabethan writer who turned to continental authorities on Latin would obviously find a recognition of how unsatisfactory the sixteenth-century pronunciations of Latin were for the reading of verse, and an awareness of the fact that quantitative verse ought to be based on audible features of the language. He might come across a passage which spelled out clearly the relationship between the length of vowels and the length of syllables which his school grammar had failed to describe and which his pronunciation completely obscured, and he might acquire a fuller understanding of the traditional theory of durational quantity and pitch accent. Most of the discussions he would be likely to encounter would confirm his view that Latin verse and Latin prose should be read in the same way. But the problems posed by quantitative metre would by no means be solved for him – we have seen that some of them remain unsolved today – and the ideas implanted at school, though some of them would be shown up for the misunderstandings they were, would probably continue to influence his appreciation of Latin verse and his approach to Latin metre. We shall find that both the grammar-school misapprehension and the scholarly theories played a part in the attempt to create in English an equivalent of the metres of Latin poetry.

in the habit of teaching their pupils to lengthen the penultimate syllables in all disyllables. So they recite this line of Catullus thus:...For my part, I find it remarkable that there could be anyone who could listen to, and could endure, that disgusting mode of recitation.'

[1] Kabell (1960) discusses and quotes from a manuscript of late sixteenth-century Spanish origin which gives hundreds of examples of Latin hexameters and pentameters with their accent markings, all of which show normal prose accentuation (pp. 36–7).

PART TWO

English verse and classical metre

7

Attitudes towards accentual verse

'A playne and simple manner of wryting'

Let us imagine an educated Englishman in the 1560s or 1570s who, as a result of his grammar-school training in Latin, holds attitudes towards metre of the kind I have described turning his attention towards English poetry of his time. One difference would be immediately apparent to him: lines of English verse had no metre, as he understood it; there was no complex pattern of syllables of different types, and hence no intellectual pleasure to be gained from observing how the pattern was kept and the rules obeyed, and no resulting sense of admiration for the skilful poet who, following the extensive and detailed precepts established by tradition and authority, had made from the loose and disordered flux of words a carefully constructed artefact. In short, there was no art of English poetry. And if he had learned his lessons thoroughly, he might go on to say to himself that, lacking metre, it of necessity lacked sweetness and harmony, and he might persuade himself that it actually sounded harsh and discordant. Nor should we be too quick to assume that such a judgement would merely be the conclusion of a theoretical argument: he might well *feel*, as he read Gascoigne after Virgil, that the words were clumsily and unsystematically heaped up one after the other, and this felt disorder would probably be expressed in terms of the *sound* of the verse, since the beauties of metrical arrangement were nearly always expressed in these terms, however visual or intellectual the response really was. We have seen how quantity was always defined in terms of the sound of syllables, though in fact it bore no relation to it; and quantitative patterns were thought of as manipulations of the sounds of words to make harmonious lines. But English poets took no account of quantity: how could their verses be harmonious?

To be sure, their poetry was slightly more ordered than prose. English poets at least observed the principle of number: they counted the total number of syllables in every line, and kept it constant. But number without proportion, lines without divisions and subdivisions in an ordered system, were not enough to make a poem metrical – and the hexameter showed that a constant number of syllables was not even a prerequisite. Towards the end of the 1560s George Puttenham wrote part of his *Arte of English Poesie*,[1] in which he tried to show that English poetry, though 'we have no such feete or times or stirres in our meeters, by whose *simpathie*, or pleasant conveniencie with th'eare, we could take any delight' (Smith, II, 72), was nevertheless an art. In Book II, 'Of Proportion Poetical', he discussed the five types of proportion that do exist in English verse: the number of lines in the stanza, the number of syllables in the line, the rhymes, the spacing and patterning of the rhymes, and the use of lines of different length to make visual shapes. The amount of detail he goes into makes it dreary reading, and may seem unnecessary, but it was, in fact, crucial to his argument that 'there may be an art of our English poesie, aswell as there is of the Latine and Greeke', since art is, as Puttenham defines it, 'but a certaine order of rules prescribed by reason, and gathered by experience' (Smith, II, 5). The rules had to be shown to be detailed and extensive, allowing simultaneously for great variety and rigorous order, and our imaginary Englishman, less committed to the cause of vernacular verse, might well have felt that Puttenham's rules failed to match those of Latin and Greek prosody. He would not, in fact, have had an opportunity to read Puttenham's arguments until 1589, when the book was published with some modifications, including the addition of several chapters to Book II, which reveal that he is not as unusual in his attitudes to metre as might have appeared in the 1560s, for he puts forward

---

[1] On the dating of Puttenham's *Arte*, see the introduction by Willcock and Walker to their edition, pp. xliv–liii.

a system whereby 'the use of the Greeke and Latine feete might be brought into our vulgar poesie', so as to 'make in our meetres a more pleasant numerositie then now is' (Smith, II, 117).

Unlike Puttenham, our Elizabethan might find that the rules governing English verse were too simple: counting the number of syllables in a line neither offered a challenge to the poet's skill, nor gave satisfaction to the learned reader. He might, it is true, be aware that there is more to the construction of a line of traditional verse than a certain number of syllables; if he had ever tried writing poetry in English he would have found that some combinations of words sounded right, and others not; but obvious as it may seem to us, there is no reason to assume that he would have realised that his sense of rightness or wrongness depended on the alternation of stressed and unstressed syllables. As we have seen, the notion of 'accent' in Latin was a complicated and confused one, combining purely visual with purely aural features, and its transposition to English would not have been a simple matter. Furthermore, even if he did realise the importance of stress in English verse, whatever name he gave to it, he would find its function in the line very different from that of quantity in the Latin line. He might, for instance, read Gascoigne's pioneering and perceptive work on English metre, *Certayne Notes of Instruction*, published in 1575 (Smith, I, 46–57), and find that it only confirmed him in his feeling that English verse had no metre. Gascoigne understands the role of stress, which he identifies with the Latin accents, though the way he does this testifies to the wholly unobvious nature of the parallel: he identifies English stress with the Latin *grave* accent, probably because a stressed syllable seemed 'heavy', though this is just the opposite of the Latin practice. But to the man who regarded Latin metre as the ideal, Gascoigne's description of the basis of English verse as residing in alternating accents would merely show up its poverty. For one thing, English accents, because they could not be accounted for by a set of rules, must have seemed arbitrary and unreliable, with nothing like the immutable status of quantity in Latin; for another, the lack of variety in metrical patterns would have contrasted unfavourably

with Latin richness. Gascoigne himself feels the second limitation strongly: 'Now a dayes in English rimes (for I dare not cal
them English verses) we use none other order but a foote of two
sillables', he says, and a little further on he elaborates on this:

> And surely I can lament that wee are fallen into suche a playne and
> simple manner of wryting, that there is none other foote used but one;
> wherby our Poemes may justly be called Rithmes, and cannot by
> any right challenge the name of a Verse.   (Smith, 1, 50)

Our Elizabethan might even find the rhythmic beat of English
verse (especially the monotonous regularity that prevailed in
the third quarter of the century) itself crude and distasteful, so
different from the sound of Latin verse, with its accentual irregularity, leavened only occasionally by bursts of rhythmicality.

What might he find advanced as a compensating glory of
English verse by a man like Puttenham? Something not only
avoided in all Latin and Greek verse, but actually dispraised by
classical authorities: rhyme. Moreover, both rhyme and accentual regularity were features of Medieval Latin verse, which a
true humanist could only regard as yet another example of the
corruption of the glories of Rome by the barbarians; and if it
was the humanist's task to cast out of the Latin language all the
medieval impurities, it was surely also his task to get rid of
rhyming accentual verse in whatever language it appeared. His
feelings about English poetry would involve feelings about the
English language; next to Latin it would seem crude and dis-
organised, without rules, without constant orthography, and
(most important as far as verse was concerned) without any
agreed division of syllables into long and short. He might well
decide that before true verse could be written, the language
itself would have to be reformed. In general, then, we would
expect him to conclude that English poetry was in a sorry state;
that what went for verse was a mere putting together of words
with a rhyme at the end which anyone could accomplish; that
the pleasure to be got from it was small compared to the delight
which Latin poetry inspired; and, if with many others he
wished to see the English language and English poetry reach
the heights of Greek and Latin, that a concerted effort was
necessary to improve the situation.

Roger Ascham: the humanist response

These attitudes are, of course, what we find repeatedly in the writings of those who concerned themselves with English verse. At the head of these writers stands Roger Ascham, whose comments on English verse in *The Scholemaster* (published posthumously in 1570) were to be echoed several times before the end of the century, comments which are worth quoting at some length as typical of the humanist's attitude to vernacular verse that we have been discussing. In the second book he mentions the metrical imperfections of Plautus and Terence, and quotes Horace to the effect that not they, but the Greeks, should serve as models for iambic verse. He continues:

This matter maketh me gladly remember my sweete tyme spent at Cambrige, and the pleasant talke which I had oft with *M. Cheke* and *M. Watson* of this fault, not onely in the olde Latin Poets, but also in our new English Rymers at this day. They wished as *Virgil* and *Horace* were not wedded to follow the faultes of former fathers (a shrewd mariage in greater matters) but by right *Imitation* of the perfit Grecians had brought Poetrie to perfitnesse also in the Latin tong, that we Englishmen likewise would acknowledge and understand rightfully our rude beggerly ryming, brought first into Italie by *Gothes* and *Hunnes*, whan all good verses and all good learning to were destroyd by them, and after caryed into France and Germanie, and at last receyved into England by men of excellent wit in deede, but of small learning and lesse judgement in that behalfe.

But now, when men know the difference, and have the examples, both of the best and of the worst, surelie to follow rather the *Gothes* in Ryming than the *Greekes* in trew versifying were even to eate ackornes with swyne, when we may freely eate wheate bread emonges men. In deede, *Chauser*, *Th. Norton* of Bristow, my L. of Surrey, *M. Wiat*, *Th. Phaer*, and other Jentlemen, in translating *Ovide*, *Palingenius*, and *Seneca*, have gonne as farre to their great praise as the copie they followed could cary them; but, if soch good wittes and forward diligence had bene directed to follow the best examples, and not have bene caryed by tyme and custome to content themselves with that barbarous and rude Ryming, emonges their other worthy praises, which they have justly deserved, this had not bene the least, to be counted emonges men of learning and skill more like unto the Grecians than unto the Gothians in handling of their verse.

(Smith, I, 29–30)

The humanist's scorn of all things medieval is obviously an important factor in the rejection by Cheke, Watson and Ascham of native metres, but perhaps more noteworthy is that this is used to support the argument that only classical metres are worthy of the attention of the *learned* man: the disappearance of 'good verses' and 'good learning' are two aspects of the same process, and accentual verse could only have been adopted in England by men of 'small learning and lesse judgement'. True art requires the sustained effort of self-education, and the resultant familiarity with the work of the best practitioners, and with the minutiae of the rules. English poets have shown themselves to be deficient in learning and skill, however great their other qualities. The implication is that accentual verse is despised because it is the product of some natural instinct, not subject to the ordering and shaping of the higher faculties working according to slowly-accumulated and painstakingly-acquired knowledge.

Before we proceed, it will be as well to clear up the confusion which tends to surround the words 'rhyme' and 'rhythm' in Elizabethan usage, as the history of these words is closely bound up with the changes in the understanding of metre in English which we are tracing. The terms *rithmi* and *rithmici versus* were used in Medieval Latin to denote accentual as opposed to quantitative verse, and because the most obvious feature of the accentual poems was their rhyming line-ends, the terms took on the additional meaning of 'rhyming verse', or simply 'rhyme'. The word entered English, via Old French, as *rime*, and from about 1560 acquired several new spellings as the result of the humanistic tendency to revert to classical orthography: *rithme*, *rythme*, *rhythme*, etc. (though the pronunciation apparently remained unchanged). When Ascham uses the word, therefore, he can mean 'rhymed verses', as when he talks of the shops being full of 'lewd and rude rymes', or rhyme itself, as when in the same sentence he remarks that ignorant people writing this kind of poetry can 'easelie stumble on every Ryme' (Smith, I, 31). But because, like many people in the sixteenth century, he saw rhyme as the essential difference between classical and modern verse, the word used in the former sense retained at the same time its meaning of 'non-quantitative verse', so that in the long passage quoted above it is as much the absence of quantitative structure as the presence of rhyme that he is attacking. He would not have been aware that this was an additional meaning: to him, as we shall see, if one's lines did not rhyme, one was attempting quantitative verse. There was simply no word, and no concept, for blank verse.

The situation became even more complicated when humanists, not content with altering the spelling, began demanding that the meaning too should be determined by the classical original. Puttenham remarks that we use *rime* 'by maner of abusion', but is willing to accept it because 'we apply it in our vulgar Poesie another way very commendably & curiously' (Smith, II, 80). He explains that

ryme is a borrowed word from the Greeks by the Latines and French, from them by us Saxon angles, and by abusion as hath bene sayd, and therefore it shall not do amisse to tell what this *rithmos* was with the Greekes...*Rithmos* or numerositie [is] a certaine flowing utteraunce by slipper words and sillables, such as the toung easily utters, and the eare with pleasure receiveth. (Smith, II, 80–1)

William Webbe, in his *Discourse of English Poetrie* (1586), is less tolerant of the English usage, as he is of the phenomenon itself:

The falling out of verses together in one like sounde is commonly called, in English, Ryme, taken from the Greeke worde 'Ρυθμός, which surely in my judgment is verye abusivelye applyed to such a sence...for Ryme is properly the just proportion of a clause or sentence, whether it be in prose or meeter, aptly comprised together. (Smith, I, 267)

There is a vagueness about these definitions which suggests, not surprisingly, that Puttenham and Webbe are not referring to a quality of verse they can actually perceive.

Gradually the two different meanings became associated with different spellings of the words: like-sounding words and verses using them were *rimes*, or, especially after about 1600, *rhymes*, while *rhythm* and similar forms were used to denote the 'flowing utterance' and 'just proportion' later to become especially associated with the accentual regularity of English verse (though the spelling *rhythm* continued to be used by some writers throughout the seventeenth century to mean rhyme). For examples, see the *OED* articles on *rhyme, rhythm, rhythmus* and *rime* (though these do not make it clear that the meaning 'measured recurrence of arsis and thesis determined by... stress' is not found in the sixteenth century). It is worth noting, too, that when used in the sense of 'rhymed poetry' as opposed to *verse* (that is, quantitative verse), the word carried unfavourable connotations in the seventies, so that even a champion of native metre like Gascoigne uses it in the passages quoted above (spelled *rimes* or *Rithmes*) in a disparaging sense.

Returning to Ascham, we find further evidence of the close association between learning and good verse in his thinking: he cites as an authority for the worthlessness of rhyme '*Quintilian*, in hys learned Chapiter *de Compositione*' (Smith, 1, 30), and later remarks, 'You that prayse this Ryming, bicause ye neither have reason why to like it nor can shew learning to defend it, yet I will helpe you with the authoritie of the oldest and learnedst tyme' (Smith, 1, 32). This second 'authority' is the example of Simmias Rhodius, whom Ascham erroneously believed to have written 'a book in ryming *Greke* verses'; both author and book were 'so forgotten by men, and consumed by tyme, as scarse the name of either is kept in memorie of learnyng' (Smith, 1, 32). The same stress on learning is evident in the following passage:

This mislyking of Ryming beginneth not now of any newfangle singularitie, but hath bene long misliked of many, and that of men of greatest learnyng and deepest judgement. And soch that defend it do so, either for lacke of knowledge what is best, or els of verie envie that any should performe that in learnyng, whereunto they, as I sayd before, either for ignorance can not, or for idlenes will not, labor to attaine unto.   (Smith, 1, 31–2)

True verse, then, requires both deep learning and great effort, and the ease with which lines of native verse can be turned out counts strongly against it. Learning is required because Latin versifying is, as we have seen, the summit of the educational process, coming after years of training; it shows a complete grasp of Latin grammar, a thorough knowledge of prosody, and the close acquaintance with the best Latin writers needed to provide authorities for doubtful quantities (and all this, it must be remembered, is necessary to achieve nothing more than metrical correctness). English poetry, on the other hand, has no background of education, grammar books, prosody, and authorities, and naturally appeared to have nothing to do with learning, or the values embodied in a humanistic education.

What is more, the difficulty of writing Latin verse (especially at a time before the wide availability of dictionaries indicating quantities at a glance) meant that only someone with something important to say would go to the necessary trouble – or so Ascham thought. The following passage gives the heart of his argument against 'ryming', and reveals clearly his belief that native verse is simply a matter of a fixed number of syllables with a rhyme at the end:

As the worthie Poetes in *Athens* and *Rome* were more carefull to satisfie the judgement of one learned than rashe in pleasing the humor of a rude multitude, even so if men in England now had the like reverend regard to learning, skill, and judgement, and durst not presume to write except they came with the like learnyng, and also did use like diligence in searchyng out not onelie just measure in everie meter, as every ignorant person may easely do, but also trew quantitie in every foote and sillable, as onelie the learned shalbe able to do..., surelie than rash ignorant heads, which now can easely recken up fourten sillabes, and easelie stumble on every Ryme, either durst not, for lacke of such learnyng, or els would not, in avoyding such labor, be so busie as everie where they be; and shoppes in London should not be so full of lewd and rude rymes, as commonlie they are. But now the ripest of tong be readiest to write: And many dayly in setting out bookes and balettes make great shew of blossomes and buddes, in whom is neither roote of learning nor frute of wisedome at all.   (Smith, i, 31)

Ascham insists several times on the twin requirements of 'learning' and 'labor' in writing quantitative verse, and on the opposite vices which lead men to write native verse. This emphasis is quite deliberate, as can be seen when he turns on those who would attack writers who attempt quantitative verse in the vernacular: 'Wisemen shall trewlie judge that you do so, as I have sayd and say yet agayne unto you, bicause either for idlenes ye will not, or for ignorance ye can not, cum by no better your selfe' (Smith, I, 33).

Ascham's discussion of blank verse is worth looking at closely, because it shows clearly the difficulty experienced by someone with the attitudes to metre already described when he has to deal directly with the real basis of English 'rhymes', accentual regularity. The accepted theory of prosody had no room – indeed, no vocabulary – for this phenomenon, but it was too obvious a characteristic for anyone but the most imperceptive to be totally unaware of it, especially in poetry where there was no rhyme to provide an immediate focus of attention. Ascham happily ignores the accentual properties of rhymed verse, but when he reads unrhymed verse, his assumption that it must be an attempt at quantitative verse leads him to look for feet, and feet he finds, though clearly not of the right kind. Surrey in his translation of Virgil and Perez in his Spanish translation of Homer, he says,

have both, by good judgement, avoyded the fault of Ryming, yet neither of them hath fullie hit[t]e perfite and trew versifying. In deede, they observe just number, and even feete: but here is the fault, that their feete be feete without joyntes, that is to say, not distinct by trew quantitie of sillabes: And so soch feete be but numme feete, and be even as unfitte for a verse to turne and runne roundly withall as feete of brasse or wood be unweeldie to go well withall. And as a foote of wood is a plaine shew of a manifest maime, even so feete in our English versifying without quantitie and joyntes be sure signes that the verse is either borne deformed, unnaturall, and lame, and so verie unseemlie to looke upon, except to men that be gogle eyed them selves. (Smith, I, 32–3)

If we did not know what metre probably meant to Ascham, we might be surprised at his assertion that accentually regular verse is 'lame', but with an awareness of what he expected from a line of 'trew versifying', we can understand his disappointment when, on applying the rules for ascertaining the quantity of syllables, he found that the apparent feet had no clear quantitative subdivisions. He conveys vividly the experience of reading such lines by his development of the 'foot' image: to him they seem stiff and awkward compared to classical verse – instead of being continually aware of the succession of longs and shorts giving the whole line form and variety, he merely has an awareness that the line is divided into a certain number of units. The quantitative subdivisions of classical feet enable the line to move at a varying pace, like joints in human feet, but non-quantitative verse lacks this capacity, and instead stumps heavily forward like a man with a wooden leg. Ascham is perhaps in part reacting against the feeling of unvarying repetition resulting from accentual regularity, in contrast to the ever-changing accentual pattern of classical verse, and to this extent he is talking about an audible property of the lines, though without really being aware of its nature. However, he is also clearly translating his intellectual apprehension of quantitative patterns into something felt about the movement of classical lines, and he therefore feels that accentual verse lacks this movement. As I have pointed out, though the longs and shorts of Latin verse had no phonetic reality in the pronunciation of the time, boys were taught to think of them as durational subdivisions of the line, and once this became ingrained habit, it no doubt became quite possible to respond to them as if they were. Puttenham also thinks of human feet in describing the movement of classical verse:

A foote by his sence naturall is a member of office and function, and serveth to three purposes, that is to say, to go, to runne, & to stand still; so as he must be sometimes swift, sometimes slow, sometime unegally marching or peradventure steddy.   (Smith, ii, 70)

He too finds native English verse lacking in feet of this kind, and admits that this is its one area of inferiority to classical verse. Neither Puttenham nor Ascham shows an awareness of the fact that if they are responding to anything actually present in the verse, it is to a visual property – though it is tempting to take Ascham's choice of image, the lame man who is 'unseemlie to looke upon', as an unconscious admission of the greater importance of the eye than the ear in his response.

These, then are the attitudes towards English metre of a highly-regarded humanist scholar in the late 1560s. As we have seen, they are entirely explicable once the relevant background is understood; and it must not be forgotten that at the time there was no corpus of English poetry to match that of the classics and to raise doubts about the correctness of an analysis which placed native English metre on such a low level. We can assume, therefore, that Ascham's views were common among educated Englishmen at this time (we know that Cheke and Bishop Watson had shared them at an earlier date when all three were at Cambridge). The next forty years, however, were to see great changes, largely owing to the way in which English poets proved by their works that Ascham was wrong. Nevertheless, many of the factors which produced Ascham's attitudes remained in existence, notably the grammar-school education with its stress on the classics and the particular conception of Latin metre which it inculcated, and it is not surprising to find writers continuing to express similar opinions – especially writers who, like Ascham, combined great reverence for the classics with a wish to raise English poetry to as high a level as possible.

'*The rakehellye route of our ragged rymers*'

Thus the attacks on 'ryming' continued. Ascham's suggestion that such verse was a medieval debasement of classical perfection was echoed by Blenerhasset in the 'Induction' following his 'Complaint of Cadwallader' in the *Second Part of the Mirror for Magistrates* (1578):

> It is greate marvaile that these ripewitted Gentlemen of *England* have not left of their Gotish kinde of ryming, (for the rude *Gothes* brought that kind of writing fyrst),[1] & imitated the learned Latines & greekes.　　　　　　　　　　　　　　　　　　　(p. 450)

The idea was more forcibly expressed by Webbe in 1586:

> That Poetry was in small price among them [the English after the Norman conquest], it is very manifest, and no great marvayle, for even that light of Greeke and Latine Poets which they had they much contemned, as appeareth by theyr rude versifying, which of long time was used (a barbarous use it was), wherin they converted the naturall property of the sweete Latine verse to be a balde kinde of ryming, thinking nothing to be learnedly written in verse which fell not out in ryme.　　　　　　　　　　　　(Smith, I, 239–40)

---

[1] I correct the misplaced parenthesis, which Campbell, though she corrects a similar error on the same page, leaves in its original position (after 'greekes').

Protestant humanists might see a further reason for disliking medieval verse (and often, therefore, any rhymed verse) in its association with the monastic orders. Ascham's attitude towards the orders can be gauged from his remarks in Book I of *The Scholemaster*:

In our forefathers tyme, whan Papistrie, as a standyng poole, covered and overflowed all England, fewe bookes were read in our tong, savyng certaine bookes of Chevalrie, as they sayd, for pastime and pleasure, which, as some say, were made in Monasteries, by idle Monkes or wanton Chanons. (Smith, I, 3)

Even Puttenham, trying to defend rhyming verse by proving that it is 'the most universall', grows less enthusiastic when he comes to medieval verse, and has a low estimate of the situation in which it was produced, and of the period in general:

The Christian Religion became through the excessive authoritie of Popes and deepe devotion of Princes strongly fortified and established by erection of orders *Monastical*, in which many simple clerks for devotion sake & sanctitie were received more then for any learning; by which occasion & the solitarinesse of their life waxing studious without discipline or instruction by any good methode, some of them grew to be historiographers, some Poets; and following either the barbarous rudenes of the time, or els their own idle inventions, all that they wrote to the favor or prayse of Princes they did it in such maner of minstrelsie, and thought themselves no small fooles when they could make their verses goe all in ryme.

(Smith, II, 12–13)

But he clearly enjoys their verse, though he is careful not to praise it too highly, and quotes many examples, reserving most of his criticism for the 'rable of Monkes' themselves, concluding: 'Thus what in writing of rymes and registring of lyes was the Clergy of that fabulous age wholly occupied' (Smith, II, 15).

Thomas Campion, in his *Observations in the Art of English Poesie* (1602), like Puttenham, attacks the general decay of learning in the Middle Ages, and the orders which he associates with it, but he has no doubts about their verse:

Learning, after the declining of the *Romaine* Empire and the pollution of their language through the conquest of the *Barbarians*, lay most pitifully deformed till the time of *Erasmus, Rewcline*, Sir *Thomas More*, and other learned men of that age, who brought the Latine toong again to light, redeeming it with much labour out of the hands of the illiterate Monks and Friers...In those lack-learning times, and in barbarized Italy, began that vulgar and easie kind of Poesie which is now in use throughout most parts of Christendome, which we abusively call Rime and Meeter.   (Smith, II, 329)

The feeling that the general standard of vernacular poetry was abysmally low, and this was in part attributable to the ease with which anyone, no matter how ignorant or idle, could write a technically satisfactory line of rhyming verse, remained common. Vernon Hall (1945) argues that 'the greater part of the argument [against rhyme] is based on social snobbishness' (p. 201, and see the whole chapter, entitled 'Scorn for the People', pp. 197–202), but it is worth remembering that the élite in this case was seen as an élite of the learned and diligent (however much these qualities were identified with the aristocracy), and that the motive was the desire to raise the standard of vernacular verse. In the Dedication prefixed to his quantitative translation of the *Aeneid*, published in 1582, Richard Stanyhurst, with typical vigour, presents the argument clearly:

Good God, what a frye of such wooden *rythmours* dooth swarme in stacioners shops, who neaver enstructed in any grammar schoole, not atayning too thee paringes of thee Latin or Greeke tongue, yeet lyke blynd bayards rush on forward, fostring theyre vayne conceites wyth such overweening silly follyes, as they reck not too bee condemned of thee learned for ignorant, so they bee commended of the ignorant for learned. Thee reddyest way therefore too flap theese droanes from thee sweete senting hives of *Poëtrye* is for thee learned too applye theym selves wholye (yf they be delighted wyth that veyne) too thee true making of verses in such wise as thee *Greekes* and *Latins*, thee fathers of knowledge, have doone, and too leave too theese doltish coystrels theyre rude rythming and balducktoom ballads.   (Smith, I, 141)

As usual, it is the learning and labour necessary to write quantitative verses which are to guarantee that the new poetry will be better than the old. Webbe, whose debt to Ascham sometimes extends to faithful repetition of phrases, merely elaborates on the latter's account of the ease with which rhyming verse can be written, but is worth quoting for the maliciousness of his abuse:

If I let passe the uncountable rabble of ryming Ballet makers and compylers of sencelesse sonets, who be most busy to stuffe every stall full of grosse devises and unlearned Pamphlets, I trust I shall with the best sort be held excused. For though many such can frame an Alehouse song of five or sixe score verses, hobbling uppon some tune of a Northern Jygge, or Robyn hoode, or La lubber etc., and perhappes observe just number of sillables, eyght in one line, sixe in an other, and there withall an A to make a jercke in the ende: yet if these might be accounted Poets...surely we shall shortly have whole swarmes of Poets: and every one that can frame a Booke in Ryme, though for want of matter it be but in commendations of Copper noses or Bottle Ale, wyll catch at the Garlande due to Poets; whose potticall, poeticall (I should say), heades I would wyshe at their worshipfull comencements might in steede of Lawrell be gorgiously garnished with fayre greene Barley, in token of their good affection to our Englishe Malt. (Smith, I, 246)

But Webbe is writing in 1586, when it was not so easy to dismiss English verse written in the native metrical tradition, and he has to admit that he cannot 'utterly dissalowe' this 'rude kinde of verse' (Smith, I, 266).

The anonymous writer of *The First Booke of the Preservation of King Henry the vii* (1599, reprinted by Collier in 1866), in quantitative hexameters, ignores the even more obvious success of accentual metres by the end of the century (though he does 'confesse and acknowledge that we have many excellent and singular good Poets in this our age', Smith, I, 377), and carries on the battle, with the same weapons as before. Poets claim, he says, that they do not attempt quantitative verse in English because 'our speach is not copious enough';

but this is the trew cause why they do not so; *Hoc opus, hic labor est,* which the chiefe Doctors and best learned of them all, cannot deny. And perhappes some of the best of them, that are curious carpers and reprehenders of this trew metrified verse, though skilful in other arts, cannot formally compose the like. (p. 4)

He uses his own adaptation of the classical hexameter to extol quantitative verse in English, and to make the usual attack on rhymers (and we may note the characteristic emphasis on the skilful craftsmanship necessary for true metre):

You fine metricians, that verses skilfully compile,

(As fine artificers hard iron do refile on an anvile)
This verse irregular, this rustick rythmery bannish,
Which doth abase poetry; such verse, such meter abolish,
For lily milke-white swannes flote on streams cleare as a
    crystall,
And in a fowle mud-y lake donguehill duckes strive for an
    offall.
Both Greekes and Latinists such verselesse verse did abandon,
Whose verse is purifi'd, as gould is try'd by the touchstone.
As vineger doth aford no pleasant taste to the palate,
So wordes unmetrifi'd, which rythmers rudely promulgate,
Bringe no delight to the wits, nor sound with a grace in a
    man's eare.
Every worthie poet will such rude rythmery forbear.

(p. 9)

But in spite of this, he admits that, faced with the achievement
of Elizabethan poetry, he cannot 'utterly discommend or
condemne' native metres (p. 11). Finally, Campion uses the
argument once again in 1602: 'The facilitie and popularitie of
Rime creates as many Poets as a hot sommer flies' (Smith, II,
330).

Such attacks are not confined, however, to advocates of
quantitative verse in English (and I am leaving aside the
attacks on poetry as a whole, which do not concern us): for example, in E. K.'s 'Epistle Dedicatory' to Spenser's *Shepheardes
Calender* (1579) occurs the following passage (the second half
of which was later approvingly quoted by Webbe), in which
the writer attempts to argue that Spenser's verse has the learning and organisation which readers would have expected from
Latin verse, and which is lacking in most English poetry:

Now, for the knitting of sentences, whych they call the joynts and
members therof, and for al the compasse of the speach, it is round
without roughnesse, and learned wythout hardnes, such indeede as
may be perceived of the leaste, understoode of the moste, but
judged onely of the learned. For what in most English wryters useth
to be loose, and as it were ungyrt, in this Authour is well grounded,
finely framed, and strongly trussed up together. In regard wherof,
I scorne and spue out the rakehellye route of our ragged rymers (for
so themselves use to hunt the letter) which without learning boste,

without judgement jangle, without reason rage and fome, as if some instinct of Poeticall spirite had newly ravished them above the meaneness of commen capacitie.   (Smith, I, 130–1)

E. K.'s estimate of the English poetry of the 1570s is given in terms very similar to those used by the writers we have been discussing (there is, for instance, the same emphasis on learning, and the same abuse of 'rymers'), so it is not surprising to find Spenser, who probably held similar opinions, saying in a letter to Harvey in the same year: 'I am, of late, more in love wyth my Englishe Versifying than with Ryming' (Smith, I, 89) – 'versifying' being, of course, the term for writing in quantitative metre. E. K.'s dedication, moreover, is addressed to Gabriel Harvey, and in his gloss on Spenser's May eclogue, he quotes a couplet in English hexameters composed by Spenser himself, 'ex tempore in bed', as Spenser reminds Harvey in another letter, 'the last time we lay togither in Westminster' (Smith, I, 99). Thus *The Shepheardes Calender* is a product of the movement to improve English poetry by imparting to it some of the qualities of classical verse – though Spenser, experimenting in this work with a wide variety of purely accentual metres, was trying an alternative to quantitative versifying.

'Artificial Verses'

A quality of classical verse closely associated with its 'learned-ness' was its 'artificiality', in the Elizabethan sense. In the first two of his lines quoted above, the author of *The Preservation* gives an indication of the great importance of the poet's role as artificer, especially his function of turning the crude substance of language into carefully organised metrical verse. The gap between the Elizabethan attitude to this quality and our own is perhaps felt most strongly when we read the 'trick-poems' and 'figure-poems' which were so popular during the Renais-sance. For example, poems which can be read both horizontally and vertically occur frequently, as do poems whose shapes mirror their subjects.[1] For Puttenham this use of shapes was one form

---

[1] For the former, see the examples and Rollins' notes in his editions of *The Phoenix Nest*, an anthology brought out in 1593 by one R. S. (pp. 71–2, 173–8), and of Davison's *Poetical Rhapsody* (1602–21, I, 223; II, 184–5); for the latter, see the *Poetical Rhapsody* (I, 180; II, 158–60), Church (1946), and J. W. Bennett's intro-

of 'proportion' which could make up for the lack of quantitative organisation in English verse, and he gives several examples (Smith, II, 95–105). Richard Willes achieved fame as a poet (among those who praised him were Spenser and Abraham Fraunce – see Seaton's introduction to Fraunce's *Arcadian Rhetorike*, 1588, pp. xli–li) on the strength of his *Poematum Liber* (1573), consisting of a collection of trick-poems, figure-poems, puzzle-poems, pattern-poems and the like, mostly in Latin, sometimes on the most serious religious topics, and followed by *De Re Poetica*, the first formal defence of poetry to be published in England, and an elaborate commentary on the poems (chiefly on their forms), the whole book being intended to raise the standard of poetry in England (see Fowler's introduction to his separate edition of *De Re Poetica*). Some scholars, however, disliked such excesses (they were, after all, a continuation of a tradition which flourished in medieval Latin poetry). Harvey, for instance, refers to figure-poems as 'ridiculous and madd gugawes and crockchettes' (Smith, I, 126), and says that Willes himself turned against them. But that they had a fascination for many Elizabethans with sound poetic judgement is quite clear, and this aspect of Elizabethan taste is no doubt related to the widespread admiration of classical metre and the tendency to disparage the native tradition of versification as insufficiently 'artificial' (it is hardly fortuitous that much of the non-quantitative verse in Sidney's *Arcadia* aims at artificiality by other means – complicated rhyme-schemes, 'reporting' poems, sestinas and the like – or that Fraunce, the most prolific of the quantitative poets, should devote several pages of his *Arcadian Rhetorike* to 'a number of conceited verses' of this kind, whose 'grace & delicacie' had impressed him – see pp. 53–63).

Puttenham's defence of English poetry is largely devoted to a demonstration that it admits of skilful, 'artificial' handling, both in the matter of 'proportion', which I have already mentioned, and of 'ornament', to which the third and last book is devoted. Ornament in poetry – that is, the use of rhetorical

duction to Blenerhasset's *Revelation of the True Minerva* (1582, pp. xiii–xvi). The importance of the sense of sight in the response to this kind of verse, incidentally, constitutes another link with quantitative verse as understood by the Elizabethans.

schemes and tropes – is compared to fine clothing, which hides the limb from sight, 'that is from the common course of ordinary speach and capacitie of the vulgar judgement, and yet being artificially handled must needes yeld it much more bewtie and commendation' (Smith, II, 142–3) (notice that an 'artificial' poem escapes the stigma of being widely appreciated among the populace). But it was the metre, in particular, which had to exhibit this quality (for this set it apart from rhetorically ornate prose), and Puttenham admits that 'artificial' verse *par excellence* is classical verse:

Our maner of vulgar Poesie is more ancient then the artificiall of the Greeks and Latines, ours comming by instinct of nature, which was before Art or observation, and used with the savage and un-civill, who were before all science or civilitie, even as the naked by prioritie of time is before the clothed, and the ignorant before the learned. (Smith, II, 11)

His ideal, however, is a union of nature and art, and he avoids making what seems the obvious conclusion by claiming, unusually for a Renaissance humanist, that nature is entirely obscured in classical verse.

More common, however, is the feeling that the native tradition of English verse is lacking in the 'artificiality' which is the glory of quantitative verse; thus Harvey in a letter to Spenser can refer to 'our new famous enterprise for the Exchanging of Barbarous and Balductum Rymes with Artificial Verses, the one being in manner of pure and fine Goulde, the other but counterfet and base ylfavoured Copper' (Smith, I, 101). By 1586 there is too much good accentual poetry for Webbe to dismiss it as easily, but he says of it:

I can be content to esteeme it as a thing the perfection whereof is very commendable, yet so as wyth others I could wysh it were by men of learning and ability bettered, and made more artificiall, according to the woorthines of our speeche. (Smith, I, 267)

Notice again the link between 'learning' and 'artificiality', which is also in evidence when Campion, in the Dedication of his *Observations* (1602), says 'The vulgar and unarteficiall custome of riming hath, I know, deter'd many excellent wits from the exercise of English poesy' (Smith, II, 327). With 'artificiality' so important a criterion, it is not surprising that so many writers – some of them excellent poets – were dissatisfied with the native metrical tradition, nor that discussions of metre bulk so large in the critical writings of the time.[1]

'A straunge metre'

We noted earlier that Ascham thought of rhymed accentual verse merely as a fixed number of syllables with a rhyme at the end, and when he came to blank verse he found it very difficult to comprehend. In spite of relatively clear accounts of the function of accent in English verse, first from Gascoigne and then from Puttenham, Ascham's misunderstanding continued to find expression, so firmly embedded in many minds was the conception of metre gained from the study of Latin. This, of course, is closely linked with the feeling that English verse lacked 'artificiality'. Someone writing a line of ordinary English verse was engaged in an activity quite different from that of writing quantitative verse: he had to string words together, paying no attention to their spelling or the characteristics of their syllables, or to such matters as elision, caesura, and feet, until the line sounded right. In the case of ballad-metres (including their long-line forms, poulter's measure and fourteeners), there was no need for any conscious apprehension of what this 'rightness' consisted in: these patterns of three or four stresses a line or half-line have a prominent and immediately appreciable rhythm which could easily have been produced without any awareness of the phenomenon of stress. The other common metre was the iambic pentameter, the composer of which was more likely to be consciously aware that he was

---

[1] The desire for 'artificiality' in Elizabethan verse has, of course, often been commented on without special reference to metrical properties. C. S. Lewis, for instance, states that Elizabethan poets 'are never concerned solely to communicate an experience; they are also concerned – usually more concerned – to fabricate a novel, attractive, intricate object, a dainty device' (1954, p. 271), and the anonymous author of an article on 'Elizabethan Decoration' (1937) remarks that 'the Elizabethan poet saw words as jewels inviting him to relate them in geometrical patterns' (p. 485). See also Tuve (1947), especially pp. 27–40 on 'Imitation and Images as Artifice,' and Buxton (1963) for full discussions of this topic. The question of quantitative verse and the wider perspective of sixteenth-century taste is discussed in the following chapter.

using five units to a line, but he would quite probably not have a clear idea of what these units were – once again, any incorrectness in the line would be immediately evident from the *sound*, a situation totally unlike that of classical metre. The more technically conscious poets probably counted the total number of syllables in the line, but even this would not have been necessary to produce metrically correct lines.

The one point where the vernacular poet might be involved in a procedure similar to those of quantitative versifying would be at the end of the line, where he would have to search his memory – or his books – for words that rhymed, but even there it was largely a matter of getting it to *sound* right. It is not surprising that to someone judging by the standards of classical metre, as an Elizabethan understood it, this kind of verse seemed barbarous. Unless he was a practising poet in the native tradition, as Gascoigne was, it would be quite likely that a reader of such verse, though he would recognise some sort of regularity, would not become conscious of the alternating pattern in the syllables, or the fixed number of stresses. In looking at the verse (and his Latin training would make him look rather than read and listen if he was interested in the metre), he would notice a fixed number of syllables, and he would of course be immediately conscious of the rhyme, visually as well as aurally prominent, but he would see nothing to indicate the accentual pattern. And if he did become aware that in reading the verse there was a beat occurring so many times in each line, he would be very likely to shrug this off as having nothing to do with the metre, just as he ignored the accentual pattern in a Latin hexameter when he was considering its metrical structure.

Accustomed as we are to the notion of accentual metrical patterns, it is difficult to imagine this state of mind, but there is evidence for it in other comments on blank verse. The title-page of Surrey's blank-verse translation of the *Fourth Boke of Virgill* (1554?) describes it as 'drawne into a straunge metre'; Harvey's description of lines of blank verse – 'those that stand uppon the number, not in meter' (Smith, I, 126) – reminds one of Ascham's misconceptions; and Meres in 1598 repeats

Ascham's remarks on Surrey and Perez almost word for word (Smith, II, 314–15). Webbe, in the passage quoted on p. 103 above, gives an account of metre in the native tradition which ignores the role of accent ('just number of sillables, eyght in one line, sixe in an other, and there withall an A to make a jercke in the ende', Smith, I, 246), though his discussion of accentual metre later in the work (Smith, I, 266–78) suggests that he was more fully aware of the role of accent than this would indicate, and that he is here merely repeating, with embellishments, Ascham's comments quoted on p. 97 above. He also follows Ascham in his belief that Surrey was attempting quantitative verse in his translation of the *Aeneid*, but shows even greater confusion in assuming that he was trying to write hexameters in English, in discussing which he says: 'The first that attempted to practise thys verse in English should seeme to be the Earle of *Surry*, who translated some part of *Virgill* into verse indeede, but without regard of true quantity of sillables' (Smith, I, 283). Webbe is no doubt here taking over Ascham's statement that the feet in Surrey's verses are 'not distinct by trew quantitie of sillabes' (see above, p. 98), and his confusion may be the result of a misunderstanding of Ascham rather than an attempt at reading Surrey; his use of the words 'true quantity' is particularly unfortunate, in view of his use of the same words to mean 'accent' (see, for example, Smith, I, 268) – which is, of course, precisely what Surrey *does* observe. As late as 1599, the *Preservation* poet thinks of rhymed accentual verse as a certain number of syllables with a rhyme at the end, and, because (following Fraunce) he accepts rhyme as a legitimate device in quantitative verse (in the attenuated, and classically less reprehensible, form of similar unstressed endings), he refers to it throughout his preface as 'rythme prose', which, as usual, he regards as being within everyone's ability, attacking those 'whose bookes are stuft with lines of prose, with a rythme in the end; which every fidler or piper can make upon a theame given' (Smith, I, 377).

These responses are not, as has often been suggested, mere classical pedantry; they reflect a real inability to appreciate one type of metre as a result of preconceptions based on another type (or rather, the misunderstanding of another type). The same preconceptions are evident in Blenerhasset's comments on his 'Complaint of Cadwallader' in *The Second Part of the Mirror for Magistrates* (1578), in which he describes the metre of the poem – actually in unrhymed accentual alexandrines – as follows:

It agreeth very wel with the *Roman* verse called *Iambus,* which consisteth on sixe feete, every foote on two syllables, one short and an other long, so proper for the Englishe toung, that it is great marvaile that these ripewitted Gentlemen of *England* have not left of their Gotish kinde of ryming. (p. 450)

I have already mentioned Blenerhasset's disparaging attitude to rhyme, but what is more unusual about this passage is the unhesitating identification of quantitative and accentual feet, and of 'long' and 'short' with stressed and unstressed syllables, something which Ascham was far too conscientious a classicist to do. The point I wish to make at this stage, however, is that it is only when the lines are not rhymed that Blenerhasset makes this identification; he seems to imply that by removing rhyme he has actually added a new structural principle, the iambic foot.

'A delight to the mindes'

The frequent attacks on native verse, then, are not as perverse as one might at first assume (especially in the period before the full flowering of Elizabethan poetry); they are the natural outcome of the conception of metre we have discussed. One reason why these attacks have appeared puzzling to many people is perhaps the unawareness of the Elizabethans themselves of the nature of their response to metre: as we have seen, they nearly always thought and wrote of metre as a property of sound, following, of course, the statements of classical writers on the subject. This appears, for instance, in the frequent comparison of metrical to musical qualities (though we must remember that the appreciation of music itself involved a response to the order, harmony and skill embodied in it), and in the notion of *rhythmos* as a product of the quantitative organisation of verse, as described by Puttenham, who says that the use of quantitative feet by the Greeks and Romans

brought their meetres to have a marvelous good grace, which was in Greeke called ῥυθμός; whence we have derived this word ryme, but improperly & not wel, because we have no such feete or times or stirres in our meeters, by whose *simpathie*, or pleasant conveniencie with th'eare, we could take any delight: this *rithmus* of theirs is not therfore our rime, but a certaine musicall numerositie in utterance.

(Smith, II, 72)

The qualities which they really valued in classical metre, however, emerge clearly from the emphasis on learning, difficulty, skill and 'artificiality' in the statements we have been discussing, and occasionally a suggestion of the intellectual basis of their response to metre is given directly, as when Ascham, referring to a line of Homer's subsequently translated into Latin by Horace and into English quantitative verse by Watson, says that he will 'set forth that one verse in all three tonges, for an Example to good wittes, that shall delite in like learned exercise' (*English Works*, p. 224). The *Preservation* poet claims that 'scanning rythmery verses' (that is, his type of English quantitative verse with partial rhymes) 'bringes a delight to the *mindes*' (p. 6), whereas

> wordes unmetrifi'd, which rythmers rudely promulgate,
> Bringe no delight to the *wits*, nor sound with a grace in a
> man's eare. (p. 9)

My italics indicate the significant words, though note that he by no means relinquishes the belief that quantitative verse sounds better. When, however, he lists 'foure commodities' which 'this trew kinde of Hexametred and Pentametred verse will bring unto us', he does not mention its supposed superiority in sound, and in the only reference to its inherent qualities he mentions just those characteristics of the Elizabethan response to metre that we have been discussing:

First, it will enrich our speach with good and significant wordes: Secondly, it will bring a delight and pleasure to the skilfull Reader, when he seeth them formally compyled: And, thirdly, it will incourage and learne the good and godly Students that affect Poetry, and are naturally enclyned thereunto, to make the like: Fourthly, it will direct a trew Idioma, and will teach trew Orthography.[1]

(Smith, I, 378)

The feeling that English accentual verse, with its lack of attention to the details of language (especially the written language), is crude and 'unartificial' by comparison with quantitative verse is perhaps best summed up by Stanyhurst: 'Thee ods beetweene *verses* and *rythme* is verye great. For, in thee one, everye *foote*, everye *word*, everye *syllable*, yea every *letter* is too bee observed: in thee oother, thee last *woord* is onlye too bee heeded' (Smith, I, 140).

I ought perhaps to emphasise at this point that the attitudes I have been describing are seldom untempered by other conconsiderations, and that this becomes truer as the native metrical tradition proves itself capable of scaling greater and greater heights. I shall later discuss the way in which individual writers attempt to compromise between the qualities they see in classical metre and those they see in native metre, and trace the increasing importance accorded to the latter in the combination. But to appreciate the triumph of the accentual tradition in the last two decades of the century, one needs first to be aware of the habits of thought which this tradition challenged, and to realise how firm a hold these habits had on those who had undergone the humanist-inspired training of the Elizabethan grammar school.

[1] The first and fourth of these advantages illustrate the close link between the desire to raise the standard of English verse by using classical metres and the feeling that the English language itself is in need of reform. The inconsistency of English spelling would have been particularly noticeable when compared with the regularity of Latin, and though it gave the quantitative poet a certain amount of freedom, it added to the difficulty of achieving agreement on rules. Many supporters of the quantitative movement advocated or used a regularised orthography; Baïf, for instance, used a reformed system based on one which Ramus had adopted from Louis Meigret (see Ong, *Ramus, Method, and the Decay of Dialogue*, 1958, p. 32), and Harvey, who may also have been influenced by Ramus in this respect, as in many others, states, 'There is no one more regular and justifiable direction, eyther for the assured and infallible Certaintie of our English Artificiall Prosodye particularly, or generally to bring our Language into Arte and to frame a Grammer or Rhetorike thereof, than first of all universally to agree upon ONE AND THE SAME ORTOGRAPHIE, in all pointes conformable and proportionate to our COMMON NATURAL PROSODYE [i.e. pronunciation]' (Smith, I, 102). For a full study of changing attitudes towards the vernacular during the Renaissance, see Jones (1953).

8

The quantitative movement – causes

There was an obvious remedy to be sought by those who felt that English verse lacked all the qualities with which quantitative verse was imbued by its metrical structure, a remedy discussed by Ascham, Cheke and Watson in their 'pleasant talk' at Cambridge, and attempted by a large number of poets from then until the end of the century and beyond. The quantitative[1] experiments of the sixteenth century have often been treated as a minor byway explored only by crackpots or poets in a trivial mood, but we can see that the reasons for attempting the experiment were far from trivial, and it is only the distorting effect of hindsight which makes us assume a doomed venture was never seriously intended. Far from being an aberration, the experiments were the natural result of the attitudes to verse and metre inculcated by the grammar schools, and that poets should make these attempts was rendered all the more inevitable by a number of other factors, which I shall discuss in this chapter.

Renaissance attitudes to art

We have already seen how the Elizabethan desire for 'artificiality' resulted in dissatisfaction with accentual verse, but to understand fully the appeal of quantitative metre it will be necessary to consider briefly some further aspects of Renaissance attitudes to art (always remembering that we are concerned with only one or two of the strands that make up Renaissance

---

[1] I have used the word 'quantitative' throughout when referring to vernacular verse to mean verse which attempts to imitate in some way the metrical properties of quantitative verse in Latin and Greek. As we shall see, such verse was never truly quantitative, though the method of imitation determined how closely it approached its model. Similarly, 'quantitative poets' in the vernacular receive the epithet by virtue of their intentions, not their accomplishments.

taste and aesthetic thought, albeit prominent ones). The importance of proportion and harmony to Renaissance theories of art needs no demonstration, but a quotation from Willes's *De Re Poetica* (1573) will indicate how central these notions were to theories of metre (and, conversely, how important a role metre played in the theoretical justification of poetry):

Metri origo a Deo opt. max. est, quippe qui hunc mundum & quaecunque eius ambitu continentur, certa ratione, quasi metro composuit, usque adeo ut harmoniam in coelestibus terrenisque rebus Pythagoras confirmarit. quo enim pacto mundus consisteret, nisi certa ratione ac definitis numeris ageretur? omnia quoque instrumenta, quibus utimur, mensura quadam .i. metro fiunt. quod si hoc caeteris in rebus accidit, quanto magis in oratione, quae res omnes interpretatur?[1]

(ed. Fowler, pp. 62, 64)

The comparison of the artist's creation of harmony with God's creation of the universe was a commonplace (see Røstvig, 1970, pp. 32–6, and Fowler, 1970, pp. 15–17), and had been used by Augustine with specific reference to quantitative metre (see Christopher Butler, 1970, pp. 96–7); and the mention of Pythagoras hints at the importance of metre within the tradition of numerological thought, whose influence on Renaissance literature has been brought out in several recent works – see especially those by the three writers just mentioned. Quantitative metre, with its theory of exact proportions of duration, its attention to every letter, and its careful and testable patterning, obviously accords with these ideas much more than accentual verse, particularly as it was understood in the sixteenth century. The motives which encouraged poets like Spenser and Sidney to organise poems on strict numerological principles (see Hieatt, 1960, and Fowler, 1970, pp. 161–82) were similar in many respects to those which lay behind their experiments in quantita-

[1] 'The source of metre is Almighty God, inasmuch as he created this universe and everything contained within its sphere according to a fixed plan, as it were by measure; so much so that Pythagoras has affirmed that there is harmony in heavenly and earthly things. By what means could the universe endure, if it were not kept in motion in accordance with a fixed plan and strict harmony? All the instruments which we use are made with certain proportions, that is by measure. If this occurs in other things, how much more so in language, which gives expression to all things?'

tive verse – most notably, a desire to fulfil the poet's function as creator of order and proportion.

One characteristic of the numerological structure of many Elizabethan poems that strikes the modern reader as particularly odd is the fact that it is not directly perceptible as part of the experience of reading, but is a matter of counting and calculating in a separate intellectual operation. The conclusions reached in this operation can then be borne in mind during the reading, and related to the content of the poem; but the two cannot be simultaneously experienced in the way which we usually demand today. The similarities with the reading of quantitative verse as I have described it need not be spelled out; it is obvious that a reader who accepted – and valued – complex numerological structures apprehended only by means of a mechanical calculation separate from the act of reading would see no obstacle in complex metrical structures whose appreciation was equally dependent on mental operations external to a direct response to the poem.[1]

As I have mentioned, it is quite possible that a reader of quantitative verse assumed nevertheless that the harmonious patterning of syllables contributed to the beauty of the verse, even though it was not something he could point to directly in the sound. An analogy can be found in Renaissance architectural theory, discussed in detail by Wittkower (1962); for instance, he says of the ratios which Alberti recommended between the height and diameter of round churches:

It is obvious that such mathematical relations between plan and section cannot be correctly perceived when one walks about in a building. Alberti knew that, of course, quite as well as we do. We must therefore conclude that the harmonic perfection of the geometrical scheme represents an absolute value, independent of our subjective and transitory perception...For Alberti – as for other

---

[1] This way of reading was of course a continuation of medieval traditions; numerological structure is present in much medieval poetry (see, for instance, Hieatt's study of *Sir Gawain and the Green Knight*, 1970), and part of the enjoyment of Latin verse in classical metres had no doubt for a long time been the intellectual apprehension of an underlying pattern. Medieval music provides similar examples; Bukofzer (1942) discusses musical devices which the ear cannot perceive, like reversed melodies or repeated patterns of note-values, where 'the

Renaissance artists – this man-created harmony was a visible echo of a celestial and universally valid harmony.[1]   (p. 8)

Other features which architectural theory shared with the quantitative movement were the complexity of some of the systems used, the attempt to follow classical rules (the most important authority in architecture being Vitruvius), and the falling out of favour of this approach in the seventeenth century (see Wittkower, especially pp. 13–16, 102–16, 142–54).

Associated with these attitudes towards poetry and architecture is the more general question of that aspect of sixteenth-century taste called *maniera* or Mannerism.[2] Many of the characteristics of this approach to art as described, for instance, by Shearman (1967) have obvious connections with the admiration of quantitative verse (and we are now dealing less with theories about art than with responses to works of art themselves): the enjoyment of 'artificiality' (p. 18), of 'works of art that are polished, rarefied and idealized away from the natural' (p. 19), and of 'those kinds of complexity and invention that are the result of deliberately raising more difficulties, so that dexterity may be displayed in overcoming them' (p. 21). Shearman also mentions Vignola's alignment of the steps and grottoes of the Farnese Gardens with the Basilica of Maxentius, 'a relationship that is appreciable only on an intellectual level, for he did not give us any point from which the elements may be seen in this dramatic conjunction' (p. 125). Rowland (1964), discussing Mannerism in painting, music and poetry, similarly makes statements that could be used of the Elizabethan appreciation of quantitative verse, as when he says of the music of Gesualdo and the painting of Rosso and Pontormo, 'the connoisseur who can perceive the intricate formal patterns is all the more conscious of the skill of the

intellect is the sole link between...two forms', and draws an analogy with the architectural proportions of medieval cathedrals (pp. 176–80).

[1] It is interesting to note that Alberti, who stands at the head of the Renaissance experiments in quantitative metres (see below, p. 123), occupies a similar position with regard to the Renaissance tradition of architectural proportion.

[2] 'Mannerism' is used by some with the same meaning as *maniera*, but its use by others to refer to a somewhat different aspect of sixteenth-century style makes it less suitable for what I am concerned with here (see the discussion of the two applications of the term by Pevsner, 1968, pp. 11–12).

artist in having imposed a pattern upon elements that in themselves have little cohesive force' (p. 47), or when he sums up as follows:

'Unreadable' is an accurate term to describe Mannerist structure, because it is more obvious to the mind than it is to the eye or the ear. It is a structure which always emerges when a work is studied, but is seldom obvious because of the complication and refinement of the very elements which constitute it. Only those sensitive to this type of structure can perceive it. (p. 78)

These attitudes to art help to explain the value that Elizabethans attached to quantitative verse as they understood it; and the quantitative movement in turn affords an interesting, and in many respects extreme, example of an important aspect of sixteenth-century taste.

One could perhaps consider here as another factor working in favour of quantitative experiments the tendency to react to the visual as well as the aural properties of poetry, though we have already discussed the way such an approach was the inevitable result of the sixteenth-century pronunciation of Latin, and we noted its manifestation in the popularity of figure-poems. It is important to remember, however, that a poet attempting quantitative verse in English would not be as discouraged by a harsh-sounding result as we are when we read it, since he would be more conscious of the quantitative patterns laid out on the page, and correspondingly less aware of the sound as an isolated entity.[1] Ing (1951) discusses the Elizabethan tendency to respond to visual forms, and relates it to the ideas expressed in Pico's *Liber de Imaginatione*, in which the claim is made that sight is the most important of the senses (pp. 27–8, 88–96), though I would prefer to locate it at the level of unconscious habit rather than consciously-held theory, which all too often

---

[1] An interesting parallel to this way of reading verse exists in the system of medieval Latin prosody aptly called 'Scheinprosodie', in which no distinction is made between long and short vowels in open syllables, the only important rule being that a syllable long by position may not count as short (see Norberg, 1958, p. 10). This is obviously the result of a pronunciation which does not distinguish between classically long and short vowels, so that position assumes an all-important role, and quantity becomes more than ever a question of which syllables *look* long or short.

had little to do with the actual response to works of art (see also Ong, 1962, pp. 68–87, and Fowler, 1970, pp. 17–19).

Classical and Biblical precedents

A further source of encouragement to the experimenters was the example of the Romans, who had done with Greek metrical forms precisely what the English quantitative poets were trying to do with Latin ones. Webbe, for example, realising that English quantitative verses had not been an immediate success, derives comfort from his knowledge of the experience of the Latin poets:

I am fully and certainlie perswaded that if the true kind of versifying in immitation of Greekes and Latines had beene practised in the English tongue, and put in ure from time to tyme by our Poets, who might have continually beene mending and pollyshing the same, every one according to their severall giftes, it would long ere this have aspyred to as full perfection as in anie other tongue whatsoever. For why may I not thinke so of our English, seeing that among the Romaines a long time, yea even till the dayes of *Tully*, they esteemed not the Latine Poetrie almost worth any thing in respecte of the Greeke, as appeareth in the Oration *pro Archia Poeta*; yet afterwardes it increased in credite more and more, and that in short space, so that in *Virgilles* time wherein were they not comparable with the Greekes? So likewise now it seemeth not currant for an English verse to runne upon true quantity and those feete which the Latines use, because it is straunge, and the other barbarous custome, beeing within compasse of every base witt, hath worne it out of credite or estimation. (Smith, 1, 278)

Nor is the parallel a wholly illegitimate one: we have already considered the possibility that quantitative verse in Latin (as opposed to Greek) had some of the artificiality that it has in English, although it obviously corresponded more closely to the phonetic structure of Latin than it does to English. Moreover, sixteenth-century poets had no reason to doubt that quantity was a universal property of language – it was, after all, no more obviously present in the sound of English words than in Latin ones. The Roman precedent, then, was a strong, and to some extent valid, reason for attempting the same thing in English.

The humanist concept of 'imitation' was, of course, central to the whole quantitative movement. The style, the subject-matter, the rhetorical embellishments, and the metre of the classical authors were all held up as models for conscious imitation when versifying in Latin, and it was only natural that the writing of English poetry should be based on the same principle. Thus Ascham's discussion of English quantitative metre occurs in a section of *The Scholemaster* headed 'Imitatio', and it is the imitation by the golden Latin poets of the Greeks rather than their Latin predecessors which gives Ascham an example he would like to see followed with regard to English poetry (see above, p. 93).

But apart from the classical models, many Elizabethan quantitative poets believed they were following a further, and to many an even more important, example. Baroway, in two interesting articles (1933, 1935), has shown that it was a common belief in Elizabethan England that parts of the Bible were in quantitative verse, a belief which had its origins in the first-century writings of Philo Judaeus and Flavius Josephus, who, trying to impress their Greek-reading public, misled the Church into regarding Biblical verse as quantitative. This view was accepted by Jerome, who was particularly influential during the Renaissance, and in England we find it echoed in the writings of Barnabe Googe (1565, sig. (‡) 2r–v), Richard Willes (1573, ed. Fowler, pp. 64, 66), and Thomas Lodge (1579, Smith, I, 71) (the fact that quantitative verse was not expected to have audible patterning naturally made it easier for the misunderstanding to gain currency). The most important part of the Bible in this respect, because the most obviously in verse of some sort, was the psalms, and a good idea of how fitting it seemed that the psalms should be in a strict metre is given by a passage in a sermon preached by Donne in 1618:

He gives us our instruction...in *Psalms*, which is also a limited, and a restrained form; Not in an *Oration*, not in *Prose*, but in *Psalms*; which is such a form as is both curious, and requires diligence in the making, and then when it is made, can have nothing, no syllable taken from it, nor added to it: Therefore is Gods will delivered to us in *Psalms*, that we might have it more cheerfully, and that we might have it more certainly, because where all the words are numbred,

and measured, and weighed, the whole work is the lesse subject to
falsification, either by substraction or addition.

(Sermons, II, 49–50)

Not surprisingly, then, translations of the psalms form an important part of the Renaissance attempts at quantitative verse
in the vernacular. Jean-Antoine de Baïf, for instance, made
quantitative French translations of the first seventy-eight
psalms between 1567 and 1569, and then of the whole Psalter
in 1573, including new versions of the ones already translated
(see Yates, 1947, p. 65). Quantitative translations of the psalms
into English were undertaken by Stanyhurst, Fraunce and the
Countess of Pembroke, all of whom no doubt shared the common assumption that Biblical verse was, of all poetry, 'the
chiefe both in antiquitie and excellencie', (Sidney, *An Apologie
for Poetrie*, Smith, I, 158).

Continental influences

Finally, English quantitative poets may have been encouraged
in their endeavour by an awareness of continental precedents.
Someone who supported the movement in France, and who
had a wide following in England, was Ramus, and it is likely
that many Elizabethans read and were impressed by the passage
in his French grammar in which he expresses this support. It
first occurs in the 1562 *Gramerę*, written in Ramus' improved
orthography, and is expanded in the 1572 edition, the nor-
mally-spelt *Grammaire*. Ramus' exhortation to French poets is
similar in tone and substance to the English equivalents we
have looked at, except that he is more sympathetic to the native
tradition (perhaps partly because in France this did not mean
the accentual alternation which made English native verse
sound so different from classical verse). He recommends French
verse on a quantitative basis and continues:

A ceste cause fauldroit supplier aux muses Francoyses dentreprendre
ce labeur, non pas pour abolir la rithme, qui est fort plaisante &
delectable, mais affin que leur patrie fust esgallee a la Graece & a
lItalie touchant la prosodie en quantite & accent. Et hardiment le
premier gentil esprit, qui remplira ses vers mesures dune bonne
& riche poesie, il sera le premier poete des Francois, comme

Homere & Livius ont este de Grecs & des Latins, devant lesquels ny avoit ny en Grece, ny en Italie aultre poesie que de rithmes.

(1572, pp. 43–4)

Harvey was an ardent follower of Ramus (see, for example, his *Ciceronianus*, 1577, and the introduction by H. S. Wilson, as well as Wilson, 1945, 1948), and he may well have been encouraged by these remarks to attempt quantitative verse in English. Another English writer who might have been influenced by Ramus in this respect is Sidney, whose friendship with the French scholar received testimony in the dedication by de Banos of the posthumous *Petri Rami Commentariorum de Religione Christiana* to Sidney (see Osborn, 1972, p. 51). Sidney was in Paris in 1573, when the second edition of the *Grammaire* was published by André Wechel, with whom he stayed for several months after both had left Paris following the massacre of St Bartholomew (in which Ramus himself was killed). But Sidney, of all the quantitative poets the one most in touch with continental developments in scholarship and literature, was almost certainly influenced and encouraged by another French manifestation of the quantitative movement, the writing and performing of 'measured verse and music' by Baïf and his followers. Sidney's stay in Paris was at a time when Baïf's 'Académie de Poésie et de Musique' was flourishing, and the two men had a common friend in the neo-Latin poet Daniel Rogers (for an account of Rogers' role as a link between French and English poetic circles, see Phillips, 1965, and for a detailed study of Rogers and his connections with Sidney, see Van Dorsten, 1962). Sidney's concern with the connections between quantitative verse and music (unusual in the English discussions) probably reflects this influence.

In general, however, it is difficult to tell how aware the Elizabethans were of the experiments in metre that had been carried out in other countries. Ascham, referring presumably to his discussions with Cheke and Watson, and Watson's quantitative verses in English written 'a good while ago, in Cambrige' (*English Works*, p. 224), says, 'I rejoyce that even poore England prevented *Italie*, first in spying out, than in seekyng to amend this fault in learnyng' (Smith, I, 34). This means that

Ascham is ignorant not only of the experiments in vernacular quantitative verse by Leon Battista Alberti and Leonardo di Pietro Dati read as part of a competition organised by the former in 1441, but also of Claudio Tolomei's 'Accademia della Nuova Poesia', founded in 1538 to promote Italian quantitative verse, which produced a collection entitled *Versi, et regole de la nuova poesia toscana* in 1539 (probably compiled by Cosimo Pallavicino — see Baxter, 1901, pp. 13–17). He does, however, mention 'that worthie *Senese Felice Figliucci*' (Smith, I, 33), who made some translations into quantitative verse in his commentary on Aristotle's *Ethics* in 1551. Daniel, in his *Defence of Ryme* (1603), does mention Tolomei (whom he believes to be the initiator of Italian quantitative versification) (Smith, II, 368), though of course to attack him. One of the earliest quantitative poems to appear in English was James Sandford's translation of a French quantitative poem by Estienne Jodelle (see p. 195 below). Fraunce, the most prolific and one of the most successful of the quantitative poets, left no discussion of his method, but in his *Arcadian Rhetorike* (1588), based largely on the standard Ramist rhetoric written by Talaeus, he writes as though quantitative verse were the norm in modern European vernaculars. Thus in his chapter on metre (pp. 27–33) he not only gives Latin and Greek examples of quantitative feet, but English, Italian, French and Spanish ones as well; and when he comes to the kinds of metre, where Talaeus (writing of course in Latin) gives Latin examples, Fraunce adds quantitative lines in English, French and Italian. The foreign authors whom he identifies by name are 'Comes de Alcinois' (i.e., Conte d'Alsinois, an anagram employed by Nicolas Denisot), Estienne Jodelle, and Remi Belleau, but for the former two Fraunce is indebted to a collection of literary curiosities by Estienne Tabourot, entitled *Les Bigarrures* (see Seaton's introduction to *The Arcadian Rhetorike*, pp. xxviii–xxxii). Apart from these few indications, there is little evidence that the English quantitative poets were conscious of continental precedents — though this may be because of a reluctance to admit that such an obviously praiseworthy venture had its origins outside England. We ought to note, however, that *within* the country the example of the illustrious forefathers of the movement – first Ascham and his humanist associates at Cambridge, then at a later stage Sidney, Spenser and Harvey (who for all the abuse he attracted from some quarters was a highly-regarded scholar) – played an important part in encouraging later writers. Webbe's praise of the hexameters by Watson in Ascham's *Scholemaster* as a 'famous *Distichon*, which is common in the mouthes of all men' and his remark that 'the great company of famous verses of thys sort which Master *Harvey* made is not unknowne to any' (Smith, I, 283, 284), and Stanyhurst's claim to have 'taken upon mee too execute soom part of mayster *Askam* his wyl' in writing quantitative verse (Smith, I, 137), indicate this clearly. The influence of Sidney's example on later quantitative poets will become abundantly evident in later chapters.

It would seem, then, that with the possible exception of Ramus, and to a more limited extent, Baïf, the numerous writers on the continent who discussed and attempted quantitative verse in the vernacular did not markedly influence the growth of the movement in England, and that the simultaneous appearance in several countries of similar movements was chiefly the result of a shared intellectual background – for most of the causes dealt with in this and earlier chapters would have been operative throughout Europe, from the unclassical pronunciation of Latin and the humanist educational programme to the tendency towards visual responses and the taste for artifice and ornament.

9

The quantitative movement – magnitude

Geographical and chronological extent

The flourishing in several countries of quantitative movements during the sixteenth century, often with little contact between them, shows that the English experiments were far from being the freakish craze they have often been taken for.[1] The earliest quantitative verse to be written in a modern vernacular appears to have been the Italian experiments of 1441 by Alberti and Dati mentioned in the previous chapter. The *Versi, et regole* of 1539 has also been referred to; this contained quantitative verse in Italian by no less than twenty-four named poets, among them Claudio Tolomei, Antonio Renieri, Annibale Caro, and Dionigi Atanagi, as well as several anonymous contributions. Numerous other Italian poets attempted classical imitations during the Renaissance (Carducci's anthology of 1881 contains examples by forty-two writers of the fifteenth and sixteenth centuries); they included Figliucci (whose work was, as we have seen, known to Ascham), Apollonio Filareto, Luigi Alamanni, Luigi Groto, Girolamo Fracastoro, and Lodovico Paterno. A large number of French writers also attempted or defended quantitative metres in the vernacular, beginning with a treatise by Michel de Boteauville in 1497. Among the sixteenth-century participants in the movement were Jodelle, Denisot and Belleau (mentioned above in connection with

[1] The most complete published survey of the quantitative movement as a European phenomenon is given by Kabell (1960, ch. 6); in an unpublished dissertation, Park (1968) also deals with experiments in several countries. Two other dissertations, Underdown (1961) and Dunn (1967), include surveys of the Italian and French experiments; for a more detailed account of the latter see de Thomasson (1937). The German experiments are dealt with fully by Bennett (1963).

Fraunce), Estienne Pasquier, Nicolas Rapin, Agrippa d'Aubigné, Marc Claude de Buttet, Jacques Peletier, Claude de Boissiere, and Jacques de la Taille; and perhaps the most successful of all the Renaissance experiments were those carried out in conjunction with music by the 'Académie de Poésie et de Musique' of Baïf and Courville. Nor was Germany immune from the desire to improve her native metres by classical imitations. The earliest was Conrad Gesner in 1555, and other sixteenth-century supporters of the new metres were Johann Clajus, Sixt Birken, Johann Fischart, Bartolomäus Ringwald, Johann Kolross and Hermann Haberer (see Bennett, 1963, pp. 20–1, 39–41, 117, 233–4). Quantitative experiments in Spain began with a poem in sapphics by Antonio Agustín in 1540, and several other writers made the attempt during the sixteenth century, including Francisco de Salinas, Diego Girón, and Alonso Pinciano Lopez (see Kabell, 1960, pp. 161–6, and Park, 1968, ch. 5). Žirmunskij (tr. Brown, 1966) mentions that in Russia Meletij Smotrickij tried in 1619 to base a quantitative system on orthography (p. 208, n. 19). The Netherlands and the Scandinavian countries saw quantitative movements of their own during the Renaissance (Kabell, pp. 183–8, 197–204), and experiments are also recorded in Hungarian and Czech (Park, p. iii, n. 2). It is clear that, though nearly all such experiments were by their very nature bound to fail and be quickly buried, throughout Europe the attempt to naturalise quantitative metre was being made again and again during the sixteenth century – and in some countries, notably Italy and Germany, well beyond. This suggests how obvious a step it was for someone concerned about the quality of vernacular verse to take, and how necessary it was for the attempt to be made, and to be seen to be hopeless, for the vernacular tradition to go ahead in full confidence, supported not only by the common people, but also by the well-educated élite who considered it their duty to carry the torch passed on by antiquity.

When we look at the quantitative verse written in English during the Renaissance, it comes as no surprise that poets as expert as Sidney and Spenser, having made the attempt, turned their full attention to the native tradition, or that later poets, seeing the failure of the movement, ridiculed quantitative verse or used it only in a light-hearted or satirical manner. If anything, it is the longevity of the movement in England which is notable, though commentators have usually stressed its shortness, as Smith does in the introduction to his collection of essays:

Not the least remarkable feature of this special controversy, and of the poets' experimental interest in it, is its brief life, which begins and ends within the limits of these volumes. When Daniel struck his blow the craze was at the point of death, for Campion, who incited Daniel, was a belated theorist; and the curious preface to the *First Booke of the Preservation of King Henry the VII* is the enthusiasm of a monomaniac out of touch with the times. (I, xlvii)

It is true that the movement goes back no further than the discussions by Ascham, Watson and Cheke in the 1540s, but since it was so much a product of Renaissance humanism coupled with a new faith in the vernacular, a combination which these men were among the first to exhibit, this is not to be wondered at. It is less true that it did not survive Daniel's attack in 1603: Jonson's comments in his *English Grammar* (published in 1640) show that the feeling that English metre lacked art compared to classical metre was by no means dead, especially in those minds most sympathetic to classical ideals:

Here order would require to speake of the *Quantitie* of *Syllabes*, their speciall *Prerogative* among the *Latines* and *Greekes*: whereof so much as is constant, and derived from *Nature*, hath beene handled already. The other which growes by *Position*, and placing of letters, as yet (not through *default* of our *Tongue*, being able enough to receive it, but our owne carelesnesse, being negligent to give it) is ruled by no *Art*. The principall cause whereof seemeth to be this; because our *Verses* and *Rythmes* (as it is almost with all other people, whose *Language* is spoken at this day) are *naturall*, and such whereof *Aristotle* speaketh,... made of a *naturall*, and *voluntarie* composition, without regard to the *Quantitie* of *Syllabes*.

This would ask a larger time and field, then is here given, for the examination: but since I am assigned to this Province; that it is the *lot* of my *age*, after thirty yeares conversation with men, to be *elementarius Senex*: I will promise, and obtaine so much of my selfe, as to give, in the heele of the booke, some spurre and incitement to that which I so reasonably seeke. Not that I would have the *vulgar*, and *practis'd* way of making, abolish'd and abdicated, (being both sweet and delightfull, and much taking the eare) but, to the end our *Tongue* may be equall to those of the renowned Countries, *Italy*, and *Greece*, touching this particular. (*Works*, VIII, 500–1)

Though Jonson never fulfilled his promise, it is clear from this passage that, for all his understanding and mastery of accentual verse, he felt the same disparity between the classical and native traditions of metre that Ascham had discussed with his friends nearly a century earlier. He was too good a poet to be impressed by the results of the movement up to then (his judgement, expressed to Drummond, that Fraunce 'in his English Hexameters was a Foole', *Works*, I, 133, probably went for the other quantitative poets too), but he clung to the belief that, in theory, English verse could be made truly 'artificial'. Understandably, his references to 'natural' verse do not carry the implications of inferiority that they might have done at an earlier period, as the final sentence indicates – though it is in fact translated from Ramus' remarks in his *Grammaire* of 1572 (see above, p. 121). Jonson is also more aware than earlier writers on the subject of the great difference between quantity as a matter of the sound of vowels (which is 'constant, and derived from *Nature*', and which he tries to give an account of earlier in the book), and quantity as a matter of the 'placing of letters' – in other words, not a property of the sound of the line but a pattern arrived at by following accepted rules. English, like all languages, contains the former, but the latter has to be devised and applied by men; and to Jonson, as to the other writers we have been considering, this does not mean at all that the former is therefore superior.

That the desire to naturalise quantitative verse did not die out altogether is also evident from occasional attempts during the seventeenth century; for instance, Robert Chamberlain included a poem in hexameters in his *Nocturnall Lucubrations* of 1638 (sig. H2*v*), and a commendatory poem by John Hockenhull prefaced to the second edition of Barker's *Art of Angling* (1657, sig. A6) is also in hexameters. Milton, too, wished to create in English an equivalent of Latin metres; the note on the verse prefaced to *Paradise Lost* echoes many sixteenth-century writers in its attacks on rhyme as 'the Invention of a barbarous Age' and in its praise of 'apt Numbers' and 'fit quantity of Syllables', and the introductory note to his translation of Horace's Fifth Ode of Book I states that it is 'rendred almost word for word without Rhyme according to the Latin Measure, as near as the Language will permit' – though Shawcross (1968), in attempting to prove that the Ode and the *Samson Agonistes* choruses are based on a quantitative system like that of the Elizabethan experimenters, finds so many irregularities that he unintentionally demonstrates that they are not (for a useful discussion of the metrical problems raised by the Ode, see Weismiller, 1972, pp. 1023–6).[1]

The Elizabethan experiments: a survey

Though it is certainly true that the movement lost its force after about 1600, a constant stream of works using or defending quantitative metres appeared between the late 1570s and that date, and a chronological survey of these will be the best way of demonstrating the hold which the movement gained in Elizabethan England (the nature of the individual contributions will be discussed, with more detailed bibliographical references, in Part Three). Watson's lines written in the 1540s and quoted by Ascham in *The Scholemaster* and Ascham's own quantitative translations in *Toxophilus* (1545) were the earliest of the English attempts,[2] but they had no immediate successors. James Sandford published some quantitative verse in various languages,

[1] The eighteenth century also saw a few isolated attempts at imitating classical metres, chiefly sapphics, but it was only at the end of the century that it became a widespread practice once more. This time, however, there was no thought of following the rules of Latin prosody as the Elizabethans had done; the basic principle was the replacement of ictus by stress, and the immediate inspiration was the German verse written according to this sytem by Klopstock and others. Among the English poets who wrote verse of this kind during the nineteenth century were Coleridge, Southey, Clough, Longfellow, and Kingsley. In the second half of the century a number of writers attempted more strictly quantitative verse in imitation of what they took to be classical metre; these included Tennyson, C. B. Cayley, Robinson Ellis, and W. J. Stone. For bibliographical details of both these schools see Omond (1921), Appendix A (on 'quantitative' imitations) and Appendix B (on accentual imitations). In this century, such writers as Bridges, Pound, MacNeice and Auden have used classically-derived metres in English.

[2] The nearest approach to an imitation of classical metre that we have from the pen of John Cheke, the other participant in the discussions at St John's, is a

including English, in his *Houres of recreation* (1576), but the movement did not really get under way until Sidney started writing quantitative poems for the *Arcadia*, probably between 1577 and 1580, and discussing the subject with Drant, Dyer and Spenser.[1] In 1580 Harvey published the letters which had passed between Spenser and himself that year and the previous year, largely on the subject of quantitative verse, in which it appears that Harvey had previously attempted to interest Spenser in the project but had failed. Sidney and Dyer, however, were more persuasive (Drant had died in 1578), and the letters contain quantitative verse by Spenser as well as by Harvey (and by Harvey's brother John).[2] Sidney's influence can also be seen in Greville's single attempt at quantitative verse (*Caelica*, vi), perhaps written at this time, as well as in the quantitative verse by James Reshoulde and Robert Mills included, along with many of Sidney's poems (including some in quantitative verse), in MS Rawlinson poet. 85, an anthology compiled in the late 1580s. Sidney's example was all-important in Fraunce's career as a quantitative poet – it was Sidney who paid for Fraunce's education at St John's, Cambridge (a college whose connection with the quantitative movement goes back to the discussions held there by three of its members – Ascham, Cheke and Watson – in the 1540s), and all but one of Fraunce's works were dedicated to members of the Sidney family, the exception being a dedication to Dyer. Fraunce's success is a measure of the strength of the movement at this

group of several poems in the Arundel Harington MS (which also contains a transcript of Spenser's quantitative 'Iambicum Trimetrum'), all in unrhymed alexandrines (Hughey, 1960, I, 332–5). They have an accentual iambic structure.

[1] John Grange's *Golden Aphroditis* (1577) includes among its crude fourteeners some lines which appear to be meant as hexameters (sig. L4*v*), but they in fact have no quantitative basis. Another figure who belongs to the quantitative movement by virtue of his intentions is Thomas Blenerhasset; we have seen that he thought of his accentual alexandrines published in 1578 as imitations of Latin iambic verse, and in *A Revelation of the True Minerva* (1582) (a work containing much 'conceited verse') he included two short passages which must be intended as hexameters (sig. A4) and elegiacs (sig. A4*v*), although they have no quantitative structure and are only partially imitations of the Latin accentual schemes.

[2] The exact nature of the group referred to as the 'Areopagus' by Spenser in these letters has never been established, nor is it certain how closely acquainted Spenser and Sidney were. There is no evidence of a formal body like the Baïf Academy, and it must be remembered that Spenser's reference, and Harvey's

time: *The Lamentations of Amyntas*, a translation into English hexameters of the Latin poem *Amyntas* by Thomas Watson (not to be confused with the Thomas Watson mentioned by Ascham), was first published in 1587 and went through further editions in 1588, 1589 and 1596, as well as appearing in *The Countess of Pembrokes Yvychurch* in 1591, together with more quantitative verse by Fraunce, including a translation of Virgil, which had first appeared in his *Lawiers Logike* of 1588. He also published *The Countess of Pembrokes Emanuel* in 1591, containing a long poem on the life of Christ and several translations of psalms, all in hexameters, and *The Third part of the Countess of Pembrokes Yvychurch: Entituled, Amintas Dale* in 1592. Among those who praised his quantitative verse were Spenser, Harvey, Meres, Nashe and Peele (see Koller, 1940, p. 108); and selections were reprinted in Allot's *Englands Parnassus* in 1600.

Meanwhile, Stanyhurst had in 1582 published his translation in hexameters of *Thee First Foure Bookes of Virgil his Aeneis*, containing 'oother poëtical divises' also in quantitative verse, and 1586 saw the appearance of Webbe's treatise including a defence of, and some attempts at, quantitative verse. Byrd's *Psalmes, Sonets, & songs of sadnes and pietie*, containing the settings of two quantitative poems, was published in 1588,[1] and even a Marprelate pamphlet of that year, *An Epistle to the Terrible Priests of the Convocation House*, contains two epitaphs written in English hexameters of a crude kind (p. 24). The Protestant *Mar-Martine* of 1589 contains similar hexameters in reply – see McKerrow, 1902, p. 149. Puttenham's *Arte of English Poesie*, with its suggested method of using quantitative metres in English (which is among the sections of the book probably written in about 1584–5), appeared in 1589, and the following year saw the first appearance in print of Sidney's quantitative verse in the first edition of the *Arcadia*, though all but two of the

comment on it, are in a light-hearted tone which gives no reason for taking the name as anything but a joke. For discussions of the question see Fletcher (1898–9), Maynadier (1909), Long (1914), Fulton (1916), T. P. Harrison (1930), and Phillips (1965), and for a summary of the whole controversy, see Spenser's *Prose Works*, pp. 479–80. A useful account of the activities of those associated with the group is given by Gair in an unpublished dissertation (1969, ch. 4).

[1] It has not, to my knowledge, been noticed that song no. xxxiv is a setting of a quantitative poem in aristophanics, very similar to Sidney's own 'When to my

quantitative poems were omitted by the editors. Robert Greene published works containing quantitative poems in 1590, 1591 and 1593, while Campion's earliest attempt at quantitative verse, apparently in imitation of Sidney, appeared in Newman's surreptitious quarto of *Astrophel and Stella* in 1591. In 1593 *The Phoenix Nest* appeared, containing three poems in stanzas based on the sapphic, one or two of them probably by Lodge. 1593 was also the year in which the second edition of the *Arcadia* was published, the composite text which was to remain the standard version until this century, and which restored Sidney's quantitative poems to the Eclogues. This may well have given an added impetus to the writing of quantitative verse: the following year witnessed the publication of quantitative poems by Barnfield, Dickenson, and the unknown author of *Greenes Funeralls*, who identified himself only as R. B. Barnfield's poem, 'Hellens Rape', which appeared in *The Affectionate Shepheard*, was (though metrically exact) satirical in intent, but this fact itself gives an indication of the widespread familiarity with quantitative metres which Barnfield must have counted on. Dickenson's poems were contained in his *Arisbas*, which was followed in 1596 by *The Shepheardes Complaint* and in 1598 by *Greene in Conceipt*, in both of which Dickenson included more quantitative verse. Francis Sabie's quantitative eclogues, entitled *Pan's Pipe*, appeared in 1595, and though they are extremely crude, they constitute a serious, extended attempt to use several kinds of classical metre in English. His *Flora's Fortune*, containing some further lines of quantitative verse, also appeared in 1595, and 1596 saw the publication of Peter Colse's *Penelopes Complaint*, which included some quantitative sapphics. At about the same time Richard Carew was writing *The Excellency of the English Tongue*, and remarking,

And in a worde, to close up these prooffes of our copiousnes, looke into our Imitacione of all sortes of verses affoorded by any other Language, and you shall finde that *Sr. Phillip Sidney, Mr. Stanihurst*, and divers moe, have made use how farre wee are within compasse of a fore imagined impossibility in that behalff. (Smith, II, 292)

deadly pleasure.' The setting, like that of the other quantitative poem in the volume, 'Constant *Penelope...*' (no. xxiii), reflects the quantitative structure.

When he included Carew's treatise in the 1614 edition of his *Remains*, Camden inserted 'Maister Puttenham' between the other two names (Smith, II, 444–5), confirming that it is quantitative verse that is here being held up for admiration, and suggesting that Camden shared his admiration. It was also in the 1590s that Sidney's sister, the Countess of Pembroke, was translating into English the psalms which her brother had left untranslated when he died (we know that she had started by 1593 and had completed the task by 1600 – see Rathmell, 1963, pp. xxvi–xxvii), including several in a wide variety of classical metres on the model of the *Arcadia* quantitative verse. *The First Booke of the Preservation of King Henry the vii* came out in 1599, and though the author failed to appreciate that the quantitative movement had, by comparison with the native tradition, proved to be unsuccessful, he is hardly the 'monomaniac out of touch with the times' that he appears to Smith to be.

It is clear, then, that the 1590s saw much activity in the field of quantitative versifying (enough for Peele to include a parody of English hexameters in his *Old Wives Tale* of 1595, *Life and Works*, III, 410); nor did it end completely with the century. In 1601 Campion published, with Rosseter, *A Booke of Ayres*, and included a poem in quantitative sapphics with a setting which exactly mirrored the quantities. In his introduction, he states:

The Lyricke Poets among the Greekes and Latines were the first inventers of Ayres, tying themselves strictly to the number and value of their sillables, of which sort, you shall find here onely one song in Saphike verse; the rest are after the fascion of the time, eare-pleasing rimes without Arte. (*Works*, ed. Davis, p. 15)

This shows that exactly the same considerations were impelling Campion towards quantitative experiments as had been operative for sixty years: the sense that traditional verse lacked art, and that it pleased only the ear (not that Campion underestimated the importance of that in the way that others had done), and not, presumably, the mind of the learned reader. The following year he published his *Observations in the Art of English Poesie* (which may in fact have originally been written in 1591 – see G. B. Harrison, 1927, pp. 279–80), in which he put forward his proposals for an adaptation of classical metres which would combine the pleasing sound of English native verse with the intellectual rigour of the classical tradition. There remained, however, a market for the older kind of quantitative verse, for Davison published his *Poetical Rhapsody* in 1602 with the following title-page announcement: 'Containing, Diverse Sonnets, Odes, Elegies, Madrigalls, and other Poesies, both in Rime, and Measured Verse' – most of the measured (that is, quantitative) verse having been written some twenty years previously. Moreover, this market apparently lasted well into the new century; not only did further editions of 1608 and 1611 continue to print the quantitative poems, but the rearranged 1621 edition, while dropping some of the accentual poems of the earlier editions, added two more quantitative ones.

Further parodies of English hexameters appeared in an anonymous play, *The Second Part of the Return from Parnassus* (first acted in 1601 or 1602; ed. Leishman, 1949), II.ii, and in Marston's *Malcontent* (1604), I.i; in the first play they are spoken, appropriately enough, by a character called Academico from St John's College (with the assistance of an Echo), and in the second the lines, spoken by Sinklo, are based on John Harvey's verse in his brother's letter to Spenser. However, that such verse could still be used with the most serious intent is evident from the appearance of 'A Motive in Hexameters' by L. G. in *Sorrowes Joy*, a collection of poems on the death of Elizabeth and the accession of James in 1603. Finally, we may note that Alexander Gil, in his *Logonomia Anglica* (first edition 1619, second edition 1621), though in no doubt about the superiority of the native tradition, includes a chapter 'De Metro' (pp. 136–41) in which he discusses in some detail the ascertaining of quantities in English, and, with examples from the quantitative verse of Sidney, Stanyhurst and Harvey, common metrical licences. Stanyhurst and Sidney are again quoted in the final chapter, 'De Carminibus ad numeros Latinorum poetarum compositis' (pp. 148–53), as well as the anonymous writer of the 'Phaleuciacks' in Davison's *Poetical Rhapsody*, but for the most part the chapter is based on Campion's quantitative metres and his illustrations of them. I do not wish to suggest that the quantitative movement retained much force after 1600, but the mere fact that it did not die out altogether indicates the continuing influence of the lessons in Latin prosody drummed into grammar-school pupils and the inescapable appeal of classical versification.

10

The quantitative movement – characteristics

We are now in a position to explain many of the features of the quantitative movement which have puzzled writers on the subject.[1] The problem hitherto has been, in part, simply that lines of quantitative verse do not have the audible patterning of longs and shorts that we would expect if we had no knowledge of the background already discussed. So, when Ascham refers to a hexameter as follows:

Which verse...was not made at the first, more naturallie in *Greke* by *Homere*, nor after turned more aptelie into *Latin* by *Horace*, than it was a good while ago, in Cambrige, translated into English, both plainlie for the sense, and roundlie for the verse, by one of the best Scholers, that ever S. Johns College bred, *M. Watson*,

(*English Works*, p. 224)

we might expect something more obviously metrical than what follows (the scansion is my addition):

$$- \quad \cup \cup | - \quad - | - \quad \cup \cup | - \quad - | \quad - \quad \cup \cup | - \; -$$
All travellers do gladly report great prayse of Ulysses,
$$- \quad \cup \quad \cup | \quad - \quad \cup \cup | \quad - \quad - | - \quad - \quad | - \quad \cup \cup | \; - \; -$$
For that he knew many mens maners, and saw many Cities.

[1] Most commentators on the English quantitative movement have expressed perplexity at, or have misunderstood or ignored, the characteristics discussed in this chapter (usually because of an unawareness of the background considered in Part One above). McKerrow's study (1901–2) remains one of the most perceptive; he deduces from the experiments that 'quantity was not an affair of pronunciation, of actual length in time; it was merely that conventionally established attribute of a syllable that determined where it could be placed in verse' (1901, p. 176), but instead of finding support for this idea in the Elizabethan approach to Latin verse, he goes on to argue that the quantitative poets intended their verse to be read in such a way as to make the quantities audible. Willcock (1934) gives an excellent account of some of the habits of thought underlying the experiments, including the attitudes towards accentual verse (and see above, p. 75), but she is puzzled by such things as the 'farce of manipulating the

Commentators have been perplexed by these lines, and many similar ones by other poets, because they are not examples of either of the two kinds of 'quantitative' verse which constitute the majority of the classical imitations of the nineteenth and twentieth centuries. They do not attempt to replace the quantitative patterning of the classical metre by accentual patterning, as, for instance, in this hexameter from Clough's *Amours de Voyage*:

Shortly, an Englishman comes, who says he has been to
St Peter's,

but freely allow stressed syllables to count as short (*trăvellers, mǎny*), and unstressed syllables to count as long, even when in ictus position (*travellērs, manērs*). Nor is their structure based on a theory of syllabic duration which ignores stress, as in the following hexameter by Bridges from his *Epistle I to L.M.: Wintry Delights*:

My solace in solitude, when broken roads barricade me,

since we would expect a lax vowel to be a sign of a short syllable, especially when followed by a single consonant, but instead we have *mān ers* and *Cĭties*. They even appear to contradict Latin rules, since position is ignored in *travĕllers*. It is tempting to conclude, as Willcock (1934) does, that these lines 'betray the confusion of ideas in this early period' (p. 2), but such a conclusion is the result of reading the lines with the wrong presuppositions about the Elizabethan conception of metre. We

spelling' (p. 5) and the notion of 'pre-election'. Hendrickson (1949) ignores most of these problems, but stresses (and in fact exaggerates) the faithfulness with which some of the experiments follow the Latin accentual patterns. Kabell (1960) also overlooks the existence of the 'scanning' method of reading Latin verse, and its effects, but gives the best account of the non-phonetic nature of the Renaissance conception of quantity, and the reasons for it. Of the three doctoral dissertations on the quantitative movement mentioned earlier, only Park (1968) discusses the background of Latin pronunciation and prosody in any detail, and much of his argument is difficult to accept. These are the most important studies to have appeared; for the sake of completeness I have included many others in the bibliography, and nearly all of these testify in some measure to the widespread misunderstanding of the quantitative movement (for a fuller discussion of previous accounts, see Attridge, 1971, ch. 11).

shall return later to this example and to the question of audible quantity, but I should first like to discuss other features of the movement which appear strange and which have not yet been adequately explained. These are: the great importance attached to rules, and in particular the debate about accent and quantity which often accompanies discussions about rules; the arbitrary nature of the decisions about quantities of syllables; and the use of variations in spelling to achieve desired quantities.

'*Certaine Lawes and rules of Quantities*'

Firstly, we can now see why the question of rules was so important – rules, that is, which are basically concerned with ascertaining the quantity of syllables (higher-order rules like those governing the composition of the foot and the line are of a different nature and do not present the same kind of problem, since they do not purport to be about something inherent in the language). In classical Latin versifying, rules at this level would have played a relatively minor part, since quantity was perceived immediately, presumably by all native speakers; but when quantity ceased to have any relation to the language as pronounced, it became entirely a matter of rules, agreed upon, learned, and applied. They are, in a sense, arbitrary, and hence it is of vital importance to the success of the experiment that there be general agreement among all writers and readers on the smallest details. If there are no carefully-codified and widely-accepted rules, metre simply does not exist, except as a private game.

Since in theory quantity was thought of as an actual property of languages, the arbitrariness of the rules could not be fully accepted by the Elizabethans, though the practical necessity of agreement on rules sometimes resulted in formulations which come near to an acceptance of it. Thus Spenser writes to Harvey: 'They have, by autho[ri]tie of their whole Senate, prescribed certaine Lawes and rules of Quantities of English sillables for English Verse' (Smith, 1, 89), choosing to use a metaphor which carries a suggestion of the conventional nature of the rules. This question continues to play a major part in the correspondence: Spenser enjoys Harvey's experimental verse, but his pleasure is marred by the fact that 'once or twice you make a breache in Maister DRANTS Rules' (Smith, 1, 90). Harvey's answer does not indicate any dissatisfaction with the idea of reading verse with rules in mind – he merely rejects Drant as an authority, since he has not seen Drant's rules, which 'may as wel be either unsufficient or faultie as otherwise' (Smith, 1, 97). Harvey has a stronger sense than most that the rules ought to answer to something in the language, and fears that Drant's rules may be incorrect, but Spenser, more alive to the practicalities of the situation if less conscious of the contradictions which it involved, is more concerned with the problem of getting agreement on a set of rules, so that quantitative poetry can be written and read:

I would hartily wish you would either send me the Rules and Precepts of Arte, which you observe in Quantities, or else followe mine, that M. Philip Sidney gave me, being the very same which M. Drant devised, but enlarged with M. Sidney's own judgement, and augmented with my Observations, that we might both accorde and agree in one, leaste we overthrowe one an other and be overthrown of the rest. (Smith, 1, 99–100)

Sidney's comment in the *Apologie* on the Book of Psalms is also revealing: 'It is fully written in meeter, as all learned Hebricians agree, although the rules be not yet fully found' (Smith, 1, 155). It seems to him quite natural that one should not be able to appreciate the metre of a body of verse if one does not know the rules governing it. In the single leaf which survives of *Certen observacons for Latyne and Englyshe versyfyinge* (1589), H. B. states that in this book he has 'looked into the versifying rules' (that is, of Latin), and continues:

And, because I am informed that many young gentlemen are greatly delited with English versifying, after the commendable examples of the Earle of Surrey, my L. Buckhurst, sir Philip Sydney, sir Thomas Wyat, Master Arthure Golding, master B. G. master A. N. and other such worthy men, and yet knowe no better rules to be directed by in making their Poems and songs than the uncertaine & variable judgement of the eare: I have to further them and other in so liberall a studie, and so good an exercise, added certaine praecepts concerning English verses also. (sig. A2 *r–v*)

The plight of would-be poets who find they have only their ear to go by is not one to command immediate sympathy now, but it is a striking comment on the habitual approach to versifying at this time.

Since there was no reason for believing that the Latin rules were not universal (admittedly, they bore no relation to spoken English, but the situation was no different in Elizabethan Latin), the quantitative poets naturally tried to adopt them for use in English versifying. In general, they satisfied the obvious requirements for quantitative rules: they allowed one to know immediately by rules like position and diphthong the quantity of a substantial proportion of syllables, they were consonant with the conception of the poem as a visible artefact in that they relied on the printed and not the spoken word, they were sufficiently complex to deter the ignorant, and, most important, they were firmly embedded as part of the learning acquired by all Elizabethans who had been through grammar school.

We would expect the most important rule to be position: it is unambiguous, visual (not only in that it relies on the spelling of the word, but also in that it involves the actual *length* of the printed word), and, as we saw in Chapter 4, it was the most important of the Latin rules. It is easily transferred to English, and it serves to determine the quantity of a large number of syllables. So we find that the first of the list of rules for 'English measurde verses' which occur in the St John's manuscript of Sidney's *Old Arcadia* (first published by Ringler in 1950, and given in an emended form in his edition of the *Poems*, p. 391) is 'Consonant before consonant allwayes longe, except a mute and a liquide (as "rĕfrayne") suche indiffrent'. In Sidney's practice, too, as Ringler points out, 'the Latin rule of length by position overrides all others' (*Poems*, pp. 391–2). Even Campion, in spite of his sensitivity to the sound of English, follows his statement that 'above all the accent of our words is diligently to be observ'd' by the proviso: 'Neither can I remember any impediment except position that can alter the accent of any sillable in our English verse' (Smith, II, 351).[1]

---

[1] Since the renewal of the debate about truly quantitative verse in English in the nineteenth century, the question of whether 'position made length' has been

Apart from position, there were two other rules which could easily be transposed and which enabled one to ascertain quantity directly from the printed syllable: 'vowel before vowel' and 'diphthong' (the latter, we must remember, nearly always meant two letters, not two sounds; thus in Elizabethan Latin *ae* and *oe*, though pronounced as *e*, were still called diphthongs). We have seen that Lily gives these rules after the rule of position, all three being rules which apply to all syllables. The other Latin rules, however, pose problems when applied to English, and it is with these problems that much of the discussion of quantitative verse is concerned. At first sight, derivation seems to be a useful rule, if you take it to mean that all words derived from Latin should have the same quantities as their originals: the laboriously-acquired knowledge of Latin quantities could thus be transferred to the vernacular and the differences in pronunciation would not, of course, have been regarded as very important. It was, in fact, part of the system of German quantitative verse put forward in the seventeenth century by Adamus Bythnerus (see Park, 1968, pp. 96–8), but English, with its much greater stock of Latin-derived words, posed greater problems, and attempts to follow the rule would result in frequent clashes with the other rules. The Elizabethan experimenters saw how much words had changed in spelling, so why not in quantity? Thus Sidney's rules include the stipulation that 'For the wordes derived out of Latin and other Languages, they are measured as they are dennisinde in englishe and not as before they came over Sea' (*Poems*, p. 391). That Sidney feels it is necessary to counter the supposition that derivation from Latin should determine English quantities shows that he is aware of its plausibility as a rule, and the same note of warning is struck in other writers. Stanyhurst starts his Preface 'Too thee learned reader' as follows:

In thee observation of quantitees of syllables, soom happlye wyl bee

much discussed. There are those who hold with Saintsbury (1906–10, III, 412–13) that position has no effect on quantity in English (except perhaps to shorten the preceding vowel-sound), and those who, like Stone (in his study of classical metres in English, reprinted by an approving Bridges in 1901, pp. 159–62), believe that they can detect lengthening in a syllable ending in two consonants. See also p. 143, n. 1, below.

so stieflie tyed too thee ordinaunces of thee Latins, as what shal seeme too swarve from theyre maximes they wyl not stick too skore up for errours. In which resolution such curious *Priscianistes* dooe attribute greater prerogative too thee Latin tongue than reason wyl affurd, and lesse libertye too oure language than nature may permit.

(Smith, I, 141–2)

Some of the examples he gives make it clear that he is in part thinking of quantity by derivation from Latin: 'The first of *Breviter* is short, thee first of *briefly* wyth us must bee long. Lykewise, *sonans* is short, yeet *sowning* in English must bee long' (Smith, I, 142). Stanyhurst is here facing the problem of contradictory rules, and asserting that diphthong (in *briefly*) and position (in *sowning*) override derivation from Latin. But when other rules allow, he feels that derivation should have some weight:

Such woordes as proceede from thee Latin, and bee not altred by oure English, in theym I observe thee quantitie of thee Latin. As *Honest, Honor*: a few I excepted, as thee first of *apeered*, *aventure*, *aproched* I make short, althogh they are long in Latin, as *Appareo*, *Advenio*, *Appropinquo*: for which, and percase a few such woordes, I must crave pardon of thee curteous reader.   (Smith, I, 144–5)

And his uneasiness at altering the original Latin quantity is shown by the lengths to which he will go to defend some of his decisions:

Yeet in theese *dirivations* of termes I would not bee doomde by everye reaching herrault, that in roaming wise wyl attempt too fetche thee petit degree of woordes, I know not from what aunce-toure. As I make thee first of *River* short, a Wrangler may imagin yt should bee long, by reason of *Rivus*, of which yt seemeth too bee derived. And yeet forsooth *rivus* is but a *brooke*, and not a *river*.

(Smith, I, 145)

The rule of derivation could be used in English in a way closer to its original use; thus Campion gives the rule, 'Derivatives hold the quantities of their primitives, as *dĕvōut*, *dĕvōutelie*' (Smith, II, 352). But this involves further contradictions, as Stanyhurst discovers:

Honoure in English is short, as wyth thee Latins; yeet *dishonour* must bee long by thee formoure maxime [the penultimate rule]: which is contrary too an oother ground of thee Latins, whereby they prescribe that thee *primative* and *derivative*, thee *simple* and *compound*, bee of one quantitye. But that rule of al oothers must be abandoned from thee English. (Smith, 1, 142–3)

Of Lily's other rules, 'Regula' has no equivalent, and authority can have no application until a body of verse exists (though, as we shall see, it soon came to play a part in English versifying). The Latin rule of preposition provides a model for some rules governing *pre-*, *pro-*, and *de-* given by the *Preservation* poet (pp. 12–13). Rules depending on Latin inflections do not of course apply, and the detailed rules concerning final syllables in Latin can only be partially transferred, as in the *Preservation* poet's rule that 'All words ending in O are indifferent' (p. 12) (compare, for instance, '*O* in the end of a word is common', *Latine Grammar of P. Ramus*, 1585, p. 11).

The penultimate rule

We saw in Chapter 5 that one of the most useful rules was not part of Lily's list: the 'penultimate rule', whereby a stressed penultimate is long, an unstressed penultimate short.[1] In the pronunciation of English even more than in the pronunciation of Latin, the position of the stress was something which every Englishman knew immediately, so we should not be surprised to find that this rule played an important part in the English experiments, even if it was accorded little theoretical recognition. Thus Sidney does not include it in his rules, but it is clear

---

[1] This is the only explicit attention paid to the role of accent in determining quantity by the stricter experimenters, but even they often allow greater coincidence of accent and quantity than this rule would provide for, no doubt partly as a result of their familiarity with the rhythm produced by the 'scanning' method of delivery. In the debate of the late nineteenth and early twentieth century on classical imitations, the effect of accent on quantity was much disputed; some believed that in English quantity and stress were inseparable (for instance, Mayor, 1886; Omond, 1897; and Saintsbury, 1906–10), while others argued, like Stone (1901), that 'accent and quantity are two entirely separate things, neither affecting the other in the smallest degree' (p. 117), among them being Cayley (1862–3) and Monro (1872). The complex question of the factors which determine the duration of syllables (probably more complex than any of these writers suspected – see Lehiste, 1970, pp. 6–53 for a review of recent research) and the problem of the relationship between actual and perceived duration (a problem which they do not even consider) are in fact not of great importance, since, as we have seen, quantity in Latin was not simply a matter of duration.

from his examples of words with different scansions in English and Latin that this is because he took the rule for granted and assumed that his readers would: 'we say not "fortūnate" tho the Latin saye "fortūna", nor "usūry" but "ūsury" in the first' (*Poems*, p. 391). In other words, we know that the penultimate syllables of the English words *fortunate* and *usury* are not long because if they were they would, by the penultimate rule, be stressed; and they are therefore different in quantity from the equivalent syllables in the Latin words. In Chapter 5 we saw that some writers on Latin make no distinction between quantity and stress when they are talking about the penultimate syllable, and Sidney is almost doing this here: he is assuming that we will instinctively make the transition from one to the other, and it is no doubt because he is hardly conscious of this transition that he feels no need to make an explicit rule about it. (This is not, of course, to say that he confused stress and quantity, merely that at this point in the word to talk of one is to talk of the other.) Naturally this way of thinking did lead to confusions, not always of a minor nature like Sidney's 'we say..."ūsury" in the first', where he is actually referring to stress, not quantity (since a length diacritic on the ante-penultimate does not immediately indicate a stress, as it does on the penultimate), but for the most part identification between stress and quantity occurs only when the penultimate syllable is in question. Ignorance of the penultimate rule and its habitual use has caused many modern commentators to misunderstand the discussions of quantitative verse, and to assume a 'confusion' where there is none, and it will be useful to look at the point in some detail.

The *Preservation* poet's comment is similar to Sidney's:

The Latin and the English quantitie in some wordes are not alike, but are meerely dissonant. And we are to follow our naturall pre-nuntiation and accent in words, yet following the Latin as neare as we may, observing the right euphonia; as, for exampel, we say in Latin, orâtor, long in ra; but in English we make ra, in orator, short.

(p. 12)

He too makes no explicit mention of the penultimate rule, and seems to step from stress to quantity in the penultimate syllable

without considering the reasons for doing so, though by marking the relevant syllable in the Latin word with a circumflex
accent (indicating a stressed syllable which is long by nature)
he gives at least an implicit indication. The type of word
chosen by both him and Sidney was obviously one in which
difference in quantity between Latin and English was particularly noticeable, and this was no doubt because, for once,
difference in quantity was actually perceptible as difference in
pronunciation.

The *Preservation* poet writes, 'I reverence Stanihurst; who
being but an Irish man, did first attempt to translate those
foure bookes of Eneados' (p. 4), and it is perhaps from the
Preface of that work that his example comes. Stanyhurst gives
other examples, and finally states the penultimate rule
explicitly:

Also in thee midest of a woord wee differ soomtymes from the
Romans. As in Latin wee pronounce *Orâtor, Audîtor, Magîster* long:
in English, *Orâtoure, Audîtoure, Magĭstrat* short. Lykewise wee
pronounce *Praepăro, compăro* short in Latin, and *prepâred* and *com-
pâred* long in English. Agayne the infallibelist rule that thee Latins
have for thee quantitye of middle syllables is this. *Penultima acuta
producitur, ut virtûtis; penultima gravata corripitur, ut sanguĭnis.*[1]

(Smith, I, 142)

He goes on to state that this overrides derivation (see the quotation above, pp. 142–3).

When the penultimate rule clashes with the rule of position,
the problem posed is a more serious one; which is to be ignored,
the evidence of the extra consonant on the page, or the evidence of the stress in the voice? The tendency to use the
penultimate rule unconsciously, and to think that the stress on a
penultimate syllable *was* its quantity, made it especially difficult
to ignore; on the other hand, position was the most important
and the most useful of all the rules. The discussion occupies
many pages in the quantitative theorising of the time, though
it has often been misinterpreted. The best-known occurrence

---

[1] 'A penultimate syllable with an acute accent is lengthened, as in *virtûtis*; a
penultimate syllable with a grave accent is shortened, as in *sanguĭnis*.'

is in the Spenser/Harvey letters; Spenser plunges into the argument and proposes a bold solution:

The onely or chiefest hardnesse, whych seemeth, is in the Accente; whyche sometime gapeth, and, as it were, yawneth ilfavouredly, comming shorte of that it should, and sometime exceeding the measure of the Number, as in Carpenter the middle sillable, being used short in speache, when it shall be read long in Verse, seemeth like a lame Gosling that draweth one legge after hir: and Heaven, beeing used shorte as one sillable, when it is in Verse stretched out with a *Diastole*, is like a lame Dogge that holdes up one legge. But it is to be wonne with Custome, and rough words must be subdued with Use. For why, a Gods name, may not we, as else the Greekes, have the kingdome of oure owne Language, and measure our Accentes by the sounde, reserving the Quantitie to the Verse?

(Smith, i, 98–9)

Judging by the fact that it refers to the problems posed by both 'Carpenter' and 'Heaven', the word 'Accente' in the first sentence must mean 'pronunciation' rather than 'stress' (unless the problem of 'heaven' was an afterthought). It is not the fact that syllables long by position do not sound long that Spenser is worried about, as is usually thought – after all, Latin syllables which are long by position would have sounded exactly the same – but the problem of the penultimate rule clashing with the rule of position. The important thing about *carpenter* is that it is one of many English words (several other examples occur in the writings on quantitative verse) in which the penultimate syllable is, by Latin standards, long by position and short by the penultimate rule. Spenser gives position priority, but then, having decided that the syllable is long, makes the usual instinctive jump from penultimate quantity to penultimate stress, and assumes that it must also be stressed. But if *carpenter* is stressed on the penultimate, it 'seemeth like a lame Gosling'. The case of *heaven* is simpler: the normal Elizabethan pronunciation appears to have been as one syllable, but Spenser, again going by the word as it appears before his eyes rather than as it sounds in his ears, feels that it must count as two syllables in a line of verse, and if this is so it must be pronounced as two syllables when that line is read –

hence the 'lame Dogge'. The solution lies with 'Custome' and 'Use': an oddity ceases to be odd if it becomes common enough, and Spenser is clearly proposing to continue using incorrect pronunciation where necessary in English quantitative verse. The final sentence is difficult to understand precisely; out of its context it might seem to mean, as has been suggested by Hendrickson and others who perhaps find it difficult to accept that Harvey was more sensitive on this point than Spenser, 'normal accents for speech or pronunciation, quantity for the construction of the verse' (Hendrickson, 1949, p. 251). However, this plainly contradicts the rest of the passage (and is certainly not what Harvey takes it to mean, as we shall see); perhaps Spenser means that we should for ordinary purposes be guided in our pronunciation ('Accentes') by the normal sound, using special 'quantitative' pronunciations only when reading verse. He seems, not surprisingly, to have been alone in holding this view, and in any case it affected only a tiny proportion of words; so there are no grounds for seeing this, as McKerrow (1901) does, as proof that the quantitative poets used a special means of reading to bring out the quantitative pattern of their verse (p. 177).

As we might expect, Harvey's response is one of horror at the idea of distorting normal English pronunciation. But it must be noted that, like Spenser, he is here concerned only with the specific case of the word in which the penultimate syllable is unstressed and followed by two consonants, of which he manages to find numerous examples:

You shal never have my subscription or consent (though you should charge me wyth the authoritie of five hundreth Maister DRANTS) to make your *Carpĕnter*, our *Carpĕnter*, an inche longer or bigger than God and his Englishe people have made him...Never heard I any that durst presume so much over the Englishe (excepting a fewe suche stammerers as have not the masterie of their owne Tongues) as to alter the Quantitie of any one sillable, otherwise than oure common speache and generall receyved Custome woulde beare them oute. Woulde not I laughe, thinke you, to heare MESTER IMMERITO come in baldely with his *Majēstie, Royāltie, Honēstie, Sciēnces, Facūlties, Excēllent, Tavērnour, Manfūlly, Faithfūlly,* and a

thousande the like, in steade of *Majĕstie, Royăltie, Honĕstie,* and so
forth. (Smith, I, 117–18)

As with many other writers, Harvey's application of the penultimate rule is instinctive and hardly conscious;[1] he marks
penultimates as long to indicate that they are long and stressed,
and when he refers to the audible altering of quantity he means,
of course, the quantity of the penultimate syllable – the only
time such an alteration *is* audible. He does not even conceive
of the possibility of scanning a penultimate syllable as long and
yet stressing the antepenultimate, and in this he is in agreement with Spenser; they differ in that Spenser is for both length
and stress on the penultimate, Harvey for neither. Clearly,
neither of them thought in terms of a rule for penultimate
syllables which may contradict another rule (as Stanyhurst,
more clear-sightedly, did); a stressed penultimate syllable *was*
a long syllable. We traced in Chapters 4 and 5 the way in
which grammar-school Latin training would have encouraged
this identification; this does not mean, however, that the common claim that Harvey confused accent and quantity is true.
As his quantitative verse shows, he was fully aware of the
distinction, and the only occasions on which he talks about one
in terms of the other are when the framework of Latin rules
within which he is working makes it possible to do so.

Harvey is prepared, then, to allow the penultimate law
(which he thinks of as 'pronunciation') to override position in
cases where they conflict. He also makes it clear that it overrides the diphthong rule as well:

And trowe you anye coulde forbeare the byting of his lippe or
smyling in his Sleeve, if a jolly fellowe and greate Clarke (as it
might be youre selfe) reading a fewe Verses unto him, for his owne
credit and commendation, should nowe and then tell him of
bargaĭneth, follōwing, harrōwing, thoroūghly, or the like, in steade of
bargaĭneth, follōwing, harrōwing, and the reste? (Smith, I, 118)

---

[1] In Harvey's copy of Gascoigne's *Certayne Notes* there is a marginal annotation
which indicates that the writer has understood Gascoigne's unusually perceptive
remarks about accent, and the easiest way he can represent this to himself is in
terms of the penultimate rule: 'The naturall and ordinary Emphasis of every
word, as violĕntly: not violēntly.' (Smith does not identify the hand as Harvey's,
but Moore Smith includes it in his collection of Harvey's marginalia without
comment, 1913, p. 168.)

Having quoted authorities from lines of English quantitative verse by Watson and Ascham (probably the first use of the rule of authority in the English quantitative movement) he goes on to a consideration of other problems connected with the penultimate rule, weaving into his comments several more words which show that it overrides cases of position and diphthong occurring together, and the rule of derivation from Latin. He makes an exception of only one type of word – *violently*, *diligently*, *magnificently*, and *indifferently* are the examples he gives – and though he does not realise it, this is probably because the penultimate syllable had a secondary stress in his pronunciation (see Dobson, 1968, II, 445–6), which meant that if it was long and therefore stressed in verse it would not sound as odd as the mispronunciation of *carpenter* and similar words. In replying to Spenser's remarks about *heaven* he takes a common-sense view, again based on his conviction that the pronunciation of English should not be altered: if a word is pronounced as one syllable, it ought to be spelled as one. This problem, however, was not as grave as the clash of rules in the penultimate syllable, which continued to exercise the minds of those who sought to determine quantity in English.[1]

As we have seen, Stanyhurst states the penultimate rule explicitly. He goes on to discuss instances of its clashing with other rules, first derivation (within English), then position:

Buckler is long; yeet *swashbuckler* is short. And albeyt that woord bee long by *position*, yeet doubtlesse thee natural dialect of English wyl not allow of that rule in middle syllables, but yt must bee of force with us excepted, where thee natural pronuntiation wyl so have yt.

(Smith, I, 143)

Like Harvey, whom he goes on to mention, he is more ready to contradict the rule of position than the penultimate rule, and though he is more aware than Harvey that it is a matter of

---

[1] In 1582 Spenser's schoolmaster at Merchant Taylors' School, Richard Mulcaster, brought out his *First Part of the Elementarie*, in which he attempted a defence and description of the English language. His discussion of quantity in English suggests that he would have sided against his former pupil in the debate with Harvey, for among his examples of the 'short time' is *carpenter*, and he explicitly denies that position has any force when in conflict with the penultimate rule: 'A number of our derivatives ar short in their last syllab save one, even where the

deciding between two rules, he too seems to feel that the penultimate rule, because it is based on pronunciation, is the more
important (this attitude may be partly the result of the uncertain orthography of English, of which both Harvey and
Stanyhurst were very aware; in contrast to Latin, English
pronunciation probably seemed a more reliable foundation than
spelling when rules contradicted one another). In fact, Stanyhurst does at times write as if stress and quantity in the penultimate syllable were the same thing, as when he says that in
English we pronounce '*Orătoure*' and similar words short
(Smith, I, 142); and he even applies the rule, apparently
without realising it, to the antepenultimate syllable of the word
planetary, which, presumably because it is an unstressed
syllable after the main stress, he feels is short (Smith, I, 144).
However, it is once more necessary to stress that Stanyhurst,
like Harvey, is writing not about accent and the rule of position
in general, but about their occurrence at a specific point in a
particular type of word, and that it is not true to say, as Omond
(1921) does, that he borrowed from Harvey's letters 'their
unfortunate confusion of accent with quantity' (p. 12).

Webbe seems less willing than Harvey and Stanyhurst to
tamper with the rule of position, and offers an alternative
solution, the use of the variable orthography to avoid the clash:

> The myddle sillables, which are not very many, come for the most
> part under the precinct of *Position*, whereof some of them will not
> possibly abide the touch, and therfore must needes be a little
> wrested: such as commonly the Adverbs of three sillables, as
> *mournfully*, *spyghtfully*, and such like words, derived of this Adjective
> *full*: and therfore if there be great occasion to use them, they must be
> reformed by detracting onely (*l*) and then they stand meetely
> currant, as *mournfuly*.   (Smith, I, 282)

This solution is applicable, of course, to only one kind of conflict between penultimate rule and position, though it was no
doubt a particularly worrying one for the quantitative poet.

vowell cummeth befor two consonants whether the same or other, as *perfĭtnesse*,
travĕlling, *pevĭshnesse*' (p. 149). It is interesting to note that even a schoolmaster of
the calibre of Mulcaster finds it extremely difficult to relate the theory of Latin
'Prosodia' to the actualities of a living language: he identifies accent with vowel-
tenseness, and thinks of quantity almost entirely in terms of the penultimate
rule, so that it becomes virtually identified with stress.

Campion's remarks on this conflict of rules have also frequently been misunderstood, but his example makes it clear that he is concerned with precisely the same difficulty that worried Spenser, Harvey, Stanyhurst and Webbe:

Neither can I remember any impediment except position that can alter the accent of any sillable in our English verse. For though we accent the second of *Trumpington* short, yet is it naturally long, and so of necessity must be held of every composer.

(Smith, II, 351–2)

The question of what Campion means by 'accent' is a complex one, and will be discussed in Chapter 15, but it is clear that he is considering the clash of position and the penultimate rule, and, unlike Harvey and Stanyhurst, putting forward the view that position makes a syllable 'naturally long' even when it is in normal speech an unstressed penultimate. But whether, like Spenser, he envisages a special pronunciation of such words in verse is not clear: the phrase 'alter the accent' suggests that perhaps he does, in which case 'naturally long' does not mean 'of greater actual duration because of the extra consonant' but 'ideally speaking, stressed and therefore long'.

Finally, we may look at the discussion of this problem by Alexander Gil in his *Logonomia Anglica*, first published in 1619. Gil has read most, if not all, of the discussions and experiments involving quantitative metre published during Elizabeth's reign, and in the chapters on metre in this work he attempts to combine as many of these views as he can, before rejecting quantitative verse in favour of the accentual tradition. Thus in discussing quantity in English he accepts Harvey's and Stanyhurst's view that an unstressed penultimate is short, even if the rule of position applies to it, but tries to lay down a rule for exceptions to this principle which will prevent it from contradicting Campion's comments (the English words are in Gil's phonetic orthography, but in this paragraph are easily read):

In diversis dictionibus positio saepe valet ut apud Latinos: at, in eâdem dictione, accentus positioni praevalet; ita ut in trissyllabis, accentus in primâ sonorâ naturâ aut positione longâ, abbreviet utrasque sequentes: ut, in *Chéstertun, Wímbldun*. Nec quisquam, qui

Anglicé novit, negare audebit *Ténterden stŭpl* esse carmen Adonicum
[that is, — ᵕ ᵕ | — ᵕ]. nam hîc adeo violentus est accentus, ut etiam
in diversis dictionibus positionem auferat. Idipsum affirmabis, si
Sussexios audias in *Wáterdoun fórrest.* Adeo clarus est accentus in
primo trissyllabo, licet positione non elevetur. Hîc tamen cautelâ
opus, nam si ad positionem *l. n.* vel *ng*, concurrat, media syllaba
producitur: ut, *Sémpringam, Trúmpingtun, A'bington, Wímundam,
Wílfulnes,* &c.[1]   (p. 138)

Gil is perhaps trying to distinguish between unstressed vowels
which retain the quality of stressed vowels, and those which
are reduced, but his view is essentially an attempt to combine
the observations of Harvey and Stanyhurst on the one hand
and Campion on the other.

'*Preelection in the first Poetes*'

These examples should be enough to indicate that an understanding of the background to the quantitative experiments
reveals more clarity of thought in the discussions of such
problems as the role of accent in English quantitative verse than
is generally realised, though it does not minimise one's awareness of the extent to which the ability to grapple directly with
the problems of English metre was hamstrung by the authority
of the Latin precedent and the imprecision inherent in the
conception of Latin metre itself. We have also seen that an
important reason why the rules are discussed at such length is
that general agreement is crucial, not merely out of a desire to
reach some 'truth' about English quantities, but because
without general agreement the very act of apprehending and
enjoying the metrical pattern of quantitative verse is impossible.
We may now consider how aware the quantitative poets were

---

[1] 'When it involves separate words, position often has an effect, as it does in
Latin; but in one and the same word, accent predominates over position, with the
result that in trisyllables an accent on an initial syllable which is sounding by
nature or long by position shortens both the following syllables, as in *Chéstertun,
Wímbldun.* Nor will anyone who knows English presume to deny that *Ténterden
stŭpl* is an adonic verse. In fact, this accent is so powerful that even in separate
words it overcomes position. You would say the same if you heard the inhabitants
of Sussex in *Wáterdoun fórrest,* so clear is the accent on the initial syllable, even
though it does not receive it by position. But here one must be careful, for if *l,
n* or *ng* contribute to position, the middle syllable is lengthened, as in *Sémpringam,
Trúmpingtun, Ábington, Wímundam, wílfulnes,* etc.'

that the success of their enterprise depended not so much on their reaching an accurate description of English, but on the acceptance by the whole movement of a system of rules which had to meet certain functional requirements but which was, in the last analysis, arbitrary; and in the course of discussing this question we shall be able to account for some further aspects of the movement which have met with modern incomprehension. I have quoted passages in which Spenser seems to be showing an awareness of this arbitrariness (see pp. 138–9 above), but he was probably not very conscious of it. The theory was, after all, that Latin quantity was inherent in the language, and the same would be assumed to hold for English; nor would the lack of correspondence between the system and the sounds of English unduly worry someone who had received his training in prosody in an Elizabethan grammar school. Thus Webbe in the following passage at first suggests something of the conventional nature of the rules – they are to be 'ratified and sette downe' by the 'famous and learned' poets (as always, an emphasis on learning) – but he then goes on to assume that the rules will reflect something in the language:

Thus much I am bolde to say in behalfe of Poetrie,...as it were by way of supplication to the famous and learned Lawreat Masters of Englande, that they would but consult one halfe howre with their heavenly Muse what credite they might winne to theyr native speeche, what enormities they might wipe out of English Poetry, what a fitte vaine they might frequent, wherein to shewe forth their worthie faculties if English Poetrie were truely reformed, and some perfect platforme or *Prosodia* of versifying were by them ratified and sette downe, eyther in immitation of Greekes and Latines, or, where it would skant abyde the touch of theyr Rules, the like observations selected and established by the naturall affectation of the speeche.   (Smith, i, 228–9)

Notice that it is the poets themselves he appeals to; this is consistent with the generally-held view that it was the poets who determined the quantities of Greek and Latin words – there is, in other words, no suggestion that quantity was something which all speakers of the language were aware of and which was simply *used* by the poets. Such an idea would

hardly occur to an Elizabethan unless he had a strong awareness of the incorrectness of his pronunciation of Latin, and
in any case would have made the achievement of the classical
poets seem a lesser one. The onus rests on the English poets to
do the same for English verse; as Webbe puts it,

Surely it is to be thought that if any one, of sound judgment and
learning, shoulde putt foorth some famous worke, contayning
dyvers formes of true verses, fitting the measures according to the
matter, it would of it selfe be a sufficient authority, without any
prescription of rules, to the most part of Poets for them to follow
and by custome to ratify.   (Smith, i, 279)

The first poets do not set out the rules; these are 'selected and
gathered severally out of theyr workes for the direction and
behoofe of their followers' (Smith, i, 279). But what is to guide
the poets in their attempt? Webbe is somewhat vague; in the
passages quoted he invokes the principle of decorum ('fitting
the measures according to the matter') or refers to the 'naturall
affectation of the speeche'. Perhaps his view is most clearly
expressed in his remark, with reference to quantitative verse,
that 'these kinde of verses would well become the speeche, if
so bee there were such Rules prescribed as woulde admitt the
placing of our aptest and fullest wordes together' (Smith, i,
281); in other words, that the poets should use their poetic
ability to devise rules (even if they do not explicitly formulate
them) which will best enable good verse to be written. Such
rules would be arbitrary in the sense I have mentioned: they
would not necessarily correspond to anything in the language,
but they would be limited by functional criteria (they should be
complex enough to allow of the exercise of skill, they should not
prevent important words from being used, and so on). Webbe's
practice, incidentally, in no way bears out this theory: he relies
heavily on the Latin rules (he admits that he has omitted 'the
best wordes' rather than 'notoriously impugne the Latine
rules', Smith, i, 281), and the poetry itself has very little to
recommend it.

Perhaps Webbe was attracted by the idea of becoming an
authority for later writers and readers; someone who made a
more valuable attempt to set the quantitative movement going

by writing an authoritative set of poems was Sidney. He produced no treatise on quantitative versifying, and his rules have survived in only one manuscript, but instead he wrote a substantial body of quantitative verse in a wide variety of metres which seems, in spite of all his disclaimers about the *Arcadia* and his poetry in general, to have been meant as a demonstration of the possibilities of this kind of verse, and as a model for later writers, in precisely the way Webbe called for.

The arbitrariness of the decisions made by the first poets is not explicitly brought out by Webbe, though it is implicit in the assumption that rules do not gradually evolve as later poets come closer to the truth, but rather that the first poets happen also to be the best poets – or, to put it in terms Webbe would never have used, that considerations about actual quantity in the language are secondary to the necessity for common agreement about rules, which alone makes the writing of poetry possible. Other writers are more explicit about the freedom of the first poets to determine the rules, which everyone else is then bound to follow, and these comments have perplexed many modern readers who have approached them with modern preconceptions about metre. Even Harvey, who is relatively forward-looking in the importance he attaches to the role of pronunciation in verse, states:

WE BEGINNERS have the start and advantage of our Followers, who are to frame and conforme both their Examples and Precepts according to that President which they have of us: as no doubt Homer or some other in *Greeke*, and ENNIUS or I know not who else in *Latine*, did prejudice and overrule those that followeth them, as well for the quantities of syllables as number of feete, and the like: their onely Examples going for current payment, and standing in steade of Lawes and Rules with the posteritie. (Smith, I, 103)

Harvey's coupling of two types of rule which we would consider to be very different, those which enable one to ascertain the quantity of syllables, and those which lay down the number and disposition of feet in different types of metrical line is revealing (and typical of the movement – Webbe makes the same easy transition from one to the other): for him both rules are prescriptive – or if they are descriptive, it is a body of verse, not a language, that they both assist in describing.

Stanyhurst, who sees himself as a forerunner in quantitativ versifying, states:

Thee meaner clarcks wyl suppose my travail in theese heroica verses too carrye no great difficultie, in that yt lay in my choise to make what word I would short or long, having no English write beefore mee in this kind of poëtrye with whose squire I should leave my syllables. (Smith, I, 137

His reply to 'theym that guesh my travaile too be easye b reason of thee libertye I had in English woordes' is not tha he is limited by the properties of the words themselves, but a follows:

As thee first applying of a woord may ease mee in thee first place, s perhaps, when I am occasioned too use thee selfe same woord el where, I may bee as much hyndered as at thee beginning I wa furthred. For example: In thee first verse of *Virgil* I mak *season* long in an oother place yt woul[d] steede mee percase more yf I made y short, and yeet I am now tyed too use yt as long. So that the ad vantage that way is not verie great. (Smith, I, 139

He is in no doubt that it rests entirely with him to decide wha the quantities of *season* are.

The most explicit of all is Puttenham, partly because h obviously feels that there *should* be a correspondence betwee pronunciation and prosody (he is, after all, a champion c accentual poetry, and is only dallying with quantitativ versifying). He says of the Greeks and Romans:

Their sillables came to be timed some of them long, some of ther short, not by reason of any evident or apparent cause in writing c sounde remaining upon one more then another, for many times the shortned the sillable of sharpe accent and made long that of the fla & therefore we must needes say it was in many of their wordes don by preelection in the first Poetes, not having regard altogether to th *ortographie* and hardnesse or softnesse of a sillable, consonant, vowel or dipthong, but at their pleasure, or as it fell out: so as he that fir put in a verse this word *Penelope*, which might be *Homer* or some othe of his antiquitie, where he made *pē* in both places long and *nĕ* and ĕ short, he might have made them otherwise and with as goo reason, nothing in the world appearing that might move them t

make such preelection more in th'one sillable then in the other, for
e, ne, and *lo* being sillables vocals be egally smoth and currant
upon the toung, and might beare aswel the long as the short time,
but it pleased the Poet otherwise.   (Smith, II, 122–3)

He also makes more explicit the kind of assumption that Webbe
seemed to be making, that the first poets are limited in their
choice of quantities by the success or otherwise of the verse
they are able to write with them:

He that first put them into a verse found, as it is to be supposed, a
more sweetnesse in his owne eare to have them so tymed, therefore
all other Poets who followed were fayne to doe the like, which made
that *Virgill,* who came many yeares after the first reception of wordes
in their severall times, was driven of necessitie to accept them in such
quantities as they were left him.   (Smith, II, 123)

He concludes that although there may be a reason for some
rules of quantity (no doubt position would seem to be based on
an actual property of the word), the kind of rule that makes the
first syllable of *cano* and *Troia* short and long respectively
stands upon bare tradition'. His discussion appears as
bewildering stupidity to anyone who is unaware of the nature
of the Elizabethan pronunciation of Latin; but it is in fact quite
an intelligent attempt to make sense of what he saw and heard,
and his method of quantitative verse in English eschews
arbitrary quantities, being based instead on an attempt to
differentiate between prominent and non-prominent syllables
in spoken English (with accent playing a major role). Puttenham's discussion of quantitative verse is therefore far from
being an expression of the attitudes I have been trying to
depict, at least in their pure form, and it is no doubt this that
enables him to see so clearly the arbitrariness of the kind of
rules that the thoroughgoing quantitative poets were trying to
set up. He is fully aware of both the necessity and the difficulty
of achieving common agreement on any proposed rules, even
with a system which, like his, is based on the sounds of the
language:

Now peradventure with us Englishmen it be somewhat too late to
admit a new invention of feete and times that our forefathers never
used nor never observed till this day, either in their measures or in

their pronuntiation, and perchaunce will seeme in us a presumptu
ous part to attempt, considering also it would be hard to find many
men to like of one mans choise in the limitation of times and
quantities of words, with which not one but every eare is to be
pleased and made a particular judge, being most truly sayd that a
multitude or comminaltie is hard to please and easie to offend.

(Smith, II, 123–4)

These suggestions and statements of the arbitrariness and
non-phonetic nature of quantity are all the more striking in
that they contradict the theory which was instilled in the
schools: that quantity is a matter of duration, and that a long
syllable is twice the length of a short. The examination of
Latin metre made necessary by an attempt to imitate it in
English would have exposed the inadequacy of that definition
to anyone who still thought it valid at a practical level; but as a
theory of quantitative verse, not to be actively tested by
pronouncing and listening to syllables, it no doubt continued
to suffice for most people.

Quantity by orthography

The third apparently odd feature of the movement that I
should like to look at is the cavalier attitude of some of the
experimenters towards spelling. I have quoted (p. 150 above)
Webbe's solution to the problem posed by words like 'mourn
fully', and in his comments on final *y* we can see again that it
is orthography, not pronunciation, that counts:

Words ending in *y* I make short without doubt, saving that I have
marked in others one difference which they use in the same, that is to
make it short in the ende ◡ of an Adverb, as *gladly*, and long in the
ende – of an Adjective, as *goodly*: but the reason is, as I take it,
because the Adjective is or should be most commonly written thus,
goodlie. (Smith, I, 282)

As we have noted with regard to Latin, the Elizabethans seldom
made a clear distinction between visual and aural properties
of words, and they often refer to one in terms which suggest the
other. Sidney's second rule, for instance, states that single
consonants are short, except 'suche as have a dowble sownd
(as "lāck", "wīll", "tīll")' (*Poems*, p. 391). As Ringler

points out, this is essentially a visual device, but it puzzles him that Sidney should allow the sound to count for so little: 'In determining natural vowel length he is sometimes guided more by spelling than by his ear and so falls into strange contradictions' (*Poems*, p. 392). Even Stanyhurst, who stresses the importance of the ear as opposed to the eye, allows the latter far more importance than one would assume from his protestations; thus, in his *prosodiá* of final syllables, he states:

E. common: yf yt bee short, I wryte yt usualy with a single E, as *the*, *me*; yf long with two, as *thee* [this is his usual spelling of the definite article], *mee*; althogh I would not wish thee quantitie of syllables too depend so much upon the gaze of thee eye as thee censure of thee eare…G. *brevia*: soomtyme long by *position* where D may bee enterserted, as *passage* is short, but yf you make yt long, *passadge* with D would bee written; albeyt, as I sayd right now, thee eare, not ortographie, must decyde thee quantitye as neere as is possible.

(Smith, I, 146)

It is clear from his examples that he is relying on purely visual differences; what is unusual is that he is to some extent aware of it and feels that it is wrong (but only when it is made glaringly obvious by a word which has alternative spellings – he has no qualms about his quantitative system in general which, in fact, is the one which takes least account of the sounds of English). The *Preservation* poet is more typical in his total unawareness that there may be something unjustifiable about altering spelling to achieve the right quantity:

And wordes having doubel consonants in the middel of dissylabels (as account, attend, applause, afford, and the like) by figure are made short, by the detraction of a letter; as acount, atend, aplause, aford.

(p. 13)

He even calls this device a 'figure'; that is, one of the legitimate licences in versifying.

Naturally, to anyone who expects metre to be an organisation of the sounds of a language, this procedure seems wholly unwarrantable. Commentators either remark on the absurdity of what Willcock (1934) calls 'the farce of manipulating the spelling' (p. 5), or deduce that some special pronunciation was used. But neither kind of reaction is justified; to an Elizabethan who had been through grammar school, the spelling of a word determined its quantity, and hence the freedom to choose between different spellings meant the power to determine the quantitative structure of a word. To someone who pronounced *ae* and *e* identically in Latin, and yet learned that the former was always long while the latter could be short, the difference between *mee* and *me* would have appeared as a difference in quantity. Apart from the relatively rare operation of the penultimate rule, it is spelling, not pronunciation, which bears an obvious and unvarying relation to quantity.

What was quantity?

Finally, the modern demand to know what quantity *was* for the Elizabethans (a demand more common now that the reformed Latin pronunciation has made the Elizabethan apprehension of Latin metre more foreign than ever before) can be seen to be misplaced. When Thompson (1961) says, 'If quantity did mean anything consistent to these men, we do not know what it was', and refers to 'whatever they may have been using for "longs" and "shorts"' as 'mysterious elements' (p. 135), he is assuming that quantitative distinctions were somehow perceived directly as the poets read their lines, presumably from the sound. As we have seen, this is the wrong place to look for 'quantity'; it is to be found in the minds of the Elizabethans, trained in the application of a complex set of rules to the graphic embodiment of lines of verse.

We shall see that some quantitative poets did in fact attempt to give greater weight to the phonetic properties of the syllable than was the case in their Latin models; but to appreciate the originality of this step, and to account for the apparent inconsistencies which remain, it is essential to understand the verse which is the result of the direct application to English of the common conception of Latin metre – verse such as the lines by Watson which we considered at the start of this chapter:

$$- \quad \cup \cup \mid - \quad -\mid - \cup \cup \mid - \quad - \mid - \quad \cup \cup \mid - \: -$$
All travellers do gladly report great prayse of Ulysses,
$$- \quad \cup \cup \mid - \quad \cup \cup \mid - \quad -\mid - \quad - \mid - \quad \cup \cup \mid - \: -$$
For that he knew many mens maners, and saw many Cities.

If we examine these lines with reference to this conception, we shall find that Ascham's admiration for them is not as odd as it initially appears to be. In the two words in which he would have *heard* a syllable as long or short (that is, words of three syllables in which the penultimate rule operates), the scansion is correct (*travĕllers*, *Ulўsses*), and with regard to the former he presumably felt, like Harvey and Stanyhurst after him, that in English the penultimate rule must take precedence over position. As for the rest of the line, quantity depended not on the sound but on the rules, and when no rule was applicable, on the decision of the poet, who, having no predecessors, could choose freely (except that he had to be consistent: thus *many* on its second appearance is scanned in the same way as on the first). Syllables like *All* and *mens* are long by position, and even if it were not followed by a consonant, *great* would no doubt remain long because of its diphthong (or, to be precise, its digraph, for it was pronounced with a long monophthong). But the first syllable of *travellers* is not governed by any rule, and in Latin an open stressed antepenultimate can be either heavy or light; moreover, in Ascham's pronunciation of Latin the vowels of such syllables (except *u*) were always short, whatever the quantity of the syllable (see Chapter 2 above). It would have seemed to him, then, as it no doubt did to Watson, that the decision regarding the quantity of this syllable was entirely in the hands of the first poet who used it. As for words like *many* and *maners*, there were no Latin models to be taken into consideration, for the pronunciation of the time made all free, stressed penultimate vowels long (see Chapter 2); so here again, the choice was the poet's.

To understand the Elizabethan experiments, we must rid ourselves of the assumption that the quantity of every syllable is determined by some feature of its structure, and remember the great faith placed in authority as a means of ascertaining quantity. This would have been a method frequently used for those syllables whose quantity we would now judge by the tenseness of the vowel; and most Elizabethan quantitative poets would have felt quite justified in deciding on the quantities of *maners* and *cities* (if they spelt them in that way) by examining, not the syllables themselves, but Watson's lines. And if they used a word which had not previously appeared in quantitative verse, they would feel no obligation to base their decision as regards its quantities on any of its structural properties if the Latin rules did not apply. To the Elizabethan mind, Watson's hexameters were not a 'very rough approximation to quantitative verse', as Hamer (1930) calls them (p. 296); they embodied in English almost exactly what the Elizabethans found in Latin verse, metrically speaking, and there is no need to postulate printer's errors or changes in pronunciation in order to explain Ascham's praise or Webbe's remark that these lines, 'if they be examined throughout, all the rules and observations of the best versifying shall bee founde to attaine the very perfection of them all' (Smith, 1, 283).

PART THREE

Quantitative poets and theorists

11

Uncompromising imitation – Richard Stanyhurst

The quantitative experiments produced very little verse which can be enjoyed by the present-day reader in the same way as the better poetry of the native Elizabethan tradition, and an understanding of the conception of metre which lay behind the quantitative movement, though it may enable us to account for the experiments and obtain a clearer idea of Elizabethan habits of thought, cannot make us appreciate English quantitative verse in the same way as an educated Elizabethan would have done. It is an approach to poetry too foreign to our own for us to adopt it ourselves, even if we acquired the necessary prosodic training; but I hope that my account will make it more difficult to dismiss the experiments as mere folly, and that it will clear the way for a greater appreciation of some of the Elizabethan verse in native metres which exhibits the same concern with skilfully contrived artifice. I shall, however, discuss briefly the participants in the movement in order to show how the theories and attitudes we have been considering received expression in verse, and how they could be either embodied in a pure form, or tempered by a concern with the qualities of the native tradition. Some of the quantitive poets are men who have a claim on our attention for their writings in other fields, and some of the quantitative verse is not without interest, even if for qualities other than those which constitute its *raison d'être*. Moreover, the history of the movement shows a development away from the strict attempt at a completely 'artificial' verse form in imitation of Latin towards a compromise which tries to incorporate the features admired in both classical and native traditions, a development which is worth tracing, as it is part of the broad advance in metrical technique and theory which enabled the Elizabethans not only to lay the foundations of modern English accentual metre, but also to produce some of the greatest works using that metre.

I should like to begin by discussing Stanyhurst because his *First Foure Bookes of Virgil his Aeneis* (1582) is, of the extended experiments in quantitative metre, the most thoroughgoing in imitating Latin metre as it appeared to the average educated Elizabethan. Some lines from Book I will serve as an example of Stanyhurst's method and style (I give the scansion of the first five; my quotations are from van der Haar's edition):

Theare stands far stretching a nouke uplandish: an Island
Theare seat, with crabknob skrude stoans hath framed
an haven.
This creeke with running passadge thee channel inhaunteth.
Heere doe lye wyde scatterd and theare clives loftelye
steaming,
And a brace of menacing ragd rocks skymounted abydeth.
Under having cabbans, where seas doo flitter in arches.
With woods and thickets close coucht they be clothed al
upward.
A cel or a cabban by nature formed, is under,
Freshe bubling fountayns and stoanseats carved ar inward:
Of Nymphes thee Nunry, wheere sea tost navye remayning
Needs not too grapple thee sands with flooke of an anchor.
Hither hath Aeneas with seavn ships gladlye repayred.

(1.167–78)

As we have seen, Stanyhurst's Dedication and Preface exemplify many of the characteristics of the Elizabethan attitude to quantitative metre that we have discussed: though he appeals to the ear, it is really the printed word on which he bases his quantities, and he believes that he is free to choose the scansion of many words, and to decide on his own spelling to achieve this. He attaches importance to the Latin rules, though he does not feel absolutely bound by them; for example, he states that syllables ending in *b, d, t, n, r,* are short (Smith, 1, 146), no doubt basing this partly on Latin practice (compare, for instance, a rule from *The Latine Grammar of P. Ramus*: 'A short syllable is...everie vowell before these letters, *r, l, t, d, m, b,* in the ende of a word', p. 9), but when this rule conflicts with the diphthong rule in words like *playne* and *youre* he makes a compromise: 'woordes eending in dipthongwise would bee common' (Smith, 1, 146). In general, however, Stanyhurst's work is remarkable for its closeness to the Latin model, and its disregard for any aural embodiment of quantity; for instance, he not only follows the Latin practice of eliding a word-final vowel when followed by an initial vowel (something which very few quantitative poets in English did), but in both rules and verse extends this, on the Latin model, to words ending in a vowel + *m* (Smith, 1, 146–7). As has been observed by many commentators, his hexameters are accentually very close to Latin hexameters, with coincidence of stress and ictus infrequent in the first four feet of the line, and nearly always present in the last two. Nor is this achieved merely by attending to the accentual pattern; it is an exact imitation of the Latin practice of preventing coincidence in the first part of the line by means of an obligatory caesura. In Stanyhurst's hexameters, the caesura is, as in Latin, nearly always the strong third-foot type (marked || in the lines scanned above), and like the Latin caesura it consists of a word-break preceded by a polysyllabic word – not merely a pause in the line, as in English verse in the native tradition and, as we shall see, in many of the other quantitative experiments. The effect of this in a Latin line is to make coincidence impossible at this point, since the first syllable of the foot, though bearing the ictus, is the final syllable of a polysyllabic word, and hence is unstressed. In order to produce the same effect on the accentual structure of an English line, the polysyllabic words have to be accentually similar to Latin words (see p. 12 above), and this is the case in Stanyhurst's *Aeneis*: the caesura is generally preceded by a paroxytone or proparoxytone word (in the lines scanned above, *strétching, crábknob, rúnning, scátterd* and *ménacing*). At the end of the line, too, Stanyhurst observes the minutiae of the Latin hexameter rules: monosyllables or pairs of disyllables occur very rarely in final position, and then only when preceded by a monosyllable. If this rule is broken in Latin, it produces a clash in the final two feet where coincidence is required; Stanyhurst, however, does occasionally break it, but without this effect, because he uses what he rarely uses elsewhere (and what did not exist in Latin): an oxytone word (one with a stress on the final syllable). Thus there are lines ending, 'gírdĕd ăbóut hēr' (1.499), 'trŭelўe rĕsólve mē' (11.163), and 'sétlĕd ămóng ūs' (11.186), where the correct quantitative and accentual pattern is maintained, even though the final word is a monosyllable. In terms of both accentual structure and word-lengths, then, Stanyhurst achieves probably as accurate an imitation of the Latin hexameter as is possible in an extended work.

To a modern reader, the quantitative structure of Stanyhurst's lines, on the other hand, seems to be far from the Latin original: words like *brace* and *lye* in the lines above can hardly be regarded as short in any phonetic sense, nor does the termination *-ing*, or the word *the* (even when spelt *thee*), seem long. But phonetic length is not in question here: the syllables are long and short in exactly the same way as the syllables of Virgil's hexameters, as read by Stanyhurst, were long and short. Robinson pronounced the first syllable of *licet* in the same way as Stanyhurst pronounced *lye*, and the first syllable of *calor* with a vowel-sound like that in Stanyhurst's *brace*, though he scanned both as short (see above, p. 28), so why should an English quantitative poet not do likewise? Though the final syllable of *potestas* is scanned long, it is pronounced by Robinson with a lax *a*, so it is not surprising that Stanyhurst feels free to scan syllables with lax vowels as long (though for the most part he prefers to scan them as short if they are open and unstressed – unless he can use the diphthong rule, as in *thee*, or position, as in *-ing*, to justify, by orthographical means, the length). Similarly, his scansions of *vïolence* (11.201) and *vānitye* (11.296) have parallels in the Elizabethan pronunciation of words like *dïes* and *clāritas*. And because digraphs, not diphthongs, are regularly long in Latin, it is on the former that Stanyhurst bases what he no doubt believes to be the 'diphthong rule': the *i* of *violence* in Elizabethan pronunciation was, as it is today, a diphthong, but because it is represented by only one letter, Stanyhurst does not feel that it contradicts the rule of vowel before vowel. On the other hand, when he says that *playne*, *fayne* and *swayne* are 'woordes eending in dipthongwise' (Smith, I, 146) he is basing this on the spelling which he gives, for the pronunciation of these words was monophthongal (see Dobson, 1968, II, 594–603), and in his verses, syllables with digraphs are usually long (some of the exceptions being covered by the rule of final consonants). These examples of non-phonetic quantity could, of course, be added to from every line of the work; and the reason for this is not that Stanyhurst had a wayward view of quantity, but that he had a very strict view: quantity in English was to be as close to quantity in Latin as he could make it. His four translations of psalms into iambic dimeters, elegiacs, asclepiads, and sapphics, and the 'Prayer too thee Trinitye' in sapphics, all appended to his *Aeneis*, have similar general characteristics: using the same quantitative system, the lines are close structural imitations of the Latin models (except that the iambics are accentually more regular), carefully observing rules of caesura and word-length. Thus his sapphics, for instance, have the characteristic accentual rhythm of the Horatian sapphic, which I shall discuss in Chapter 14.

When we try to assess Stanyhurst as a poet, we face the same difficulties which all the quantitative poets present: we cannot avoid, as we read their verse, looking for the qualities that we normally value, some of which are contradictory to those the poet himself valued. We can admire Stanyhurst for the skill with which he had produced an imitation of Latin verse as he knew it, but we cannot take pleasure in this aspect of his poetry as we read page after page of it. When we ignore the quantitative basis of the verse, and read it as we would accentual verse of the period – something which would not have pleased Stanyhurst – we find that it has moments when vocabulary and rhythm give it a vigorous directness, but that any passage of several lines is marred by the wild diction and the veering of tone that this produces, the distorted word-order (something else which the Latin model justified, of course),[1] the omissions and repetitions of words, and, in general, the feeling that the language has been so wrenched out of shape as to have lost most of the subtlety of expression it possesses. It is difficult not to agree with the adverse judgements on the verse that have repeatedly been expressed, beginning with Nashe's comments in his Preface to Greene's *Menaphon* (1589),[2] though failure to understand what Stanyhurst was attempting (and the extent to which he succeeded) has often led to exaggerated attacks on the man himself. It is worth noting, however, that most of the Elizabethan criticism is directed, deservedly, at the diction, not the metre (though if the latter could only be obtained by using such diction, the attempt itself deserves at least some of the scorn it received); and writers who actively supported the movement naturally found something to praise in Stanyhurst's metre – Puttenham remarks that Stanyhurst translated Virgil 'not uncommendably' (Smith, II, 117), though he later takes him to task for offending against decorum in his style (Smith, II, 178–9); Harvey includes him in a list of poets singled out for praise (Smith, II, 234); and the *Preservation* poet expressed his reverence for him 'as a fine, as an exquisit author', though he too seems worried by his style, and requests Stanyhurst 'with wordes significant to refile, and finely to polish' his translation (p. 5). To modern ears, particularly, Stanyhurst's rhythm does not offend, for we do not object to accentual irregularity, and the hexameters of the *Aeneis* at least escape the dactylic tripping effect of nineteenth-century accentual hexameters, and of many of the other Renaissance experiments. The frequent use

---

[1] Note, for instance, how he rearranges what would presumably be in prose 'Heere and theare doe lye wyde scatterd clives' in the fourth line quoted above – no doubt to obtain the correct caesura.

[2] Arber prints a selection of criticism in his edition of Stanyhurst's translation (1880), including Nashe's attack on Stanyhurst's 'carterlie varietie, as no hodge plowman in a countrie, but would have held as the extremitie of clownerie' (p. xviii), Joseph Hall's description of 'the forged mint that did create/New coyne of words never articulate' in *Virgidemiarum* (1597) (p. xx), and Southey's reference to Stanyhurst as the 'common sewer of the language' in *Omniana* (1812) (p. xxi). Twentieth-century criticism abounds with judgements as harsh: 'frantic gibberish' (Saintsbury, 1906–10, II, 173); 'that lumbering Jesuit' (Rollins, *Phoenix Nest*, p. xxi); 'hideous hexameters' and 'monstrosities' (A. M. Clark, 1946, p. 120); 'a crank who played with quantitative verse' (Pattison, 1948, p. 67).

of successive stresses (as in several of the lines quoted above) give the rhythm a muscularity which is prevented from becoming turgid by the scattering of unstressed syllables both alone and in pairs – a flexibility that is worlds away from the prevailing iambic jog-trot of the time, and that could have been an element in highly successful verse, had it not been achieved at such cost to style and diction. Modern critics sometimes find Stanyhurst's vigour refreshingly different from the artificiality and smoothness of the traditional Elizabethan lyric: thus Hobsbaum includes Stanyhurst in his anthology entitled *Ten Elizabethan Poets* (1969) (and, astonishingly, considers him to be one of the seven major Elizabethan poets, p. 18), and Lucie-Smith's Penguin collection of *Elizabethan Verse* (1965) contains quantitative verse by five poets, among them Stanyhurst, whose work is said to have 'an excitement of rhythm and of language' (p. 19). (The irony of Stanyhurst's being praised for avoiding the artificiality he so valued and sought for need not be commented on.) Reeves and Seymour-Smith, who include Stanyhurst in their *New Canon of English Poetry* (1967), admit that most of his experiments are 'grotesquely bad' but that at times they have 'an authentic, if quaint, power' (p. 314), a judgement with which I am in agreement. As one of the difficulties experienced by the modern reader who has no interest in the quantitative basis of Stanyhurst's verse is the idiosyncratic spelling, I quote here some lines from Book II in Hobsbaum's modernised spelling, to illustrate Stanyhurst's capacity as a poet:

> His foes old Priamus through court and city beholding
> On rusty shoulders slow clapped his unusual armour,
> And bootless morglay to his sides he belted unable.
> His life amidst the enemies with foin to finish he mindeth.
> In middle of the palace, to skies broad all open, an altar
> Stood with green laurel through long antiquity shaded.
> Now to this hold Hecuba and her daughters mournful
> > assembled
> In vain for succour gripping their mystical idols.
> Like doves in tempest clinging fast closely together
> When she saw Priamus youthly surcharged in armour

She said 'What madness thee leads, unfortunate husband,
With these mails massive to be clogged? Now whither I pray
thee?
Our state eke and persons may not thus weakly be shielded.
No, though my darling were present, couraged Hector.
Here pitch thy fortress: let trust be reposed in altar,
This shall us all succour, or we will jointly be murdered.'
This said, her old husband in sacred seat she reposed.

(ed. Hobsbaum, p. 75)

12

Scholarship and sensitivity –
Sir Philip Sidney

Sidney's quantitative theory

Stanyhurst was presumably unaware of, or unimpressed by, the
arguments of the scholars who wished to reform the pronunciation of Latin, for an unquestioning acceptance of the traditional
pronunciation, and the conception of Latin quantity that came
with it, underlies his imitation. Sidney, on the other hand, was
a personal friend of some of the leading scholars of Europe,
many of whom made valuable contributions to the study of
Latin prosody and pronunciation, and was highly regarded for
his own learning (for a full account see Buxton, 1964, chs. 2, 3
and 5). Among those with whom he became closely acquainted
on his European travels of 1572–5 was Sturm (see Osborn,
1972, pp. 90–2), whose perceptive comments on quantitative
verse were discussed in Chapter 3. He also met and gained
the respect of both Ramus (see above, p. 122) and Stephanus,
who later dedicated two works to Sidney (see Buxton, 1964,
pp. 56–9 and Osborn, 1972, pp. 88–9). The former's unusually
sharp understanding of the effect of the Renaissance mispronunciation of Latin and the latter's collection of essays
on the reformed pronunciation of the classical languages both
received mention in Chapter 6. Even more significant was
Sidney's friendship with Lipsius, another scholar who was
concerned at the mispronunciation of Latin, and who saw
clearly the need to give 'long' and 'short' vowels phonetic
reality (see the discussion in Chapter 6 above). They probably
first met in 1577 in Louvain, where Lipsius held a professorship,
and were together in Leyden a few months before Sidney's
death in 1586 (see Van Dorsten, 1962, pp. 119–21 and Buxton,

1964, pp. 167–8). Lipsius' *De Recta Pronunciatione Latinae Linguae* (1586) opens with an Epistle Dedicatory to Sidney, beginning:

Quaeris à me seriò, Vir illustris Philippe Sidneie, de Pronunciatu Latinae linguae quid sentiam? germanúmne & verum hunc quo nunc utimur: an alium fuisse antiquitus, qui, ut multa alia, exoleverit tenebris ignorantiae obrutus & longi aevi.[1]

(sig. *2)

Sidney's interest in the correct pronunciation of Latin may have initially been aroused by Languet, who in several of his letters to Sidney encouraged him to alter his English manner of pronunciation. We find him, for instance, writing to Sidney on 5 February 1574 (and see also his similar remarks on the same subject in other letters to Sidney quoted by Osborn, 1972, pp. 130, 145–6, 161, and 203):

Obsecro, ut aliquid tentes in emendanda tua pronuntiatione. Nihil erit excellenti tuo ingenio impossibile. Senties aliquid molestiae initio, sed mihi crede, non erit opus multo tempore ad eam rem perficiendam, & quia pauci ex vestris hominibus id curant, eo plus gloriae inde reportabis.[2]   (*Epistolae*, p. 53)

It seems likely, then, that Sidney would have been conscious of the incorrectness of the sixteenth-century pronunciations of Latin and the conception of Latin metre that this gave rise to, and that his attempt to imitate classical metres would have come closer to scholarly notions of Latin verse than Stanyhurst's; in particular, Sidney would not have been content with the totally unphonetic nature of quantity in Stanyhurst's work, since Ramus, Lipsius and others had shown that quantity in classical Rome had been perceptible to the ear.

We do not have much in the way of theory from Sidney's pen, but what we do have fulfils this expectation, as well as reflecting

---

[1] 'Are you serious in asking me, illustrious Philip Sidney, what I think about the pronunciation of the Latin language – whether the pronunciation which we now use is genuine and accurate, or whether there was a different one in ancient times which, like many other things, has passed away, overwhelmed by the darkness of ignorance and the long lapse of time?'

[2] 'I beg you to make some attempt to amend your pronunciation. Nothing can be impossible for your excellent mind. At first it will be rather troublesome, but, believe me, it will not take long to achieve; and since few of your countrymen concern themselves with this, you will win all the more glory from it.'

his probable acquaintance with the activities of the Baïf Academy in Paris (see above, p. 122). In a passage which occurs in two of the *Arcadia* manuscripts, Dicus and Lalus discuss the relative merits of accentual/rhyming and quantitative verse, and Dicus' defence of the latter rests on the assumption that it is built up of phonetically short and long syllables and hence more suitable for music. His descriptions of long and short syllables, which he believes should be matched with long and short notes, are interesting, for they concentrate on the physical characteristics of the sounds: in accentual verse, he says,

the musicke, finding it confused, is forced somtime to make a quaver of that which is ruffe and heavy in the mouth, and at an other time to hould up in a long that which, being perchaunce but a light vowell, would be gone with a breath. (*Poems*, p. 390)

A 'rough' syllable is perhaps one which is made long by position; and a 'light vowel' also must refer to the pronunciation. Dicus' argument could have been undermined by a demonstration of the fact that long and short notes go most happily with stressed and unstressed syllables, but Lalus is unaware of this, and his main defence is that 'musicke is a servaunt to poetry' and it is therefore the musician who needs to take care to match the verse. In the *Apologie*, Sidney upholds Dicus' claim: classical verse is 'more fit for Musick, both words and tune observing quantity' (Smith, 1, 204).[1] And in his set of rules for quantitative verse, Sidney's concern with pronunciation can be seen to be more than merely theoretical. Rule 2 states: 'Single consonantes comonly shorte, but suche as have a dowble sownde (as "lăck", "wĭll", "tĭll") or suche as the

---

[1] Though what we have of Sidney's theory of quantitative verse is much concerned with music, we have no evidence that this manifested itself in any practical way. Buxton believes that Sidney's experiments 'arose not from a pedantic classicism, which was far from Sidney's thought, but from an attempt to accommodate verse to music' (1964, p. 116); however, while this may to some extent be true, it seems unlikely that he would not have shared the purely poetic reasons that lay behind the experiments of Watson, Ascham, Spenser, Harvey and others – especially in view of his utilisation of the findings of Renaissance scholarship in his system for assigning quantities. If he had been involved in any attempts at sung quantitative verse, he would have come face to face with the inadequacies of his quantitative system as an organisation of the durations of English syllables

vowell before dothe produce longe (as "hāte", "debāte")'
(*Poems*, p. 391). The first exception shows that it is unwise to
assume that Sidney's intention to base quantity on pronunciation means that he was successful: he was subject to all the
influences discussed earlier, and though he may have drawn his
theory and practice a little closer than most, he certainly did
not escape the tendency to confuse graphic and phonetic
embodiments of language, or the assumption that the Latin
rules were concerned with real phonetic duration. But his
second exception does show a different approach from Stanyhurst's, and gives a rule which does not appear in the Latin
grammars: a syllable with a tense vowel is long (though the
way it is expressed – as if the vowel made the consonant long –
indicates that much imprecision remains). Rule 4 makes a
similar observation: 'Suche vowells [are] longe as the pro-
nounciacon makes longe (as "glōry", "lādy"), and suche like
as seeame to have a dipthonge sownde (as "shōw", "blōw",
"dȳe", "hȳe")' (*Poems*, p. 391). Though we cannot be certain
that Sidney's pronunciation of *show* and *blow* was really
diphthongal (a monophthongal pronunciation was common in
the late sixteenth century, especially with the vowel in final
position – see Dobson, 1968, II, 804–9), and that he was not
more influenced by the spelling than the pronunciation, he is
obviously attempting to base quantity on the phonetic character of the syllables. His attitude towards elision also contrasts
with Stanyhurst's rigorous adherence to the Latin model:
although it is an important part of Latin scansion, Sidney,
appealing to the way English is actually spoken, feels free to
employ elision or to allow hiatus 'as thadvantaige of the verse
best serves; for so in our ordinarie speache we do (for as well
we saye "thow art" as "th'art")' (*Poems*, p. 391). Sidney's
more pragmatic attitude to elision was to be far more popular
with later quantitative poets than Stanyhurst's dogmatism.

– though it would have strengthened his tendency to identify stress and quantity,
and it is quite a plausible explanation of his two poems in which complete
coincidence is achieved, as such poems are much more suited to music than his
more strict classical imitations. Two other quantitative poets who were concerned
with the problems of setting words to music were Baïf and Campion, and it is
significant that both show a high degree of coincidence in their quantitative
verse.

Sidney's quantitative practice

When it came to the actual writing of quantitative verse, Sidney had various possibilities before him. He could have departed from his theory, and worked only by the Latin rules; if he had done so, his quantitative verse would contain, as Stanyhurst's does, many stressed syllables with tense vowels scanned as short. Some lines from *OA* 13,[1] 'Lady, reservd by the heav'ns to do pastors' company honnor', in hexameters, will show that this is not so:

Then do I thinke in deed, that better it is to be private
In sorrows torments, then, tyed to the pompes of a pallace,
Nurse inwarde maladyes, which have not scope to be
    breath'd out,
But perforce disgest, all bitter juices of horror
In silence, from a man's owne selfe with company robbed.
Better yet do I live, that though by my thoughts I be plunged
Into my live's bondage, yet may disburden a passion
(Opprest with ruinouse conceites) by the helpe of an
    outcrye.

(lines 102–9)

These lines, in which the quantities are typical of Sidney's experiments, show how different his method is from Stanyhurst's. The only occurrence of a tense, stressed vowel in a short syllable is *rŭinouse* in the last line, where the Latin rule of vowel before vowel overrides any considerations of sounds, and demonstrates that Sidney is far from making 'phonetic' quantity all-important. Otherwise (and this holds for all his quantitative verse) stressed syllables containing tense vowels are long. It is evident that in addition to the Latin rules he took stress or the tenseness of the vowels, or both, into consideration. To decide which of these was the more important, we need to look at syllables in which these criteria contradict one another,

---

[1] I refer to Sidney's poems by Ringler's abbreviations – *OA*: *Old Arcadia*; *CS*: *Certain Sonnets* – and all quotations are from Ringler's edition.

that is, unstressed syllables with tense vowels and stressed syllables with lax vowels. We find that the former are nearly always short – in the lines above, over half the short, unstressed syllables have vowels which are tense – which would suggest that stress was of greater importance than tenseness. However, we must remember that, by virtue of the fact that they are unstressed, these vowels would tend to be shorter than similar vowels in stressed syllables, and some of them might have been reduced to [ə] in Sidney's pronunciation, so it is possible that even in these cases he was deciding on the basis of vowel-length, as he probably knew was the case in classical times. In the other test-case, stressed syllables with lax vowels are usually short when no Latin rule is operative, as in *mălady* in the lines above. Here vowel-tenseness is obviously a more important criterion than stress, and Sidney had many Latin precedents, not only in the Elizabethan pronunciation (which made vowels of this type lax whatever the classical quantity), but also in the reconstructed classical pronunciation. What is more, Sidney usually scans such syllables as short even when they occur in penultimate position – examples in *OA* 13 are *mĕritts* (line 155) and *prĭson* (line 163) – even though the Elizabethan pronunciation of Latin had no equivalents. It can be seen, then, that Sidney is closer to the original classical model than Stanyhurst, in that he attempted to take the tenseness of vowels into consideration in ascertaining the quantity of syllables.

But Sidney, too, had been through grammar school, and many of the old habits died hard. He probably read Latin verse with an unclassical pronunciation to the end of his life,[1] so short syllables with tense vowels and long syllables with lax vowels followed by single consonants would never have *sounded* wrong to him, though on inspection he might have decided that, by classical standards, they were incorrect. But if an

---

[1] Though he may have followed Languet's advice and adopted a continental pronunciation in preference to the English one, as Lipsius' dedication of *De Recta Pronunciatione* seems to suggest (see above, p. 174), these were, as we have seen, equally unclassical. Kabell (1960) suggests that he used a French oxytone pronunciation for words like *mŏnŭmēnt* and *crŭēll*, making accent and quantity coincide completely (pp. 174–7), but there is no need to propose such an unlikely explanation for scansions which, given the normal English pronunciation, are perfect imitations of the Latin model.

important Latin rule was in danger, he had no hesitation in going against his normal practice, thus *rŭinouse* above, and in the same poem, *vĭolence* (line 12) and *Dÿamond* (line 165). And he still felt free to include as Rule 7, 'Some wordes especially short' and as Rule 8, 'Particles used nowe long, nowe shorte' (*Poems*, p. 391). In other words, he did not really escape from the common conception of quantity as something separate from the sound of the words, over which the poet – or at least the first poet – has some degree of control; though at the same time he no doubt believed, like many others, that he was dealing with real phonetic quantity.

Oddly enough, it was probably his sensitivity to the sound of syllables which, while bringing him closer to the Latin model than Stanyhurst in the manner described above, at the same time took him further away from it in other respects. We have seen that in accentual structure Stanyhurst's hexameters are extremely close to Latin hexameters (and the accentual structure was something the Elizabethan pronunciation left undistorted). It will be seen from Sidney's lines quoted above that his hexameters have a high proportion of coincidence in all parts of the line: most of the dactyls have a dactylic accentual pattern and the spondees are more often than not accentual trochees. A comparison of 70 spondees of Stanyhurst's with the same number of Sidney's, taking those which occur in the first four feet of a number of lines selected at random (Stanyhurst, *Aeneis*, 1.169–80; IV.415–25; Sidney, *OA* 13, 1–7, 42–50, 101–7, 155–64 – 23 lines in Stanyhurst, 33 in Sidney, a difference which itself reflects the lighter rhythm of the latter's verse) yields the following figures:

Accentual pattern:	/ ×	× /	× ×	/ /
Stanyhurst:	13	27	19	11
Sidney:	48	12	5	5

Thus Sidney is much closer to an accentual imitation of classical feet, and, by using coincidence of stress and ictus rather than trying to have every long syllable stressed, he achieves a fairly regular accentual rhythm. (In the same lines, Stanyhurst has nearly twice as many 'clashing' dactyls as 'coinciding', while Sidney has over five times as many of the latter as the former; in the final two feet, however, both poets have coincidence in nearly every line.) This tendency in Sidney was no doubt partly the result of his attempt to judge quantity by sound: we have seen that he scanned unstressed syllables as short if Latin rules did not apply, presumably because they did not sound 'long' to him. But this decision alone would not result in lines as accentually regular as Sidney's are,[1] for there are many stressed syllables with lax vowels in English, which would be scanned short according to Sidney's practice as described above, and which would therefore upset the regularity. Sidney's quantitative verse, however, uses these infrequently: final syllables and monosyllables of this type are nearly always made long by a following consonant (examples in the lines quoted are *then*, *have*, *yet*), and penultimate syllables often have an alternative Elizabethan spelling with a doubled consonant which Sidney uses to obtain length by position (examples in *OA* 13 are *hōnnor*, line 1, *Pāllace*, line 4, and *pittie*, line 5). Sometimes, Sidney simply scans such syllables as long – *dēserte* (line 2), *blēmishe* (line 67), and *abōlish* (line 99) occur in this poem – though this is rare. (Words like *abāsh* (line 23), *gāther* (line 63) and *sūch* (line 155) might appear to be similar instances, but there are so many occurrences of long syllables with lax vowel + *ch*, *th*, or *sh* that Sidney must have regarded these consonants as capable of having a 'dowble sounde'.) This tendency to avoid making stressed syllables short no doubt resulted from a sense that it sounded wrong to do so; either a single syllable scanned in this way seemed unsatisfactory, or a line which was accentually irregular as a result of such scansions was found unpleasant. Antepenultimate syllables posed a greater problem: English words obeyed the same rule that made the vowels in Latin open stressed antepenultimates lax in the Elizabethan pronunciation, and the doubling of the following

---

[1] In calling quantitative lines 'accentually regular' I mean that the accents fall in such a way as to give the effect of an accentual rhythm. This will usually mean a coincidence of stress and ictus, which in the hexameter gives a regular rhythm of six stresses separated by one or two unstressed syllables. If the coincidence is between stress and length (so that quantitative spondees become accentual spondees), a less tripping rhythm is achieved in the hexameter, and this is used to good effect by some quantitative poets.

consonant was often unacceptable. Moreover, the penultimate rule ensured that the penultimate syllable was short, so if the word was to be used at all in hexameter verse, either the antepenultimate or the final syllable also had to be short. In some cases (like *rĕvĕrēnce* in *OA* 13, line 5) final length by position meant that there was no choice; and even where there was, Sidney usually preferred to scan the syllable with a lax vowel as short. He could, of course, have avoided such words altogether (which he does in *OA* 32 and *CS* 25, poems in which the feet have an accentual as well as quantitative basis, rendering stressed short syllables unacceptable); that he included them, and scanned them in this way, shows that he was far from intending an accentual imitation of the classical metre.

Sidney's use of caesura also differs from Stanyhurst's, and again results in a more rhythmical line. As can be seen in the example given, he has a regular strong caesura, usually a pause marked by punctuation, which to some extent lessens the accentual regularity of the lines;[1] but in well over half his hexameters, classical practice is contradicted by a stressed syllable immediately preceding the caesura – in other words, either a stressed monosyllable (contrary to Latin practice) or an oxytone polysyllable (of which Latin has none). This means that in Sidney's verse, unlike Stanyhurst's, the caesura loses entirely its function of ensuring a clash of stress and ictus in the first part of the line, and his liking for an immediately preceding stress (for instance, 28 of the first 35 lines of *OA* 13 have stress in this position) almost makes it into a device for ensuring coincidence. It is impossible to decide with any certainty what led to this preference for accentual regularity. It may be that in trying to judge the quantity of individual syllables by their sound he found that those which were stressed nearly always seemed long, and those that were unstressed seemed short (though he need not have consciously formulated it in such terms, of course). But this does not seem to be enough to account for the marked regularity of accentual structure, for

[1] Here again, Stanyhurst seems to reflect English grammar-school traditions while Sidney is more influenced by continental discussions (see the definitions of caesura from Bird and Fabricius quoted above, p. 63, n. 3).

Sidney could have avoided it if he had really wished to, by using Latin rules like position and vowel before vowel (which he obviously did not question, and which would have yielded many long unstressed syllables and short stressed syllables if he had desired them) to counteract the predominant coincidence which a stress-based system of quantity produces. It seems likely that Sidney's sensitivity to English poetry and its rhythms prevented him from writing lines with the accentual roughness of Stanyhurst's hexameters (and we cannot discount the possibility that somewhere at the back of his mind, in spite of his learning, was the rhythm of the Latin hexameter as he had read it 'scanningly' at school). It may be, too, that in the absence of an agreed system of quantitative prosody for English he wished his lines to be relatively easy to scan; if this was his aim, he succeeded, for the reader knows that two unstressed open syllables signal a dactyl, and the other, less common, types of dactyl are also quite easy to recognise, involving as they do words of the *mălădyes* or *rŭĭnouse* type. And as the large majority of long syllables are long by position (and most of the others have a tense, stressed vowel), scansion is much less painful a process than with Stanyhurst's hexameters. Sidney was perhaps aware that for the Romans, reading quantitative verse with appreciation of the metre was not the laborious business that it was for the Elizabethans.

In the matter of final word-lengths, Sidney is again less faithful to the Latin model. Of the 175 lines of *OA* 13, 49 go against the Latin prohibition of final monosyllables, and considerably less than half of these are of the type of which classical verse was more tolerant, ending in two monosyllables. On the other hand, the poem has only one occurrence of a line ending in the sequence monosyllable + disyllable + disyllable, which was allowed in Latin, and which had been used by Watson (and was to be used by later poets), and no occurrence of the prohibited pair of final disyllables without a preceding monosyllable. An examination of the accentual structure of the final feet of Sidney's lines reveals the reason for this inconsistency in his degree of faithfulness to the Latin model: whatever length the words that make them up, these feet in

Sidney's hexameters, with very few exceptions, exhibit perfect coincidence. In English, unlike Latin, a final monosyllable preceded by a disyllable can easily fit into the pattern $/×× | /×$ or $/×× | / /$, and Sidney nearly always uses oxytone disyllables to achieve this. On the other hand, in neither English nor Latin can a final pair of disyllables fit the pattern, as the first word must have a stressed syllable; and Sidney even avoids the variant with a preceding mono-syllable, though the classical poets were prepared to accept this degree of accentual irregularity at line-ends. So here too, Sidney is paying more attention to the accentual rhythm of his lines than to the Latin rules.[1]

The skill and pains that have gone into the writing of verse which meets such strict metrical requirements cannot but be admired, but if one reads the hexameters of *OA* 13 simply as poetry, one finds little to enjoy. The accentual structure is not regular enough to impart any sense of controlled rhythm holding the poem together, and not irregular enough to create a feeling of energetic roughness, as sometimes happens in Stanyhurst's verse. The lines tend to sprawl formlessly, with the frequent double unstressed syllables of the dactyls coming like a distressing tic, and often bringing up the same words – 'of a', 'to the', 'we do', etc. – which may be quantitatively necessary, but in any other terms are irritating padding. How-ever, Sidney's chosen method of classical imitation allows him to use more of the English language as he finds it than Stany-hurst, and though the need to meet the rigid requirements of the metre no doubt restricted his creativeness, he managed to achieve some quite effective verse, especially in lines 77–115,

---

[1] It is interesting to note that of the very few lines of *OA* 13 without coincidence in the final two feet, three (lines 12, 32, and 40) were emended by the editors of the 1593 *Arcadia*, even though this meant quite substantial changes in wording. Either of the known editors, Hugh Sanford, a classical scholar of some standing (see Godshalk, 1964, pp. 177–8), or the Countess of Pembroke (whose sensitivity to accentual rhythm is evident in her own quantitative hexameters, to be discussed in ch. 14), could have been responsible. This, at least, seems to me to be the most likely explanation of the variants; Ringler, in arguing that the 1593 edition embodies earlier authorial versions of lines like 12 and 32 (Sidney, *Poems*, p. 374), has overlooked the importance of the accentual pattern in quantitative hexameters, for his theory would mean that Sidney made alterations which turned perfectly correct hexameters into accentually incorrect ones.

of which the following are a sample (and see also the lines quoted above). Cleofila is speaking:

> Let not a puppet abuse thy sprite, Kings' Crownes do not
>   helpe them
> From the cruell headache, nor shooes of golde doo the gowt
>   heale,
> And preciouse couches full oft are shak't with a feaver.
> If then a boddily evill in a boddily gloze be not hidden,
> Shall such morning deaws be an ease to the heate of a love's
>   fire?
> *Dorus.* O glittring miseries of man, if this be the fortune
> Of those fortune lulls, so small rest rests in a kingdome.
> What marvaile tho a Prince transforme himselfe to a Pastor?
> Come from marble bowers, many times the gay harbor of
>   anguish,
> Unto a silly caban, though weake, yet stronger against woes.

(lines 84–93)

Sidney's quantitative poems

I have used *OA* 13 to illustrate my points about Sidney's quantitative verse, as it is a long poem in hexameters, but they apply equally well to all of his quantitative experiments, allowing for a greater number of errors in some poems which may be his earliest attempts.[1] *OA* 11, 'Fortune, Nature, Love, long have contended about me', and *OA* 74, 'Unto the caitife wretch, whom long affliction holdeth', are in elegiacs, in which the hexameters are very similar to those of *OA* 13. The pentameters are constructed on similar principles: the classical insistence on final disyllables is not complied with, but the classical tendency towards coincidence in the second hemistich is followed (especially in *OA* 11), coincidence in the first hemistich being less predominant; the caesura is regularly a pause, and in most lines marked by punctuation; and Sidney's

---

[1] The number of errors in the quantitative verse by Sidney and others has often been exaggerated by commentators as a result of their unawareness that a final vowel followed by a word beginning with two consonants, though usually avoided (see p. 17, n. 1 above), was sometimes scanned as short in classical Latin, and that this was well known to Elizabethan grammarians – Lily, for instance, states that lengthening in this position is rare (1567, sig. G7*v*). Many of the 'errors of position' that Ringler claims to find in Sidney's quantitative verse are of this kind.

practice in assigning quantities is the same. *OA* 12, 'If mine eyes can speake to doo harty errande', consists of six stanzas of sapphics. Here, as in his hexameters, Sidney does not imitate the accentual structure of the Latin sapphic, even though this, as we shall see, was more regular than other metres; he writes lines which have a certain amount of accentual regularity while observing quantity strictly. The pattern is usually one of stresses on the third, the fourth or fifth, the eighth, and the tenth or eleventh syllables, and the result is one of the best of the quantitative poems, notably in lines 9–24:

> Yet dying, and dead, doo we sing her honour;
> So become our tombes monuments of her praise;
> So becomes our losse the triumph of her gayne;
>   Hers be the glory.
> If the senceless spheares doo yet hold a musique,
> If the Swanne's sweet voice be not heard, but at death,
> If the mute timber when it hath the life lost,
>   Yeldeth a lute's tune,
> Are the humane mindes priviledg'd so meanly,
> As that hatefull death can abridge them of powre,
> With the voyce of truth to recorde to all worldes,
>   That we be her spoiles?
> Thus not ending, endes the due praise of her praise;
> Fleshly vaile consumes; but a soule hath his life,
> Which is helde in love, love it is, that hath joynde
>   Life to this our soule.

The hexameter echo-poem, *OA* 31 ('Faire Rocks, goodly rivers, sweet woods, when shall I see peace?'), shows the same characteristics as the other hexameters, except that it has more errors, suggesting that it is an earlier work. *OA* 32, 'My muse what ails this ardour' is an experiment in combining accentual and quantitative structure: it scans correctly as anacreontic verse, but at the same time there is complete coincidence, and as the metre is one of regular alternations ($\smile - \smile - \smile - -$), the result is regularly rhythmical (though the stiffness of the accentual pattern produces a rather dull poem). This bears out what I have already suggested: that Sidney, unlike Stanyhurst, was concerned to find a way of writing quantitative verse which did not go against the normal English habit of regular accentuation, and later quantitative poets, especially Campion, followed up Sidney's experiment with some successful verse of this kind. The 'Phaleuciackes' of *OA* 33, 'Reason, tell me thy mind, if here be reason', were probably also influential – Davison's *Poetical Rhapsody* of 1602–21 contains several poems in this metre. They have the usual regular caesura in the form of a pause, but their accentual structure is less regular than most of Sidney's quantitative verse. *OA* 34, 'O sweet woods the delight of solitarines!' (in asclepiads) seems to be another earlier work; it has several errors of scansion, and does not take vowel-tenseness into consideration as do the other poems (*snăky*, *dŭty*, *tĭtle* would be long in later works, and *opīnions*, *vānity*, *pāradise* probably short). Nevertheless, it is an interesting poem, and one of the most successful of the experiments as poetry in its own right, partly because of its subtly varied accentual patterns which avoid the dactylic tic of the hexa-meters because of the frequent stressed short syllables and the high proportion of monosyllables, and partly because the lack of strong rhythms suits the gently languorous tone. The poem begins:

$$\bar{} \quad \bar{} \quad \bar{} \quad \breve{} \, \breve{} \bar{} \quad \bar{} \quad \breve{} \breve{} \bar{} \breve{} \bar{}$$
O sweet woods the delight of solitarines!
$$\bar{} \quad \bar{} \quad \bar{} \quad \bar{} \quad \breve{} \, \breve{} \bar{} \breve{} \quad \bar{}$$
O how much I do like your solitarines!
$$\bar{} \quad \bar{} \quad \bar{} \quad \breve{} \quad \breve{} \quad \bar{} \quad \breve{} \breve{} \bar{} \breve{} \bar{}$$
Where man's mind hath a freed consideration
$$\bar{} \quad \bar{} \quad \bar{} \quad \breve{} \, \breve{} \quad \bar{} \quad \bar{} \quad \breve{} \, \breve{} \bar{} \breve{} \bar{}$$
Of goodnes to receive lovely direction.
Where senses do behold th'order of heav'nly hoste,
And wise thoughts do behold what the creator is:
Contemplation here holdeth his only seate:
Bownded with no limitts, borne with a wing of hope
Clymes even unto the starres, Nature is under it.
Nought disturbs thy quiet, all to thy service yeeld,
Each sight draws on a thought, thought mother of science,
Sweet birds kindly do graunt harmony unto thee,
Faire trees' shade is enough fortification,
Nor danger to thy selfe if be not in thy selfe.

(lines 1–14)

Included in *Certain Sonnets* are four quantitative poems, probably written at about the same time as the *Old Arcadia*, three of which, *CS* 5 in sapphics and *CS* 13 and *CS* 14 in elegiacs, are broadly similar to the *Old Arcadia* poems, though they are less accomplished as quantitative verse. *CS* 25, 'When to my deadlie pleasure', is in aristophanics, and like *OA* 32 combines accentual and quantitative verse in a simple metrical scheme, though, interestingly, Sidney includes words where short syllables are stressed because of the Latin vowel before vowel rule (*violence* and *tied*), thus upsetting the accentual pattern (as Campion was to do in verse of a similar kind). However, the poem ends effectively with regular coincidence of stress and quantity in a rhythmically insistent monosyllabic climax:

> ‾ ∪ ∪ ‾ ∪ ‾ ‾
> Thus do I fall to rise thus,
> ‾ ∪ ∪ ‾ ∪ ‾ ‾
> Thus do I dye to live thus,
> ‾ ∪ ∪ ‾ ∪ ‾ ‾
> Changed to a change, I change not.
>
> Thus may I not be from you:
> Thus be my senses on you:
> Thus what I thinke is of you:
> Thus what I seeke is in you:
> All what I am, it is you.
>
> (lines 27–34)

Sidney's quantitative verse is not the detailed and accurate imitation of Latin verse that Hendrickson (1949) and John Thompson (1961) see it as, nor does it ignore natural length and accent as McKerrow claims (1901, p. 179); it is an extended attempt to introduce into English poetry those features of classical verse so highly admired by the Elizabethans, without losing too much of the rhythmical quality of traditional English verse. The numerous types of metre used, and the different systems employed in making imitations, show a mind consciously and carefully experimenting with the poetic potential of the English language, meeting with some success, but more failure, and no doubt discovering much in the process. The lessons learned were to benefit not only Sidney in his later verse, but Elizabethan poetry in general.

13

'Our new famous enterprise' –
Spenser, Harvey and Fraunce

Stanyhurst, in spite of the praise he received from some dedicated English hexametrists, was not a figure to initiate a new
poetic movement; Sidney very clearly was. Although Harvey
refers coyly to 'the good Aungell (whether it were Gabriell or
some other) that put so good a motion' into the heads of Sidney
and Dyer, he fully realises how much their example will 'helpe
forwarde our new famous enterprise for the Exchanging of
Barbarous and Balductum Rymes with Artificial Verses'
(Smith, I, 101). Fraunce merits consideration in this chapter as
an example of Sidney's powerful influence, and as one of the
few quantitative poets who, within the terms the movement set
itself, achieved success. Spenser too, owed his brief passion for
quantitative versifying to Sidney, but the importance of the
verse in the Spenser/Harvey letters, apart from our natural
interest in the minor writings of a great poet, lies in its direct
exemplification of the forces at work behind the movement,
untempered by thoroughgoing adherence to the Latin model
or by sensitivity to the result as English poetry.

Spenser and Harvey

Only a few poems in quantitative metres by Spenser and Harvey
survive, chiefly in the letters which passed between them in
1579–80, and which were published by Harvey in the latter
year (Smith, I, 87–122). Harvey's *Letter Book* also contains a
poem in quantitative hexameters written before 1580, part of
which was published in his *Foure Letters* of 1592 (p. 61). In
spite of numerous modern assertions that they represented
opposed approaches to the question of classical metres in

English,[1] Spenser and Harvey wrote broadly the same kind of quantitative verse. Fidelity to the Latin model varies: the Latin rules of position, vowel before vowel, and diphthong (that is, digraph) are observed quite carefully, though there are errors; the classical practice with regard to caesura is sometimes followed, sometimes not; and the restrictions on final word-lengths play no part at all. Vowel-tenseness is not taken into consideration as it is by Sidney; unstressed, lax vowels occur in long syllables without position in the verse of both writers, and stressed, tense vowels occur in short syllables. Like Stanyhurst, then, they imitate Latin quantity as they understood it, but unlike him, their imitation of classical metres does not extend to details of verse-structure. And unlike both Stanyhurst and Sidney, they do not ensure, by the use of position and other unmistakable rules, that the scansion is never in doubt. Nor is it always merely a question of two equally correct scansions: the second line of Spenser's 'Iambicum Trimetrum' (Smith, 1, 90–1), for instance, is a syllable short. This must have worried Davison, for he prints the poem in his *Poetical Rhapsody* (1, 233) with 'Thought' at the end of the second line instead of at the beginning of the third (which Harvey had criticized because it has two extra syllables). The problem is not solved, however, for the rearrangement results in the scansion 'flȳĭng thought', which contradicts both the rule of vowel before vowel and that of position. With regard to accent, the examples of neither writer reveal a clear decision as to its role in quantitative verse. Harvey's hexameters are certainly not based on coincidence as is often claimed; in general they exhibit less coincidence than Sidney's but more than Stanyhurst's (excluding the final two feet, which, following classical precedent, are nearly always accentually regular). However, this practice varies from poem to poem: 'Encomium Lauri' (Smith, 1, 106–7), for instance, has a large number of lines with complete stress/ictus coincidence, where 'A New Yeeres Gift' (Smith, 1, 104–5) has few, especially after the first four lines. It would seem that he did not pay much attention to stress – except, as we saw in

[1] See, for instance, Omond (1921, pp. 10–12), Hamer (1930, p. 297), Willcock (1934, p. 5), and Lewis (1954, pp. 364–5).

Chapter 10, when it revealed the quantity of the penultimate syllable. Thus the diphthong rule has no force in the penultimate of *unkodpĕased* and *travăiler* (Smith, 1, 108, 109), and Harvey's brother – whose quantitative verse is quoted in Harvey's second letter – scans *majestie* with a short penultimate in spite of position (Smith, 1, 113). Spenser's few hexameters also vary from a line of complete coincidence to lines with several clashes of accent and ictus in the first four feet.

The quantitative verse of both Spenser and Harvey gives the impression of hasty composition,[1] and judged as poetry, only Spenser's 'Iambicum Trimetrum' is of any value, perhaps because, being what Harvey calls a 'mixte and licentious IAMBICKE', it imposes less severe restraints than most quantitative metres – in every foot except the last, the short mora can be replaced by a long or two shorts, and the long by two shorts. I give the first nine lines, with one possible scansion of the first four:

$$\breve{} \; - \mid \breve{} \; - \mid \breve{} \; - \mid - \; - \mid \breve{} \; \breve{} \; - \mid \breve{} \; -$$
Unhappie Verse, the witnesse of my unhappie state,
$$- \quad - \mid - \quad - \mid \breve{} \; - \mid - \quad - \mid \breve{} \; - \mid \breve{} \; -$$
Make thy selfe flutt[e]ring wings of thy fast flying
$$- \quad - \mid \breve{} \; - \mid - \; \breve{} \; \breve{} \mid - \quad - \mid \breve{} \; \breve{} \; - \mid \breve{} \; -$$
Thought, and fly forth unto my Love, wheresoever she be:
$$\breve{} \; - \mid \breve{} \; - \mid - \; - \mid \breve{} \; - \mid \breve{} \; - \mid \breve{} \; -$$
Whether lying reastlesse in heavy bedde, or else
Sitting so cheerelesse at the cheerfull boorde, or else
Playing alone carelesse on hir heavenlie Virginals.
If in Bed, tell hir that my eyes can take no reste;
If at Boorde, tell hir that my mouth can eate no meate;
If at hir Virginals, tel hir I can heare no mirth.

(Smith, 1, 90–1)

The tone of Harvey's poems is light-hearted, but there is no suggestion that he is attempting to ridicule the movement, as is sometimes claimed; what mattered to Harvey was the metre, and the metre was something quite separate from the intonation and rhythm (in the modern sense) of the lines. The following

---

[1] The quantitative verse by Harvey's brother is more easily scanned, more correct, and accentually more regular than Gabriel's; it observes caesura more carefully; and it appears to use vowel-tenseness to a greater degree in the determination of quantities.

hexameter lines from his 'Speculum Tuscanismi' exhibit his characteristic tone:

No man but Minion, Stowte Lowte, Plaine swayne, quoth a
   Lording:
No wordes but valorous, no workes but woomanish onely.
For life Magnificoes, not a beck but glorious in shew,
In deede most frivolous, not a looke but Tuscanish alwayes:
His *cringing side necke, Eyes glauncing, Fisnamie smirking,*
With *forefinger kisse,* and brave *embrace to the footewarde:*
Largebelled Kodpeas'd Dublet, unkodpeased halfe hose,
Straite to the dock, like a shirte, and close to the britch, like a
   diveling,
A little Apish Hatte, cowched fast to the pate, like an Oyster...

(Smith, 1, 107–8)

We have already discussed the main points which emerge from the debate between Spenser and Harvey, and it is clear from Harvey's examples that he was not proposing a radically different kind of verse from Spenser's or Sidney's. He does, however, end his second letter on 'reformed versifying' with a general discussion of quantity, in which he puts forward the sensible view that it is not the Latin model that is all-important, but the extent to which it applies to English. And he lays the foundation for an adequate theory of accentual metre when he states:

Peradventure, uppon the diligent survewe and examination of Particulars, some the like Analogie and Uniformity might be founde oute in some other respecte, that shoulde as universally and Canonically holde amongst us as Position doeth with the Latines and Greekes.   (Smith, 1, 121)

He does not, however, think of stress as the feature of English which determines 'long' and 'short', and these hints of an English prosody faithful to the phonetic actualities of the language were never elaborated, nor did they issue in practice. But in these few paragraphs, Harvey is moving away from the conception of metre which was the natural outcome of a grammar-school education, towards the conception which was to form the basis of the great Elizabethan achievements in poetry.

Abraham Fraunce

Fraunce was the most prolific and the most popular of the Elizabethan quantitative poets. All his verse is in hexameters (except for a few asclepiads in *Yvychurch*, 1591, sig. F4*r–v*), and all of it is of basically the same type (though one departure from his normal practice is the use of partial rhyme in the section of *Emanuel* on the Nativity). My examples will be from *Amyntas* (1587), available in a convenient modern edition (ed. Dickey, 1967), published together with the Latin original by Watson. His method is close to that of his master, Sidney: scrupulous attention to the rules of position, vowel before vowel, diphthong (which meant that all digraphs were long, with the exception of *-ie* and *-ee* in word-final position), and penultimate syllable; a relaxation of the Latin rules of elision; scansion of unstressed open syllables as short and stressed syllables with tense vowels as long; regular occurrence of a strong third-foot caesura marked by a pause, and very often by punctuation; and the liberal use of unmistakably long syllables to make scansion certain and relatively simple. Like Sidney, he usually ensures that a stressed syllable with a lax vowel is made long by position, and he has the same kind of exception: stressed antepenultimates like *pĭtiles* and *mĭseries* and, more rarely, stressed initial syllables of disyllables, like *prētie* and *mănie*. In one respect his imitation is stricter than Sidney's: he obeys Latin restrictions on final word-length. Two disyllables seldom occur, and then only with a preceding monosyllable in the approved manner, as first used in English by Watson (thus 'thȳ bŏnȳ Phīlĭs', VIII.104 and 'sō mănĭe ōffrīngs', IX.78); and, as in Latin, the few final monosyllables are nearly always the second of a pair. He does not go as far as Stanyhurst in imitating the Latin model, however; he uses oxytones freely in the first part of the line, and does not observe pre-caesural restrictions on word-length and accentual position, but in the final feet he does eschew oxytones – like Stanyhurst, the only exceptions are the rare occasions on which he breaks the rule of final word-length (thus 'Ĭ bĕsēech thēe', II.85 and 'līve nŏt ălōne thūs', II.88). His concern with the details of scansion can be seen in the list of 'faults escaped' where, for example, ōutrāgĭŏus is changed to *outragius* to avoid a short 'diphthong' in the last syllable, *wōfŭll* to *woful* to avoid the contradiction of position (p. xvi).

Fraunce's hexameters are, if anything, accentually even more regular than Sidney's. The rhythm is upset occasionally by the short stressed syllables, but these are not very frequent (and often accentual regularity is preserved even though the accentual 'feet' do not tally with the quantitative ones). Nearly all the dactyls are regular accentual dactyls, and very often the short syllables are of the type we have already met in Sidney's hexameters ('of the', 'to be', 'by the', etc.); furthermore, the large majority of spondees are accentual trochees. Fraunce's tendency to use rhetorical figures which involve much repetition adds to the rhythmic monotony – the following lines from *Amyntas* are by no means untypical:

> But Pan, and Fauni, but garden greene of Amintas,
> But you springs, and dales, and woods aye wont to be silent,
> Leave of your mourning, Ile give you leave to be silent,
> Leave to be silent stil, give you me leave to bee mourning,
> Leave to be mourning, stil, let this most heavie departure,
> This death of Phillis bring wished death to Amintas.

(VII.102–7)

However, one does not have to seek far to find the reasons for Fraunce's success. He combined a strict quantitative pattern, giving the intellectual satisfaction demanded by adherents to quantitative verse without too much exertion being necessary, with a rhythmicality which prevented his poetry from sounding too different from English verse in the native tradition, but which at the same time linked it with the 'scanningly' read hexameter in Latin. And at times he puts the accentual rhythm to good effect in verse which would make rewarding reading if the metrical exigencies did not constantly result in slight distortions of language and the insertion of unnecessary syllables.

Compare the accentual irregularities of the first twelve lines quoted below, where the wrenching of stresses mirrors Amyntas' state of mind as he contemplates the loss of Phillis, with the much lighter and more regular rhythm of the passage that follows a few lines later, in which Amyntas imagines a heavenly reunion:

> O dismal deaths day, with black stone still to be noted,
> Wherein no sunne shin'd, no comfort came fro the heavens,
> Wherein clustred clouds had cov'red lightsome Olympus,
> Wherein no sweete bird could finde any joy to be chirping,
> Wherein loathsome snakes from dens were loath to be creeping,
> Wherein foule skriche owles did make a detestable howling,
> And from chimney top gave woful signes of a mischiefe.
> O first day of death, last day of life to Amintas,
> Which no day shal drive from soule and hart of Amintas,
> Til Neptune dry'de up withdrawe his fludds fro the fishes,
> And skaled fishes live naked along by the sea shore,
> Till starrs fal to the ground, til light harts leap to Olympus.
> (VIII.75–86)

> Thou that abridgest breath, thou daughter dear to the
>   darknes,
> Cutt this thread of life, dispatch and bring mee to darknes,
> Infernal darknes, fit place for mournful Amintas.
> So shal Amintas walke and talke in darksome Avernus,
> So shal Amintas love with Phillis againe be renued,
> In fields Elysian Phillis shal live with Amintas.
> Thus do I wish and pray, this praying is but a pratling,
> And these wishing words but a blast, but a winde, but a
>   whistling.
> Dye then Amyntas Dye, for dead is thy bony Phillis.
> (VIII.96–104)

The movement produced little verse as good as this – which is, of course, more a censure of the movement than a commendation of Fraunce.

14

Four approaches to quantitative verse

It is possible at this stage to characterise four differing approaches to English quantitative verse, to the first three of which we can attach the names of Stanyhurst, Spenser/Harvey, and Sidney respectively, though the distinctions are far from clear-cut, and more than one method can be present in a single poem. Before going on to consider the further developments in the work of Puttenham and Campion, I shall look briefly at the other quantitative poets in terms of this framework.

The Stanyhurst approach

Stanyhurst's strict imitation of the Latin accentual patterns and restrictions on word-lengths, and his indifference to the tenseness of vowels, constitute one approach, which makes very few concessions to the native tradition of English verse and which rigorously follows through the implications of the school training in Latin prosody, without consideration of scholarly views on the subject. The result is so far removed from English verse in the native tradition and requires such a severe pruning of the normal English vocabulary, that it is not surprising that Stanyhurst had no successors. James Sandford could perhaps be considered as a predecessor on the strength of his eight-line poem in English elegiacs, published as one of 'Certayne Poemes Dedicated to the Queenes moste excellente Majestie' at the end of the second edition (1576) of his translation of Guicciardini's *L'hore di Ricreatione*, entitled *Houres of recreation*. The poem is itself a translation of Estienne Jodelle's quantitative poem 'A Madame Marguerite de France', dating from 1559 (*Oeuvres*, ed. Marty-Laveaux, II, 107), which Sandford prints, without acknowledgement, and with the slight alterations made necessary by the change in dedicatee, together with quantitative translations in Greek, Latin, Italian and English (sig. Q3v–4). It contains many stressed tense vowels in short position, and there are some signs of an attempt to imitate the Latin accentual pattern, though with nothing like Stanyhurst's strictness.

The Spenser/Harvey approach

However, it would probably be more accurate to consider Sandford as belonging to the second group: those who are concerned above all with the Latin rules of quantity, and who attempt neither an imitation of the Latin stress-patterns nor an approximation to the stress-rhythms of the native English tradition. We have seen that Ascham had no clear conception of the nature of accent and its function in verse, and it seems likely that in the fifteen lines of quantitative verse which appear in *Toxophilus* (1545) (*English Works*, pp. 4, 12, 14, 16, 24, 38, 64, 72, 75, 89, 92, 93, 104), he was not fully conscious of the stress-patterns he was producing, for some of the lines have similarities to the classical stress-pattern and others (probably the ones which had a greater influence on later writers) have a strong rhythm as a result of coincidence. Compare, for example, the following two hexameters:

What thing wants quiet and meri rest endures but a smal while.

(p. 4)

Up to the pap his stringe dyd he pul, his shafte to the hard

heed.   (p. 104)

The first has the classical pattern of clash followed by correspondence, while the second has coincidence throughout.

There are too few examples from Ascham's pen to enable one to estimate the extent to which he took vowel-tenseness into account in ascertaining quantities, but it is possible that it did play a part – in which case, Ascham looks forward to the method Sidney was to use. However, the others who belong to this group clearly ignore vowel-tenseness. We have looked at Spenser and Harvey, whose quantitative verse exhibits the same accentual variations as Ascham's, and ignores vowel-tenseness; and the two lines by Watson also seem to be of this type. Song no. xxiii in Byrd's *Psalmes, Sonets, & songs of sadnes and pietie* (1588) is in hexameters in which neither accent nor vowel-tenseness bears a consistent relation to quantity (in fact, there is less coincidence in the final two feet of the lines than in the first four) – but because it has a setting which mirrors exactly the quantities of the verse, long syllables having twice the duration of short, this is a special case (though the words and music would have been better suited if stress had coincided with quantity):

```
 –    –  | –  ∪ ∪| –  –   | –    –  | –   ∪    ∪| –  –
Constant Penelope, sends to thee careless Ulisses,
 –    –  ∪  | –   –  | –    –  | –    –  ∪ ∪| –   –
write not againe, but come sweet mate, thy self to revive me.
 –   ∪  ∪| –    –  | –     –| –  ∪ ∪  | –   ∪ ∪ ∪| –   –
Troy we do much envie, we desolate lost ladies of Greece:
 –   ∪ ∪| –    –  | –  –  | –     –  | –  ∪ ∪  | –    –
Not Priamus, nor yet all Troy can us recompence make.
```
Oh, that he had when he first toke shipping to Lacedemon,
that adulter I meane, had ben o'rewhelmed with waters:
Then had I not lien now all alone, thus quivering for cold,
nor used this complaint, nor have thought the day to be so
  long.   (sig. E3)

Perhaps we can also place in this group the work of Francis Sabie (*Pan's Pipe*, 1595, a set of poems in quantitative verse of various kinds, and *Flora's Fortune*, also 1595, containing a quantitative echo-poem on sig. B4r–v), though more because of its ineptitude than for any particular method. There are many echoes of Fraunce in the hexameters, but in the elegiacs and asclepiads something approaching the classical accentual patterns is achieved. There is little consistency, however; not only does Sabie fail to take vowel-tenseness and stress into account, but he also frequently contradicts the Latin rules of quantity – even position, which the other quantitative poets observe scrupulously.

The poets in this group, then, write quantitative verse of a type which follows naturally from the school training in Latin prosody and the conception of metre which arises out of it: as far as metre is concerned, the main requirement is that each line can be scanned according to the Latin rules, without alternative scansions being possible. The question of stress is a secondary one, if it arises consciously as a question at all. The easily recognisable stress-pattern of the final two feet of the Latin hexameter meant that an English line which lacked it sounded wrong, but apart from that, little thought was given to accentual structure. However, in the attempt to assign quantity to an individual syllable, the operation of the penultimate rule and the greater prominence of stressed syllables meant that more often than not stress and quantity would coincide, resulting in many hexameters with the characteristic dactylic-and-trochaic rhythm.

The Sidneian approach

Poets in the third group, however, seem to be more conscious of the accentual structure of the line, as well as giving vowel-tenseness an important role in decisions about quantity. The result, as we have seen in Sidney and Fraunce, is verse which is characterised by a rhythmical regularity which places it closer to the native tradition, but which never becomes complete regularity, because the concern for the Latin rules and for vowel-tenseness often results in clashes of accent and quantity. This method proved very popular, combining as it did qualities of both traditions, while appearing in its approximation to phonetic quantity to embody the theory of quantitative verse to a greater extent than Latin verse itself. Although Fraunce's *Amyntas* was written later than Sidney's quantitative verse (and took the rhythmicality of the English hexameter a stage further), it appeared in print six years earlier, so it is not surprising that the first poets outside the Sidney circle to take up this method should be closer to Fraunce than to Sidney. Webbe's *Discourse* (Smith, I, 226–302) actually appeared a year before *Amyntas*, and as he does not include Fraunce (or Sidney) in his discussion of English poets, it might seem that his hexameters, which have a high proportion of coincidence throughout and seem to take vowel-tenseness into consideration, are written according to a scheme of his own making. However, it is possible that Webbe had read some of Fraunce's verse in manuscript, for, having mentioned Abraham Fleming – himself an opponent of 'foolish rime' who attempted verse in 'due proportion and measure' (*Bucoliks*, 1589, sig. A4*v*), though not, as has been claimed, in quantitative verse – he remarks:

> To whom I would heere adjoyne one of hys name, whom I know to have excelled as well in all kinde of learning as in Poetry most especially, and would appeare so if the dainty morselles and fine poeticall inventions of hys were as common abroade as I knowe they be among some of hys freendes. (Smith, I, 244)

If it is the Christian name to which Webbe is referring, Fraunce (who, like Webbe, had been at St John's) seems a likely candidate. We should remember that because of the importance of authority as a means of ascertaining quantity, it would be quite possible for a poet writing with a knowledge of Sidney's or Fraunce's work to appear to take vowel-tenseness into account in the same way without in fact doing this consciously, and this may be true of Webb, whose attitude to authority is evident in his attempts to account for quantities he has 'marked in others' (Smith, I, 282). His translation of Virgil's first and second Eclogues begins as follows (the full text is given in Arber's edition of the *Discourse*, pp. 73–9):

```
 – ∪ ∪ |  –  – ∪∪ | – ‖– | –  | –  – ∪ ∪ | –    –
Tityrus, happilie thou lyste tumbling under a beech tree,
 –  ∪  ∪| –  –  | – ‖ – | –   –  | – ∪∪ | –  –
All in a fine oate pipe these sweete songs lustilie chaunting:
 –  –  | –   ∪  ∪| – ‖– | –   –  | –   –
We, poore soules, goe to wracke, and from these coastes be
 ∪| –  –
   remooved,
 –     – | – – | – ‖ – | – ∪  ∪ | –   ∪ ∪| –
And fro our pastures sweete: thou Tityr, at ease in a shade
 –
   plott,
 –   –  | –  ∪ ∪| – ‖ – | –   – | –  ∪ ∪|– –
Makst thicke groves to resound with songes of brave Amarillis.
                                              (Smith, I, 284)
```

(Note how, in the fourth line, Webbe ensures through his spelling 'fro' the elision by Latin rule of an unwanted vowel.) I shall discuss Webbe's sapphics later in the chapter, along with other English sapphics, as this metre poses somewhat different problems.

Another writer who produced highly rhythmical hexameters before the publication of Sidney's quantitative verse was Robert Greene, who included them in his prose works *Greenes Mourning Garment* (1590) (*Works*, IX, 151–3, 159–62), *Greenes Farewell to Folly* (1591) (*Works*, IX, 293–4), and *Mamillia* (1593) (*Works*, II, 219–20). They are all in a Frauncian vein, as the following lines, the opening of 'Hexametra ALEXIS in laudem ROSAMUNDI' from *Greenes Mourning Garment*, will indicate:

Oft have I heard my lief *Coridon* report on a love-day,
When bonny maides doe meete with the Swaines in the vally
  by *Tempe*,
How bright eyd his *Phillis* was, how lovely they glanced,
When fro th'Aarches Eben black, flew lookes as a lightning,
That set a fire with piercing flames even hearts adamantine:
Face Rose hued, Cherry red, with a silver taint like a Lilly.
Venus pride might abate, might abash with a blush to behold
  her.
Phoebus wyers compar'd to her haires unworthy the praysing.
Junoes state, and Pallas wit disgrac'd with the Graces,
That grac'd her, whom poore *Coridon* did choose for a love-
  mate:
Ah, but had *Coridon* now seene the starre that *Alexis*
Likes and loves so deare, that he melts to sighs when he sees
  her.   (pp. 151–2)

However, Greene pays less attention to vowel-tenseness than Fraunce, and so cannot be considered a true representative of the approach to quantitative verse we are now looking at. He also allows his ear for accentual rhythms to overrule his eye for Latin prosody in allowing such short syllables as 'with the' and 'in the'. It is possible that he was writing rhythmical quantitative verse before he became acquainted with Fraunce's work, as there is a stationer's entry for *Mamillia* in 1583, though there is no known copy. As already mentioned, some of the hexameters in Ascham's *Toxophilus* are of this type, so a precedent had existed since 1545.

Less rhythmical and skilful, but also basically of this kind, are the poems in hexameters by Robert Mills in MS Rawlinson poet. 85, dating from the late 1580s (see Flügel, 1891, pp. 459–61). Though Mills might have known Fraunce at Cambridge, and refers to 'Amintas' in one of the poems, he may also have been familiar with Sidney's quantitative verse, some of which was included in the same manuscript anthology (perhaps compiled by Sir John Finett – see Ringler's comments in Sidney's *Poems*, p. 558 – whose friendship with Mills is attested to in the latter's verse).

After the publication of the 1593 edition of Sidney's *Arcadia* containing the bulk of his quantitative verse, we find more poets writing hexameters of this kind without falling into a dactylic jog-trot. John Dickenson is one of the most skilful of these; his *Shepheardes Complaint* of 1596 (included by Grosart in his 1878 edition of Dickenson's *Prose and Verse*) centres round a poem in hexameters (pp. 10–13) – though with a great deal of supplementary material – and as poetry is better than most of the products of the movement. Dickenson avoids the Fraun-cian jog-trot by using successive stresses frequently and the dactylic formulae ('of a', 'to the', etc.) sparingly; he takes over Sidney's concern with vowel-tenseness, and follows him in his interpretation of the caesura as a pause, often marked by punctuation. The complaint opens as follows:

```
 –    –   |  –   –    u  u| –  ‖  –|–    –   | –   u  u|–   –
If plaints could penetrate the sun-bright top of Olympus,
 –     –    |  –    –|–  ‖  –  |  –   –|  –   u
Whose lights sweet comfort these eies, eies moist with
 u| –   –
abundance
 –    –   |  –   –  | –    ‖ –  |  –    –|–  u   u|–     –
Of down-streaming teares since wrong'd by Fancy, beheld not:
 –    –    | –      –|–  ‖ u   u|  –    –   |  –    u   u|
Or th'earth yeild passage to my voice, voice hoarse with a
 –
thousand
 –    u   u| –    –  | –   ‖ –|–   –   | –    u   u| –
More then a thousand mones, sending them down to the deep
 –
vawts,
Where PLUTO Lord of Acheron enjoyeth his Empire,
Or some blustring blasts convey by force of a whirle-wind,
These my sad laments to the wide world there to be talk'd of:
```

Gods that dwell on high, and Fiends that lurke in AVERNUS:
Men that live on earth, or saile through watery TETHYS.
Gods, whose divine shapes loves force hath oft metamorphosed,
Fiends, whose hellish hearts no remorse, no regard ever entred,
Men whom loves deepe wounds have prostrate laid at his altars,
All these would pitie me, but vaine wish can litle helpe me.

(p. 10)

When he wishes to, however, he can imitate Fraunce, and both *Arisbas* (1594) and *Greene in Conceipt* (1598) contain parodies of the Frauncian manner (*Prose and Verse*, pp. 44, 57; 127) – though the poem in the latter begins quite impressively ('As when a wave-bruisd barke, long tost by the winds in a tempest...') before descending into Frauncian word-games.

A poet who uses the Sidneian method in an extended poem in hexameters without ever lapsing into Frauncian excesses is the anonymous author of *The Preservation of King Henry the vii* (1599), which also includes several shorter poems in hexameters, elegiacs and sapphics. The *Briefe rule or prosodie* with which he prefaces the verse gives evidence of his sensitivity to the tenseness of vowels. He discusses the prefixes *pre-* and *de-* (pp. 12–13), giving examples of their occurrence as both long and short syllables, the determining factor apparently being the tenseness of the vowel; thus *prĕsident, prĕvalent, dĕdication*, but *prēmeditate, prēdominant, dēmerited, dēpopulate* (notice that quantity is in opposition to stress here, since it is the stressed vowels which are lax). He also gives examples of their occurrence as common syllables, and it seems likely that in his pronunciation these were cases where the *e* tended to be reduced, but was tense in a careful pronunciation: *prĕposterous, prĕsumptuous, dĕnunciate, dĕterminate*. This kind of observation shows greater insight into the realities of pronunciation than most of his predecessors, but by 1599 it was too late to save quantitative verse. The poetry itself is undistinguished, though the avoidance of the dactylic formulae and of Frauncian repetitions makes it more pleasant to read than much of the earlier work, and at times the lack of a regular rhythm and the counterpointing of lines and sense-units is quite skilfully used for expressive purposes, as in these lines from Edward IV's dying speech:

```
 –  ∪ ∪|–     –  | –    ||∪  ∪| –    –  | –    ∪ ∪ |– –
```
Every one, deare sonnes, in his hand here take but an arrow,
```
 –      –  |  –    –  | – ||   –   | –    –  |  – ∪∪|   –   –
```
And break them forthwith. Which they did speedily. But now
```
 –     ∪ ∪ |  –    –| –    ||  –| –      –   | – ∪ ∪| –
```
Each on a sheafe of shaftes, my sonnes, take, forcibly break
```
          –
```
   them:
```
 –     ∪ ∪| –    ∪ ∪|– || – | –     –  | –    ∪  ∪|– –
```
Which to do each did asay, but could not. Then with a solemne
```
 –     ∪ ∪| –   ||–| –   –  |  –     –  | –    –   ∪    ∪|
```
Speach thus he spake: As you could not them break, so, my
```
     – –
```
   children,

Trew fyrme and constant conjunction of many brethren
No body can dissolve. Therefore, live frendly together.
If so be you seperate your selves each from another,
Then shall your enemies (as a prey snatcht up of a tyger)
You (disagreeing so) with a small force easily conquer.

                                             (pp. 52–3)

Not surprisingly, the Sidneian method is used by the Countess
of Pembroke in her psalms in quantitative metres, written at
some time in the 1590s (that is, at the same time as her preparation of the 1593 *Arcadia*, which included Sidney's quantitative
poems), though with less attention to the tenseness of vowels.
The manuscripts (edited by Rathmell, 1963, 1964) contain ten
quantitative poems, two of which are versions which the
Countess apparently rejected. Several are, as regards metre,
imitations of poems in the *Arcadia*: Psalm 121 is in phalaecian
hendecasyllables very similar to those of Sidney's *OA* 33; the
alternative version of Psalm 122 (see Rathmell, 1964, p. 501)
is in asclepiadic verse like that of *OA* 34; and Psalm 127
(incorrectly scanned by Samuel Woodford, who transcribed the
Countess' own manuscript in 1695 with comments on the
quantitative metres) is in anacreontics, closely modelled on *OA*
32, which, as we have seen, is one of the rare occasions on which
Sidney made stress and quantity coincide, a feature which the
Countess' imitation preserves. The hexameters of Psalm 122
show a substantial degree of coincidence, and careful attention
to vowel-tenseness. Psalm 120 is an interesting combination of
the regularity achieved by the method of *OA* 32 with the
irregularity typical of classical stress-patterns: it observes

coincidence of stress and quantity, but it is in alcaic stanzas, which involve three different types of line, so that no sense of accentual regularity is set up. A departure from Sidney's model is shown in Psalm 123, in elegiacs, for Sidney goes against the classical practice of ending the pentameters with disyllables, in order to achieve a higher degree of coincidence at the line-end than was possible in Latin. The Countess, however, follows the Latin model closely, and ends the pentameters with disyllables beginning with short, but stressed, syllables. Psalm 124 is in iambics, a comparison of which with Spenser's 'Iambicum Trimetrum' again brings out the greater attention paid by the Sidney/Fraunce group to native English stress-rhythms, for the Countess, while avoiding complete coincidence, keeps to a rhythm which is basically iambic, whereas Spenser's lines are only noticeably iambic in rhythm in the final two feet.

None of the quantitative psalms I have mentioned, nor the one in sapphics (which I shall return to), has much poetic merit, but the other two do at times rise above this level. Psalm 126 achieves this at the expense of metrical regularity: it is difficult to derive any consistent quantitative pattern from it (Woodford's scansion is incorrect), the stresses form no pattern, and the line-lengths vary throughout the poem. The first two stanzas are the best, striking as they do a note of personal intensity foreign to the conception of poetry as artifice which lay behind the quantitative experiments:

> When long absent from lovly Sion
> By the Lords conduct home we returned,
> We our sences scarsly beleeving
> Thought meere visions moved our fancy.

> Then in our merry mouthes laughter abounded,
> Tongues with gladness lowdly resounded
> While thus wondring Nations whispered:
> God with them most roially dealeth.

The hexameters of the alternative version of Psalm 89 combine quantitative strictness with rhythmic interest and poetic power. The method is still basically that of Sidney and Fraunce;

however, in spite of the tendency to scan all stressed syllables as long, the high proportion of accentual spondees results in a much weightier rhythm than the dactylic canter so typical of this kind of hexameter, and the skilful avoidance of the dactylic formulae beloved of hexametrists contributes to the muscularity of the rhythm. The result is 88 lines of verse which, although it does not attempt Stanyhurst's precise imitation of the Latin accentual structure (the caesuras are the Sidneian type), transplants the Latin sequence of clash followed by coincidence into English and which, when allowances are made for errors in transcription, can probably be considered as the most successful Elizabethan attempt to naturalise the hexameter – though it is still, of course, far inferior to the best verse of the native tradition. I give the first thirty lines:

‒   ‒ |‒   ‒ |‒ ‖ ‒ | ‒   ‒ |‒ ∪ ∪| ‒ ‒
Gods boundles bownties gods promise ever abyding
‒   ∪ ∪|‒   ‒|‒ ‒ | ‒ | ‒ ∪ ∪| ‒ ‒
shall bee my songs eternall them[e] still gladly recording
‒ ∪ ∪|‒ ‒|‒ ‖   ‒ |‒   ∪ ∪ |‒ ∪ ∪ |‒ ‒
of fowloing ages, while ranged in absolute order
‒   ‒ | ‒   ‒ | ‒ ‖‒ | ‒   ‒ | ‒ ∪ ∪ |‒ ‒
gold armed squadrons of stares shall muster in heaven
‒   ‒ | ‒ ‒ |‒ ‖ ‒ | ‒ | ‒ ∪ ∪ |‒ ‒
yea this soaner I think starres best ordered order
‒   ∪ ∪|‒ ‒ |‒ ‖ ‒|‒   ‒ | ‒ ∪ ∪ | ‒ ‒
shall to disorder fall, confusd in contrary courses
then that league be reverst, that sacred treaty repealed
thus by thy selfe sometime confirmd thus sworn to thy David
while earth, while waters, while palace of heavn abideth
stablish I will thy elected seed and loftily seated
on throne will hold them, till endles eternities ending
O father high heavens at thee most worthily wonder
O father earth dwellers, whose hearts on god bee reposed
Bend to thy thruthe their praise, when so their company
    meeteth
who is above that may compare with mighty Jehova?
who can among th exalted train of glorious angells
like to Jehova be found? all him with an awfull obeisance
terrible acknowlege, and flock affrighted abowt him,
thow comander of hosts, indeed most mighty Jehova
seest not a match in powr in verity knowst not an equall
Thow of foaming seas, dost still the tumultous outcries
thow their high swelling, dost coole with lowly residing

prowd Pharoa hath felt thee: all enemies all thy resisters
felt thy revendging hand, disperst & bloudily wounded
thow thow only the fownder of earth, and former of heaven
framer of all this vawted rownd, which hanged on hindges
north and south sustain this benignity, Thabor and hermon
that where sunn falleth, this where his charrit ariseth
testify with praises: thee, thee, all oly belongeth
all powre, all puisance, makes earth with wonder amazed.

(BM MS Add 12047, fols. 44v–45)

The first edition in 1602 of Davison's *Poetical Rhapsody* (ed. Rollins, 1931–2) contained ten quantitative poems, one of which was Spenser's 'Iambicum Trimetrum', and the other nine of which were assigned to 'Anomos'. In his preface, Davison states that the poems 'under the Name of *Anomos*' (corrected in later editions to 'Anonymous') were written 'almost twentie yeers since' (1, 5–6), apparently basing this conclusion on the references to Sidney in some of them. The quantitative poems obviously come from different hands, and show different approaches to quantitative versifying, though the most predominant influence is that of Sidney. One of them, no. 132 ('An Epigram to Sir Phillip Sydney in Elegicall Verse, Translated out of Jodelle, the French Poet'), dates from even earlier: it is Sandford's translation of Jodelle's poem of 1559 from the 1576 *Houres of recreation*, slightly altered once again to become a poem in praise of Sidney. Of the others, the first of the four poems in 'Phaleuciacks' (phalaecian hendecasyllables), no. 79, is perhaps the most enjoyable:

> – – | – ∪ ∪| –   ∪ | – ∪ | – –
> Time nor place did I want, what held me tongtide?
> – – | –   ∪ ∪| – ∪| – ∪ |– –
> What Charmes, what magicall abused Altars?
> – – | – ∪ ∪| –   ∪ | – ∪ | – –
> Wherefore wisht I so oft that hower unhappy,
> – – | – ∪ ∪| – ∪| – ∪ | – –
> When with freedom I might recount my torments,
> – – | – ∪ ∪| – ∪| – ∪ | – –
> And pleade for remedy by true lamenting?
> Dumbe, nay dead in a trance I stood amazed,
> When those looks I beheld that late I long'd for;
> No speech, no memory, no life remained,
> Now speech prateth apace, my greefe bewraying,

> Now bootlesse memory my plaints remembreth,
> Now life moveth againe, but al availes not.
> Speech, life, and memory die altogether,
> With speech, life, memory, Love onely dies not.

All four sets of 'Phaleuciacks' (the others are nos. 87, 88, and
118) take vowel-tenseness into consideration in the Sidneian
manner, and are very similar to Sidney's *OA* 33 in the same
metre, though with a higher proportion of coincidence,
especially in the later three. The one in rhyme, no. 88, indicates
an interesting attitude to quantitative verse; no longer is it
seen as superior to traditional verse (an assumption which
emerges in the Sandford poem – 'Age volative eates not such
verse as did to the Greekes build/Lasting praise'), but rather an
optional method of writing verse, suited to particular subjects,
as the following four lines indicate:

> Muse not, Lady, to reade so strange a Meeter;
> Strange griefe, strange remedy for ease requireth.
> When sweet Joy did abound, I writt the sweeter,
> Now that weareth away, my Muse retireth.

Of the three poems in hexameters (all on the death of Sidney),
one, no. 133, is crude, technically and poetically, though it is
the closest to Fraunce with its regular accentual pattern and its
dactylic formulae. The other two are more accomplished, and
closer to the Latin accentual scheme; the first, no. 134, has an
unstressed syllable at all line-ends except the last, and it is a
nice touch, for this last line reads, 'Dead lies his carcase, but
fame shall live to the worldes end'. The other one, no. 135,
shows much skill in achieving the correct quantities (though the
result is not so pleasing to us as it would have been to an
Elizabethan), including the following tour-de-force:

$$-\;\;\cup\cup\,|\;\;-\;\;\cup\cup\,|-\;\;-\;\;|\;-\;\;-\;|\;-\cup\cup|\;\;-\;\;-$$
Germany, France, Italy, Spaine, Denmark, Persia, Turkey,
$$-\;\;\cup\cup|\;\;-\;\;\;-\,|\;-\;\;-\;\;|\;-\;\;\;-\,|\;-\;\;\cup\;\;\;\cup\,|\;-$$
India where *Phoebus* climes from the sea to the skie-ward,
$$-\;\;\cup\cup|\;\;-\;\;\;\;-\,|-\;\;\;-|\;\;\;-\;\;\;-\;|\;-\;\;\cup\;\;\;\cup\,|\;-$$
India where *Phoebus* declines from skie to the Sea-ward,
$$-\;\;\cup\cup|\;\;-\;\;\;-\,|-\;\;\;\;-|-\;\cup\;\;\cup|-\;\cup\cup|\;\;-\;\;-$$
Tartary, Pole, Lettow, Muscovy, Bohemia, Norway...

I shall leave the sapphics in this edition and others added in the

1621 edition for later consideration. The 1621 edition also contains what appears to be a crude attempt at rhymed phalaecian hendecasyllables (no. 250).

The accentual approach

There appeared in the 1611 and 1621 editions of the *Poetical Rhapsody* a Latin poem with an English translation in hexameters (no. 248) which differs from most of the poems so far considered in that the Latin rules provide an inadequate guide to the scansion of many lines. If, however, one assumes that dactyls will be accentual dactyls and spondees will be accentual trochees, scansion becomes much more straightforward. It is a dull poem, but it does exemplify the Frauncian method taken one step further: quantitative rules are seldom broken, but they are no longer the basis of the poem, with accentual patterns serving merely as an additional consideration. This poem is an extreme example of what we can consider as the fourth type of quantitative verse of the period, in which the accentual pattern plays a more important role than in the Sidney/Fraunce type. In most of the verse of this kind, the lines remain scannable by the Latin rules alone, but what is no longer taken into consideration is the tenseness of the vowels. It is as if the stress on a syllable is felt to be a sufficient phonetic realisation of quantity; thus this type is like the third type in demanding a phonetic element of some sort in quantity, but it is, of course, closer to the native tradition. We have already seen that Ascham wrote some lines which appear to be of this kind in 1545, and that Greene's hexameters approach this method. Someone who wrote hexameters with even less concern for vowel-tenseness than Greene, but who nevertheless succeeded in producing an effective parody of Fraunce's manner, was Richard Barnfield, whose 'Hellens Rape, or A light Lanthorne for light Ladies' (appended to his *Affectionate Shepheard*, 1594; see *Poems*, pp. 39–41) has throughout its 75 lines the Frauncian jog-trot and the Frauncian word-games (although the poem is poking fun at Fraunce, the latter's influence pervades the whole book – see Morris, 1963, ch. 2). That Barnfield was interested in the stress-rhythm itself is suggested by the fact that even when quantity and stress do not coincide, the stresses frequently form a dactylic-and-trochaic rhythm of their own, contradicting the foot-divisions of the quantitative structure. The opening twelve lines will give the flavour of Barnfield's parody (which for the most part observes the quantitative rules strictly:

Lovely a Lasse, so loved a Lasse, and (alas) such a loving
Lasse, for a while (but a while) was none such a sweet bonny
   Love-Lasse
As *Helen, Maenelaus* loving, lov'd, lovlie a love-lasse,
Till spightfull Fortune from a love-lasse made her a love-lesse
Wife. From a wise woman to a witles wanton abandond,
When her mate (unawares) made warres in *Peloponessus,*
Adultrous *Paris* (then a Boy) kept sheepe as a shepheard
On *Ida* Mountaine, unknowne to the King for a Keeper
Of sheep, on *Ida* Mountaine, as a Boy, as a shepheard:
Yet such sheep he kept, and was so seemelie a shepheard,
Seemlie a Boy, so seemlie a youth, so seemlie a Younker,
That on *Ida* was not such a Boy, such a youth, such a
   Younker.   (*Poems*, p. 39)

Barnfield may be the 'R. B.' whose *Greenes Funeralls* was published in 1594 without the author's knowledge (see McKerrow's discussion of the authorship in his edition, pp. vii–x, and the argument in favour of Barnfield by Morris, 1963, ch. 6), for the work contains four poems in quantitative metre (Sonnets vii, viii, xi, xii) which bear some resemblance to 'Hellens Rape' (as well as two quantitative poems by Stanyhurst, Sonnets xiii and xiv, acknowledged as such). Sonnet iv, in accentual verse, seems to deliver a judgement on quantitative versifying which could well be Barnfield's: it ends with two stanzas calling on 'sweete Amyntas', probably Fraunce, to 'come and teach this fond A-Mint-Asse', whom Morris identifies as Harvey – and the lesson is presumably to be one on writing quantitative verse. However, the quantitative poems are much cruder, metrically and poetically, than 'Hellens Rape', and if they are by Barnfield, it is not surprising that he did not admit to writing them. They belong firmly to this group, because they take no account of vowel-tenseness and have marked accentual rhythms. They follow Fraunce in diction and subject-matter, as a line from Sonnet vii will indicate:

Matchles *Amintas* minde, to the minde of Matchles *Amintas*.

Sonnet xi is an interesting (though unsuccessful) experiment, for the writer has inserted couplets in rhymed accentual iambics into a poem in hexameters.

Two other poems have their place in this group. The first is song no. xxxiv in Byrd's *Psalmes, Sonets, & songs* (1588), in aristophanics. It is the first of two 'funerall Songs of that honorable Gent. Syr Phillip Sidney, Knight', and is modelled on Sidney's own *CS* 25, 'When to my deadlie pleasure', in the same metre. I give the first three stanzas:

> $-$ $\cup$ $\cup$ $-$ $-$
> Come to me griefe for ever,
> $-$ $\cup$ $\cup$ $-$ $-$
> Come to me teares day & night,
> $-$ $\cup$ $\cup$ $-$ $-$
> Come to me plaint, ah helples,
> $-$ $\cup$ $\cup$ $-$ $\cup$ $-$ $-$
> just grief, heart teares, plaint worthie.
>
> Go fro me dread to die now,
> Go fro me care to live more,
> Go fro me joyes all on earth,
> *Sidney*, O *Sidney* is dead.
>
> He whome the Court adorned,
> He whome the country courtis'd,
> He who made happie his friends,
> He that dyd good to all men.
>
> (sig. G1)

Like its model, this poem is characterised by coincidence of stress and quantity in most lines, with the result that the musical setting can at the same time reflect the quantitative structure of the verse and meet the demands of the accentual pattern (although the setting is not as completely determined by quantity as it is in 'Constant *Penelope*' in the same volume). The other poem is 'A Motive in Hexameters' by L. G., published in *Sorrowes Joy* in 1603 (reprinted in Nichols, 1828, 1, 1–24). It has the usual dactylic-and-trochaic rhythm produced by coincidence of stress and quantity:

> ‾ ‿ ‿| ‾   ‾ | ‾   ‿ ‿| ‾   ‾ | ‾ ‿
> Turne to the Lord, proud Pope, by thy bulles nought setteth
>   ‿| ‾   ‾
>   a good King.
> ‾   ‿   ‿ | ‾   ‾| ‾   ‿ ‿| ‾   ‾ | ‾   ‿ ‿
> Curse though thou dost, yet shall we be blest, for God is on
> | ‾   ‾
>   our side.
> ‾   ‿ ‿| ‾   ‾| ‾   ‿   ‿ | ‾   ‾ | ‾   ‿ ‿
> Downe to the ground thy crowne doe thou cast, and flee to the
> | ‾   ‾
>   Gospel.
> ‾   ‿   ‿| ‾   ‾| ‾   ‿ ‿| ‾   ‾ | ‾   ‿   ‿
> Downe o' thy knees submisse to our King, and hurt not his
> | ‾   ‾
>   Highnes.
> Arme not his Isles with a bull, nor curse, nor whette them
>   against him.
> God is his arme, the crowne is his owne, most due by the
>   birth-right.
> Him doe we rest in, next to the Lord, and pray for his
>   welfare.
> Haste then, ye Papists, to repent, and come to the true
>   Church.

(p. 13, lines 1–8)

Notice how a strong sense of an accentual rhythm is set up by the first four lines being metrically identical.

The sapphic

In all the verse we have discussed, the quantities are, in intention at least, correct according to the Latin rules; and, as we should expect, given the ideas about Latin metre then current, it is very rarely that an attempt is made to imitate the accentual structure of a Latin metre without giving the poem a quantitative basis. Where this would be most likely would be in imitations of the sapphic, for, as we saw in Chapter 1, the sapphic in its Horatian form is unusual in having a distinctive and fairly consistent accentual rhythm, and this is no doubt one reason why the sapphic is second only to the hexameter in popularity among the quantitative poets. However, methods of adaptation vary, and many who read and enjoyed Latin sapphics no doubt failed to realise that it was the accentual structure which gave the stanza its pleasing character. The rhythm is not one which was easily seen to be related to the native metres of English, though it is basically a simple four-stress line (with a half-line at the end of the stanza). Medieval adaptations of the sapphic keep this rhythm, even when the quantitative structure is ignored, as in the ninth-century stanza quoted by Wilkinson (1963, p. 108):

> terra marique victor honorande
>
> Caesar Auguste Hludowice, Christi
>
> dogmate clarus, decus aevi nostri,
>
> spes quoque regni...

The Protestant churches took this pattern over as a hymn-metre; it occurs, for instance, in J. Heerman's sixteenth-century hymn, 'Herzliebster Jesu, was hast du verbrochen'. An English example, quoted by Needler (1941), is Dearmer's translation of a hymn ascribed to Gregory the Great:

> Father, we praise Thee, now the night is over;
>
> Active and watchful, stand we all before thee;
>
> Singing, we offer prayer and meditation:
>
> Thus we adore thee.

(p. 16)

Musical settings of such hymns often bring out the rhythm clearly (as does Flemming's 1810 setting of Horace's own *Integer Vitae*): in its basic form it could be transcribed musically as follows:

This rhythmic pattern is present to varying degrees in the Elizabethan imitations, reflecting, no doubt, the extent to which the writer was conscious of the accentual structure of the Latin model (though we must not overlook the possibility of

medieval models, even among the humanists). Thus Stanyhurst, with his acute awareness of the Latin accentual pattern,
writes sapphics which come close to achieving this rhythm, as
the first three stanzas of his version of Psalm 4 will indicate:

$$- \ \cup \ - \ - \ - \ \| \ \cup \ \cup \ - \ \cup \ - \ -$$
When that I called, with an humbil owtcrye,
$$- \ \cup \ - \ - \ - \ \| \ \cup \ \cup \ - \ \cup \ - \ -$$
Thee God of Justice, meriting mye saulftye,
$$- \ \cup \ - \ - \ - \ \| \ \cup \ \cup \ - \ \cup \ - \ -$$
In many dangers mye weake hert upholding
$$- \ \cup \ - \ - \ -$$
    Swiftlye dyd hyre mee.

Therefor al freshly, lyke one oft enured
With thye great goodnesse, yet agayne doe crave thee,
Mercye too render, with al eeke toe graunt mee
    Gratius harckning.

Wherfore of mankind ye that are begotten,
What space and season doe ye catche for hardnesse,
Vanitee looving, toe toe fondlye searching
    Trumperye falshood.

          (*Aeneis*, 1582, ed. Arber, pp. 131–2)

(Notice that the Horatian caesura after the fifth syllable is
strictly observed, and, as in the same writer's hexameters,
preceded by an oxytone polysyllable.) Stanyhurst's other poem
in sapphics, 'A Prayer too thee Trinitye' (*Aeneis*, ed. Arber, p.
133), has the same metrical characteristics. Sidney's sapphics
(*OA* 12 and *CS* 5), on the other hand, have, like his hexameters,
a rhythm which is not that of the classical model (see above,
p. 185).

The list of those whose sapphics approach the classical rhythm
to some degree is a long one: Greville (*Caelica*, vi), James
Reshoulde (in MS Rawlinson poet. 85 – see Flügel, 1891,
pp. 458–9), Dickenson ('Dorylus his Ode', in *Arisbas*, 1594,
Prose and Verse, p. 57), the Countess of Pembroke (Psalm 125),
R. B. (*Greenes Funeralls*, 1594, Sonnet xii – though this is rather
a crude imitation), the *Preservation* poet (1599, p. 66), and the
author of poem 139, 'Sapphicks. Upon the Passion of Christ',
in Davison's *Poetical Rhapsody* (1602–21). A particularly

interesting poet in this respect is Campion, whose song in sapphic stanzas in *A Booke of Ayres* (1601) (*Works*, ed. Davis, pp. 48–9) imitates closely the Horatian rhythm:

– ∪ – –   – ∪ ∪ – ∪ – –
Come, let us sound with melody the praises
–   ∪ – –   –   ∪ ∪ –   ∪– –
Of the kings king, th'omnipotent creator,
– ∪ – – –   ∪ ∪ –   ∪ – –
Author of number, that hath all the world in
– ∪ ∪ – –
Harmonie framed.

Heav'n is his throne perpetually shining,
His devine power and glorie thence he thunders,
One in all, and all still in one abiding,
    Both Father, and Sonne.

O sacred sprite, invisible, eternall,
Ev'ry where, yet unlimited, that all things
Canst in one moment penetrate, revive me,
    O holy Spirit.[1]

                            (lines 1–12)

The stanzas are set, however, in such a way as to mask the Horatian rhythm, for Campion follows the strict principles of the Baïf Academy, also observed by Byrd in the quantitative songs mentioned above: a long syllable is given a note twice as long as a short syllable. As the accentual pattern of the sapphics does not correspond to the quantitative pattern, all the rhythmicality of the poem is lost. When he came to devise an 'English *Sapphick*' for his *Observations* of 1602, he created a stanza based on trochees which nevertheless comes quite close to the classical rhythm – it is as if, assuming that a long syllable should be a stressed one, he worked back from the basic accentual pattern of a slow start to the line and a quicker continuation to reach a quantitative pattern which would suit it:

[1] Writers of sapphics who, like Campion in this poem, followed the Sidneian principles of quantitative versifying but attempted to embody the Horatian rhythm found words with a stressed lax vowel in an open syllable invaluable, for such words provided the type of syllable needed for the sixth place in the line: one which they could regard as both short and stressed. Campion uses *mĕlody*, *omnĭpotent*, *perpĕtually*, *invĭsible*, *unlĭmited*, and *pĕnetrate* in this way.

Faiths pure shield, the Christian *Diana*,
Englands glory crownd with all devinenesse,
Live long with triumphs to blesse thy people
    At thy sight triumphing.

Loe, they sound; the Knights in order armed
Entring threat the list, adrest to combat
For their courtly loves; he, hees the wonder
    Whome *Eliza* graceth.

Their plum'd pomp the vulgar heaps detaineth,
And rough steeds; let us the still devices
Close observe, the speeches and the musicks
    Peacefull arms adorning.

But whence showres so fast this angry tempest,
Clowding dimme the place? Behold, *Eliza*
This day shines not here; this heard, the launces
    And thick heads do vanish.

                 (Smith, II, 347)

As we shall see, both Puttenham and Campion find it easier to talk of accentual patterns when they have disguised them as quantitative patterns, and this is no doubt connected with the problems raised by the sapphic: an Elizabethan could respond to the accentual rhythm, but lacked a framework within which to talk about it.

Campion's setting of 'Come, let us sound' is one example of the way in which an attempt to put the theory of longs and shorts into practice destroys the intuitively-experienced accentual rhythms, and another example is Webbe's rewriting in 1586 of Spenser's April Eclogue from *The Shepheardes Calender* in sapphics (Smith, I, 287–90), which for the most part substitutes stress for quantity (while observing the Latin rules and taking vowel-tenseness into consideration), and therefore has a stress-pattern quite unlike that of the Latin sapphic, and is completely lacking in rhythmicality. Sabie's sapphics (*Pan's Pipe*, 1595, pp. 30–2) also have no accentual rhythm, which is quite in keeping with his general inability as a poet. Peter Colse's 'Encomium upon the right worshipful sir Rafe Horsey knight, and the Lady Edith in Saphic verse' (in his *Penelopes Complaint*, 1596, ed. Grosart, pp. 162–3) is quite strictly quantitative, but has only a slight suggestion of the Horatian rhythm. We may note finally four poems which are not quantitative at all, but which attempt a loose imitation of the sapphic using the materials of the native accentual tradition only: one is Sidney's *OA* 59, 'Get hence foule Griefe, the canker of the minde', and the other three occur in *The Phoenix Nest* (1593, ed. Rollins, pp. 63–4, 75–6, 109–10). The first of these three, at least, is by Thomas Lodge:

> The fatall starre that at my birthday shined,
> Were it of Jove, or Venus in hir brightnes,
> All sad effects, sowre fruits of love divined,
>   In my Loves lightnes,
>
> Light was my Love, that all too light beleeved:
> Heavens ruthe to dwell in faire alluring faces,
> That love, that hope, that damned, and repreeved,
>   To all disgraces.
>
> Love that misled, hope that deceiv'd my seeing:
> Love hope no more, mockt with deluding object:
> Sight full of sorow, that denies the being,
>   Unto the subject.
>
> Soul leave the seat, wher thoughts with endles swelling,
> Change into teares and words of no persuasion:
> Teares turne to tongs, and spend your tunes in telling,
>   Sorowes invasion.
>
> (lines 1–16)

In all four poems, the stress-pattern, though it approaches that of the classical sapphic, is basically an accentual iambic pentameter, with frequent inversions, and with a short fourth line, and the result, however disappointing to an Elizabethan who tried to scan the poems, is more successful than the great majority of the quantitative experiments.

15

Theory and compromise – Puttenham and Campion

George Puttenham

At some time in the 1580s, Puttenham was adding several chapters on the writing of quantitative verse in English to his *Arte of English Poesie*, which was eventually published in 1589. Although he seems unaware of the findings of scholars with regard to questions of Latin pronunciation and prosody (see, for instance, his remarks on the freedom of the first poets to choose quantities, p. 156 above), he shares Sidney's desire to base English quantity on the phonetic properties of the language. But he is prepared to go much further than Sidney in effecting a compromise between the classical and native traditions, and he makes it perfectly clear that he does not wish his quantitative verse to sound very different from accentual verse:

It should prove very agreable to the eare and well according with our ordinary times and pronunciation, which no man could then justly mislike...to allow every word *polisillable* one long time of necessitie, which should be where his sharpe accent falls in our owne *ydiome* most aptly and naturally, wherein we would not follow the licence of the Greeks and Latines, who made not their sharpe accent any necessary prolongation of their times. (Smith, II, 118)

Though all stressed syllables are to be long, not all unstressed syllables are to be short, and in explaining how the quantity of these syllables is to be ascertained, Puttenham seems to be attempting a defence of the rule of position on phonetic grounds:

The other sillables of any word where the sharpe accent fell not to be accompted of such time and quantitie as his *ortographie* would best

217

beare, having regard to himselfe or to his next neighbour word bounding him on either side, namely to the smoothnes & hardnesse of the sillable in his utterance, which is occasioned altogether by his *ortographie* & scituation. (Smith, II, 118)

And when he goes on to discuss monosyllables, which pose a problem for him because he does not realise that stress patterns can operate over more than one word, he is even more explicit about the Latin rules, again with an appeal to phonetic qualities:

I would as neare as I could observe and keepe the lawes of the Greeke and Latine versifiers, that is to prolong the sillable which is written with double consonants or by dipthong or with single consonants that run hard and harshly upon the toung, and to shorten all sillables that stand upon vowels, if there were no cause of *elision*, and single consonants & such of them as are most flowing and slipper upon the toung, as *n, r, t, d, l*. (Smith, II, 120)

But Puttenham's theory of a type of verse which is both accentually and quantitatively based turns out rather differently when he comes to concrete examples. He does, it is true, give several examples of single feet which appear to illustrate the theory: *mōrnĭng, mănĕr, dĕsīre, pērsĭstĭng*, etc., but several others contradict either position (*rĕstōre, tēmpĕrănce*) or stress (*mănĭe*, which may be another instance of Watson's influence, *mănĭfōld, rĕmănēnt*) (Smith, II, 124–5). And when it comes to examples of verse, Latin rules are thrown to the winds and accentual lines are discussed in terms of classical feet. For instance, he quotes, with scansion, a '*quadrein Trimeter*':

> ‾ ˘ ˘ ‾ ˘ ‾ ˘ ˘
> Render againe mie libertie,
> ˘ ‾ ˘ ‾ ˘ ‾
> and set your captive free.
> ‾ ˘ ˘ ‾ ˘ ‾ ˘ ˘
> Glorious is the victorie
> ‾ ˘ ˘ ‾ ˘ ‾ ˘ ˘
> Conquerours use with lenitie.
> (Smith, II, 129)

It is obvious that this is merely accentual verse masquerading as quantitative – and Puttenham is not unaware of this, for he comments:

Now, againe, if ye will say to me that these two words *libertie* and *conquerours* be not precise *Dactils* by the Latine rule, so much will I confesse to, but since they go currant inough upon the tongue, and be so usually pronounced, they may passe wel inough for *Dactils* in our vulgar meeters; & that is inough for me, seeking but to fashion an art, & not to finish it.   (Smith, II, 130)

In fact, Puttenham says some perceptive things about accentual metre while talking about it as if it were quantitative, for the Latin terminology gives him a framework and a vocabulary to discuss metrical patterns that he lacked when he was discussing native metre on its own terms. Whereas, for example, he was much taken up earlier in his treatise with the identification of lines by syllable-count, he now comes close to a formulation of the principle of trisyllabic substitution, for he says of the lines quoted above,

Where ye see every verse is all of a measure, and yet unegall in number of sillables; for the second verse is but of sixe sillables, where the rest are of eight. But the reason is for that in three of the same verses are two *Dactils* a peece, which abridge two sillables in every verse, and so maketh the longest even with the shortest.

                                                      (Smith, II, 129)

But as far as English quantity is concerned, his main contribution was to insist that it should be based on the phonetic properties of the language, and to show that this meant that stress, as the most prominent feature in native English rhythms, would have to be taken into account. It is another step away from the conception of metre that sprang out of the training in Latin prosody, and a further advance towards an adequate account of the real metrical potential of the English language.

Thomas Campion

It was left to Campion to put into practice Puttenham's theory, and to write quantitative verse which at the same time uses, in a fruitful way, the traditional accentual rhythms of the English language.[1] The influence of Sidney is evident from the

---

[1] Campion's treatise has suffered particularly badly from modern misinterpretations: Vivian (Campion's *Works*, 1909, pp. lix–lxv), MacDonagh (1913), Kastendieck (1938, ch. 5), Short (1944) and Lowbury, Salter and Young (1970)

start of his poetic career: among his first poems to appear (in the selection of verse appended to Newman's surreptitious edition of *Astrophel and Stella*, 1591) was the quantitative 'Canto Secundo' ('What faire pompe have I spide of glittering Ladies', *Works*, ed. Davis, pp. 7–8), which appears to be modelled on Sidney's *OA* 34 ('O sweet woods the delight of solitarines') (see Chapter 12 above). This poem, like its model, does not take vowel-tenseness into account, but many quantities in his second quantitative poem, the song in sapphics quoted in the previous chapter, appear to be based on vowel-tenseness in the Sidneian manner (while the Horatian accentual rhythm is imitated more closely than is the case with Sidney's sapphics). So it should not be too surprising to find that the final chapter of his *Observations in the Art of English Poesie* (1602), 'Of the Quantity of English Sillables', is, to a large extent, a formalisation of the rules governing the practice of Sidney and his followers. Modern writers on Campion have sometimes been led astray by the remark made in the first paragraph of the chapter: 'Above all the accent of our words is diligently to be observ'd, for chiefly by the accent in any language the true value of the sillables is to be measured' (Smith, II, 351). This sounds like a rejection of the earlier practice of allowing some stressed syllables to be short, and a reassertion of Puttenham's view that a stressed syllable must be counted as long – and this interpretation fits in neatly with the examples of quantitative verse which Campion has given earlier in the work. But the very next sentence throws doubt on this interpretation, for he goes on to say that 'position...can alter accent' (see p. 151 above for a discussion of this passage). And a glance through the examples of scansion that he gives in the following pages will reveal several words in which stressed syllables are short or unstressed syllables long: *flȳing, gŏing, rĕmedie, hĭdeous, vărious, scăb, flĕd; florishĭng, penetrāte, fortūne, vampĭre*, and many more. A

are all hampered by an inadequate grasp of the technical aspects of quantitative metre and of the background to the Elizabethan experiments. Fenyo (1970) has the merit of taking Lily's grammar into account, but unfortunately goes no further than that work, and is consequently unaware of such things as the mispronunciation of Latin and the problems surrounding the notion of accent, and the importance of these matters to an understanding of Campion's work.

few of Campion's statements from this chapter will make his concept of 'accent' clearer:

(1) A vowell before a vowell is alwaies short, as *flïing, dïing, gŏing,* unlesse the accent alter it, in *dĕnïing.* (Smith, II, 352)

(2) All monasillables that end in a grave accent are ever long, as *wrāth, hāth,*[1] *thēse, thōse, tōoth, sōoth, thrōugh, dāy, plāy, feāte*...The like rule is to be observed in the last of disillables bearing a grave rising sound, as *devine, delaie, retire, refuse, manure,* or a grave falling sound, as *fortune, pleasure, vampire.* (Smith, II, 354)

(3) All Monasillables or Polysillables that end in single consonants ...having a sharp lively accent...are short in their last sillable, as *scăb, flĕd, pārtĕd, Gŏd, ŏf, ĭf, bāndŏg, ānguĭsh.* (Smith, II, 355)

(4) All words of two or more sillables ending with a falling accent in *y* or *ye,* as *faĭrelĭe, dĕmurelĭe, beawtĭe, pĭttĭe,* or in *ue,* as *vertuĕ, rĕscuĕ,* or in *ow,* as *fŏllŏw, hŏllŏw,* or in *e* as *parlĕ, Daphnĕ,* or in *a,* as *Mannă,* are naturally short in their last sillables...But words of two sillables ending with a rising accent in *y* or *ye,* as *denye, descrye,* or in *ue,* as *ensue,* or in *ee,* as *foresee,* or in *oe,* as *forgoe,* are long in their last sillables. (Smith, II, 354)

It will be clear that by 'accent' Campion did not mean simply stress. (1) shows that he used it at times to refer to the penulti- mate rule: the difference between *fliing* and *deniing* is, of course, that in the latter the penultimate rule makes the first *i* long and, in Campion's estimation, overrides the vowel-before-vowel rule which otherwise operates to make the first *i* short – but there is no question of the *i* being long merely because it is stressed. But we can see from (2) that, to Campion, what distinguishes a 'grave accent' is the tenseness of the vowel: all his examples have tense vowels, whereas they can be stressed ('bearing a grave rising sound') or unstressed ('bearing a grave falling sound'). A lax vowel, on the other hand, has a 'sharp lively accent' (see 3), and can also be stressed or unstressed. (This is, of course, a further example of the confu- sion caused by the treatment of accent in the Latin grammars discussed above in Chapter 4; it is interesting to note that Mulcaster, 1582, ch. 17, also identifies 'sharp' and 'flat' accents with lax and tense vowels – but the other way around.)

---

[1] In the sixteenth and seventeenth centuries, *hath,* like *have,* was often pronounced with a tense *a* – see Dobson (1968, II, 453–4).

And on top of this there is a third use of 'accent': it *can* refer to stress, for the rising and falling 'sounds' of (2) are called rising and falling *accents* in (4), where it is quite clear that vowel-tenseness is being ignored. So when Campion says, 'The first rule that is to be observed is the nature of the accent, which we must ever follow' (Smith, II, 352), he does not mean that quantity is governed by stress; he means that the rules for English quantity should be based on the *sound* of English syllables, just as the penultimate rule is based on the sound of Latin syllables, and this means taking both stress and vowel-tenseness into consideration.

It will be noticed that (2), (3) and (4) above are all concerned with monosyllables and final syllables, and it seems that Campion felt that one could know the quantity of these syllables more directly than that of the others. His rules can be summarised in the table below (though it must be remembered that position will always take precedence over these rules – the diphthong rule, on the other hand, operates only 'in the midst of a word', Smith, II, p. 352, a decision which may be the result of his observation of the practice of Sidney and Fraunce).

Examples:	*devine* *tooth*	*denie* *grow*	*follow* *thee*	*parted* *of*	*fortune* *those*	— [1] *scab*	*Manna* *a*
Stress:	+	+	−	−	−	+	−
Tenseness:	+	+	+	−	+	−	−
Final consonant:	+	−	−	+	+	+	−
Quantity:	long	long	short	short	long	short	short

(Campion does not distinguish explicitly between stressed and unstressed monosyllables, but it seems possible that this is the main factor in his decision to regard some monosyllables without final consonants and with tense vowels as long and some as short, thus *thĕy, flȳe, trŭe, sĕe, făr*, etc., but *thrōugh, dāy, plāy, flōw, grōw*, where he is perhaps imagining the second group in a context where they receive strong stress – though he may only be

---

[1] Campion gives no examples of final syllables of disyllables with a lax, stressed vowel followed by a consonant, but his scansion of words like *scăb, Gŏd, prŏp*, etc., suggests that he probably would have considered such syllables to be short.

trying to account for the practice of earlier quantitative poets, who felt free to make arbitrary decisions about monosyllables of this sort.) This table could be summed up by saying that monosyllables and final syllables containing tense vowels are long, unless *neither* stressed *nor* followed by a consonant, while those containing lax vowels are always short. As for syllables in pre-final position, Campion tries as far as possible to relate decisions about their quantity to these rules (leaving aside, that is, syllables whose quantity is known by the Latin rules of position, vowel before vowel, or diphthong). In disyllables the rule is simple: if the second syllable is unstressed, the first is long (this of course means that the quantity is determined by the stress of the initial syllable, though Campion does not put it in these terms). He does make an important qualification, however: '*ăny, măny, prĕty, hŏly*,[1] and their like are excepted' (Smith, II, 353). It is noteworthy that all these words occurred frequently in earlier quantitative verse with just this scansion, beginning with Watson's *măny*, though Campion gives only one reason for differentiating between them and words like *spīrit, flōrish*,[2] and *rīgour* which also have lax vowels, an explanation which in fact explains nothing: 'One observation which leades me to judge of the difference of these disillables...I take from the originall monasillable; which if it be grave, as *shăde*, I hold that the first of *shādie* must be long' (Smith, II, 353). Penultimate syllables in trisyllabic words pose no problem, because the Latin rule operates, but initial syllables with lax vowels show the same inconsistency: *dēsolate, dīligent, prōdigall* (though Gil gives this word with a tense *o* – see Dobson, 1968, II, 496), but *rĕmedie, bĕnefit, hĭdeous*, and similarly 'all that yeeld the like quicknes of sound' (Smith, II, 353). It is of the latter type that he gives most examples, and here again there are numerous precedents in earlier quantitative poets, including Sidney and

---

[1] There existed a pronunciation of *holy* with a lax *o* – see Dobson (1968, II, 484).

[2] Though *flourish* normally had a lax vowel in the first syllable, there is evidence of an occasional tense vowel (see Dobson, 1968, II, 493), but the same cannot be said of the other examples in this list. This pronunciation, incidentally, and that of *holy* mentioned in the previous note, may account for the examples Campion gives to illustrate the rule that initial syllables of trisyllabic words follow the quantity of the disyllabic primitives, which at first sight seem transposed: '*flōrish, flōrĭshing* long; *hŏlie, hŏlĭnes* short' (Smith, II, 353).

Fraunce, not to mention the precedents in Latin. One of the commonest of such words in earlier writers was *misery*, of which Campion makes special mention: '*mi* in *mĭser* being long hinders not the first of *mĭsery* to be short, because the sound of the *i* is a little altred' (Smith, II, 353). It is interesting that he does not relate this to his 'grave' and 'sharp' accents, which he seems to think of (as he does of the falling and rising accents) only in terms of final syllables and monosyllables.

Campion's rules, then, are for the most part an elaboration and formalisation of Sidney's, though he does make some advances towards a more phonetic conception of quantity, as when he insists that 'we must esteeme our sillables as we speake, not as we write' (Smith, II, 352) – in other words, unpronounced letters are not to count towards position or diphthong. Using these rules he could have written quantitative verse very like Sidney's or Fraunce's, but when he turned to the real business of poetry his ear for English rhythms and his skill in the native tradition (a tradition which by 1602 had produced many more masterpieces than when Sidney and Fraunce were beginning their experiments) made him very selective in applying the rules, and he produced something quite different from his predecessors. This difference, and the links that Campion has with Puttenham, begin to emerge early on in the treatise when he talks of '*Iambick* and *Trochaick* feete' with reference not to classical verse but to accentual English verse (Smith, II, 330–1). For instance, he criticises English poets for such errors as allowing the last two syllables of *destiny* to make up a complete foot in an iambic line, but does not complain about the final iambic of the same line, 'dismăll chāunce', where the classical rules are broken, but the foot is accentually correct. And the following chapters show what his aim is: to retain the traditional accentual metres (adding some variations of his own, but still on an accentual basis), but to ensure that the lines can also be scanned as quantitative verse. This is implied in the statement that 'if we examine our owne writers, we shall find they unawares hit oftentimes upon the true *Iambick* numbers, but always ayme at them as far as their eare without the guidance of arte can attain unto' (Smith, II, 333).

Campion is, as his opening chapters suggest (see the quotations in Chapter 7 above), motivated by the same desire as all the quantitative poets from Watson onwards: to introduce into English verse the 'artificiality', the attention to the properties of every syllable, the challenge posed by the task of employing a complex set of rules, that were characteristic of the Latin verse he knew and admired. But he was also a superb English poet, and he knew that the products of the quantitative movement fell far below the great works of the native tradition. He therefore avoided the English hexameter that 'hath bene oftentimes attempted in our English toong, but with passing pitifull successe' (Smith, II, 333), realising that in a scheme which used stress to determine quantity the dactyl posed an insoluble problem. He says of the hexametrists, with justifiable scorn, 'I could in this place set downe many ridiculous kinds of *Dactils* which they use, but that it is not my purpose here to incite men to laughter' (Smith, II, 333). Instead, he devises a number of metres based on iambic and trochaic feet alone, creating equivalents of, rather than merely transposing, classical metres.

Throughout, his awareness of the importance of stress shows itself. English pentameters, he remarks, sound as long as Latin hexameters or pentameters, an observation which seems to be based on a stress-count; and when he moves on to a discussion of iambic verse in English, stress plays a more direct role than it does in the rules. Like Puttenham, he gives an account of trisyllabic substitution which is substantially accurate, though it pretends to be concerned with classical feet, not stress (Smith, II, 336–7). And in his examples, he achieves virtually complete coincidence of quantity and stress throughout, something which necessitates the avoidance of a great number of words which, as we have seen from his rules, he believed to contain short but stressed syllables. The result is poetry which, read as ordinary English verse, is often very successful (in spite of the severe restrictions Campion imposed on himself by his method), but which can at the same time be scanned and seen to be quantitatively correct. The quantitative movement had at last produced poetry which could stand next to work in the native tradition, and poems given in the *Observations* as examples of quantitative metres can be read with pleasure today, poems such as 'Rose-cheekt *Lawra*, come', 'Just beguiler', and 'Follow, followe', of which the first is probably the most successful (it is an example of Campion's second kind of lyrical verse):

   ¯   ¯ | ¯ ˘ | ¯
Rose-cheekt *Lawra*, come

   ¯ | ¯ ˘| ¯   ˘| ¯
Sing thou smoothly with thy beawtie's

¯¯ | ¯ ˘| ¯ ˘| ¯¯
Silent musick, either other

     ¯ ˘| ¯ ¯
Sweetely gracing.

Lovely formes do flowe
From concent devinely framed;
Heav'n is musick, and thy beawtie's
    Birth is heavenly.

These dull notes we sing
Discords neede for helps to grace them;
Only beawty purely loving
    Knowes no discord,

But still moves delight,
Like cleare springs renu'd by flowing,
Ever perfet, ever in them-
    selves eternall.

(Smith, II, 348)

It is largely the gently expanding and contracting accentual rhythm that makes this poem flow in a way so perfectly expressive of its subject-matter (together, of course, with the placing of line-ends within grammatical segments – and, at the climax of the poem, within a single word). A less well-known example is 'An *Elegy*', which illustrates how Campion's 'English Elegeick Verse' uses a skilfully manipulated accentual rhythm as an equivalent of the Latin hexameter/pentameter couplets: the first line of the couplet is a 'licentiate Iambick' (that is, an accentual iambic with a few permissible variations), while the second consists of two 'Dimeters' and begins and ends with a stress, the change from a falling to a rising rhythm being effected within the line in subtly varying ways. I give the quantitative scansion of the first eight lines, but it will be seen that the accentual pattern is not merely the result of this scansion, but is created as a rhythmical whole in its own right, thus taking to its logical and poetically satisfying conclusion Sidney's tendency towards accentual regularity.

> ‒ ‒ | ᴗ ‒ | ᴗ ‒| ‒ ‒ | ᴗ ‒
> Constant to none, but ever false to me,
> ‒ ‒ | ‒ ᴗ | ‖ ‒ ᴗ | ᴗ | ‒
> Traiter still to love through thy faint desires,
> ᴗ ‒ | ‒ ‒| ᴗ ‒ | ‒ ‒ | ᴗ ‒
> Not hope of pittie now nor vaine redresse
> ‒ ᴗ| ‒ ᴗ | ‒ ‖‒ ᴗ| ‒ ᴗ| ‒
> Turns my griefs to teares and renu'd laments.
> ᴗ ‒ | ᴗ ‒ | ᴗ ‒ | ‒ ᴗ | ᴗ ‒
> Too well thy empty vowes and hollow thoughts
> ‒ ‒ | ‒ ᴗ | ‒ ‖‒ ᴗ | ‒ ᴗ | ‒
> Witnes both thy wrongs and remorseles hart.
> ᴗ ‒ | ᴗ ‒| ᴗ ‒ | ᴗ ‒ | ᴗ ‒
> Rue not my sorrow, but blush at my name;
> ‒ ᴗ | ‒ ᴗ | ‒ ‖ ‒ ᴗ | ‒ ᴗ|
> Let thy bloudy cheeks guilty thoughts betray.
> My flames did truly burne, thine made a shew,
> As fires painted are which no heate retayne,
> Or as the glossy *Pirop* faines to blaze,
> But toucht cold appeares and an earthy stone.
> True cullours deck thy cheeks, false foiles thy brest,
> Frailer then thy light beawty is thy minde.
> None canst thou long refuse, nor long affect,
> But turn'st feare with hopes, sorrow with delight,
> Delaying, and deluding ev'ry way
> Those whose eyes are once with thy beawty chain'd.
> Thrice happy man that entring first thy love
> Can so guide the straight raynes of his desires,
> That both he can regard thee and refraine:
> If grac't, firme he stands, if not, easely falls.
>
> (Smith, ii, 344–5)

Epilogue

The verse in the *Observations* marks the high point of the quantitative movement, but the victory, however impressive, was a pyrrhic one. By demonstrating that quantitative verse succeeds only when it is also accentual, Campion had undermined the whole enterprise, and his critics had only to point out the obvious: the 'Iambick' verse, wrote Daniel in his *Defence of Ryme* the following year, 'when all is done, reaches not by a foote, but falleth out to be the plaine ancient verse, consisting of ten sillables or five feete, which hath ever beene used amongest us time out of minde' (Smith, II, 376–7), and in 1619 Gil rewrote some of Campion's lines with rhymes, remarking of his altered versions, 'Nihil à vulgatissimis cuiusvis poetae differre videbuntur' (p. 144).[1] Campion made no attempt to answer this criticism; he could have claimed that it was precisely his strength that he had introduced into English verse all the intricacy and subtlety of classical metre without sacrificing the natural English rhythms, but perhaps he realised that to anyone who admired native poetry sufficiently, the quantitative structure would seem an unnecessary strait-jacket – and perhaps he came to agree.

Side by side with the favourable comments on quantitative verse, the last decade of the century had seen some severe criticism, and this continued into the new century. At times it was directed only at some of the products of the movement – Stanyhurst's verse being, not surprisingly, a favourite target (see above, p. 170, n. 2) – while the hope remained that in other hands the experiment might still succeed. Harvey and

[1] 'They will seem no different from the most commonplace lines of any poet at all.'

Stanyhurst were mocked by both Nashe and Peele, and yet both these authors praised Fraunce for his *Amyntas*,[1] while Jonson attacked Fraunce, yet espoused his cause (see above, pp. 127–8). Campion himself ridicules earlier attempts at quantitative verse before going on to his own (Smith, II, 333), and Gil, while not doubting that the native tradition has triumphed, devotes much space to quantity and quantitative metres in English, finding fault with Stanyhurst's experiments but praising the 'divine Sidney' for his (p. 149).

More sweeping condemnations of the whole enterprise were made on the grounds that what is appropriate for one language is not necessarily appropriate for another. In spite of his earlier praise of Fraunce, Nashe wrote in his *Strange Newes of* 1592:

The Hexamiter verse I graunt to be a Gentleman of an auncient house (so is many an english begger); yet this Clyme of ours hee cannot thrive in. Our speech is too craggy for him to set his plough in; hee goes twitching and hopping in our language like a man running upon quagmiers. (Smith, II, 240)

In *The Shadow of Night* (1594) Chapman noted the superiority of the 'native robes' of English poetry to the 'strange garments' of classical hexameters (see Smith, I, liv), and George Wither wrote in 1619, 'Poesie is a mysterie so different in every tongue, that he who hath learned all the rules of that Art in one Language, may notwithstanding be very ignorant, what is to be observed in another' (p. 62) (notice, however, that Wither does not go so far as to question the dependence of verse on rules).

For those who wished to find a traditional justification for both types of verse, the distinction made by medieval writers between *metrum* (quantitative metre) and *rhythmus* (accentual metre) was useful, especially as classical authorities – notably Quintilian – could be cited, even though they had used the terms to make a different distinction. Thus Butler writes in his *Rameae Rhetoricae* (1597):

Numerus poeticus est, rhythmus, aut metrum. Rhythmus est numerus poeticus certum syllabarum numerum (nullâ habitâ

---

[1] See Nashe, Preface to Greene's *Menaphon* (1589) (Smith, I, 315–16) and *Strange Newes* (1592) (Smith, II, 240–1); and Peele, *The Old Wives Tale* (1595) (*Life and Works*, III, 410) and *The Honour of the Garter* (1593) (*Life and Works*, I, 246).

quantitatis ratione) continens. Tales rhythmi naturales sunt in omni natione atque gente: etiam in Graeciâ ante Homerum & in Italiâ ante Andronicum reperti sunt. Hodie autem plerumque Epistrophen soni coniunctam habent.[1]   (p. 34)

This is a shortened version of Talaeus' comments in his *Rhetorica* of 1577, but Butler is less willing to admit the possibility that *metrum* can be used in the modern vernaculars. As we saw in Chapter 9, Jonson makes a similar distinction between quantitative and 'naturall' verse; he is, however, confident that English quantitative verse can be successfully written:

And, as for the difficultie, that shall never withdraw, or put me off, from the Attempt: For, neither is any excellent thing done with ease, nor the compassing of this any whit to be despaired: Especially, when *Quintilian* hath observ'd to me, by this *naturall Rythme*, that we have the other *Artificiall*, as it were by certaine *Markes*, and *footing*[*s*], first traced, and found out.   (*Works*, VIII, 501)

Such confidence is unusual for the 1630s, for there had been a marked change in sensibility – artistic and otherwise – since Spenser and Harvey had exchanged letters on 'refourmed Versifying'. Had Campion's *Observations* appeared thirty years earlier, it might have been hailed as a triumphant combination of what was best in English and Latin verse; but by 1603 the desire for poetry which demonstrated the labour and learning of the writer by its skilful patterning of letters and syllables had dwindled. Donne had travelled further along the road which Sidney had entered after leaving quantitative verse behind, and the dramatists, too, had demonstrated the power and beauty of verse which organised not conventional attributes of language learned at school but the actual sounds of the speaking voice. In writing ayres, Campion himself had taken part in the movement that replaced the madrigal, with its emphasis on contrapuntal complexity, by music more concerned with the direct expression of the feelings embodied in the text; and the flat, highly ornate style of portraiture typical of the last thirty

---

[1] 'Poetic number consists of rhythm or metre. Rhythm is poetic number made up of a fixed number of syllables without regard to quantity. Such rhythms are natural in every country and people: they occurred even in Greece before Homer and in Italy before Andronicus. Nowadays they are usually linked together by repeated sounds.'

years of the century was giving way to a more naturalistic manner, with the sitter located in a concretely-realised space and a particular moment of time.[1] It is hardly surprising, then, that even those quantitative poems which seemed successful to many Elizabethans should find less favour in the seventeenth century. King James himself was an acknowledged champion of the native tradition (see his *Schort Treatise* of 1584, Smith, I, 208–25, and especially his remarks on the inferiority of ancient verse, p. 209), so opponents of the quantitative movement could hope to meet with the King's approval: Daniel, in his prefatory epistle to the *Defence*, applauds 'our Soveraignes happy inclination this way, whereby wee are rather to expect an incoragement to go on with what we do then that any innovation should checke us', (Smith, II, 357), and after James's death, Sir John Beaumont wrote a poem 'To his Late Majesty, concerning the True Forme of English Poetry' in which rhyme is praised as 'the rellish of the Muse' (Chalmers, 1810, VI, 30–1).

It was in the seventeenth century, too, that the tradition of regarding Biblical verse as quantitative discussed in Chapter 8 above received its strongest challenge from an accentual school (see Baroway, 1935, p. 91, and 1950); thus J. J. Scaliger (1606) invokes the *rhythmus/metrum* distinction, arguing that Biblical verse is an example of the former, not the latter. In 1657, Joshua Poole can ridicule the movement, now seen as something firmly in the past, by simply quoting a hexameter:

Some, in Mr. *Johnson's* time, vainly attempted to write a Heroick poem, in imitation of the *Greeks* and *Latines*, by the measure of *Spondey* and *Dactyl*, without any regard to rime. Of that number was he, who sent him a coppy of verses beginning thus,

‾ ⏑ ⏑ ‾ ‾ ‾ ‾ ‾ ‾ ⏑ ⏑ ‾ ‾

Benjamin immortal Johnson most highlie renowned.

(The English Parnassus, sig. a4)

By 1679 the idea that Spenser should have been seriously interested in quantitative versifying had become so unacceptable that the edition of his *Works* of that year inserts an 'almost'

---

[1] See, for instance, the discussion by Mercer (1962) of the changes at this time, not only in large-scale portraiture (pp. 180, 184–5), but also in the miniature (pp. 208–9), in interior decoration (pp. 103–5, 109–15), and in sculpture (pp. 241–7).

before his statement to Harvey that Sidney and Dyer have 'drawen mee to their faction' (see Spenser's *Prose Works*, p. 251).

Along with the criticism of the quantitative experiments in terms of the poverty of the results or the inappropriateness of the metre for the English language, then, we find a more fundamental set of objections, which imply a dissatisfaction with the attitudes to art that lay behind the experiments. Such criticism, carried to its logical conclusion, would have to involve a devaluation of Latin verse itself, and some writers were prepared to go this far. There occurs, for instance, in James Howell's *New English Grammar* (1662) a passage on quantity which owes much to Talaeus and Jonson, but which suggests that the rules of quantity are not an admirable ordering of nature but an unnecessary limitation:

Touching the position or quantity of syllables, ther is no language, I know of, hath exact rules, restraints, examples and cautions to that purpose but the *Greeks* and *Latins*; ther is not so much art and trouble used in the *English* or *Spanish* (or any other *Occidental* Toung) because their metrical Compositions, Verses and Rimes are meerly derived from an instinct of Nature, such as *Aristotle* speaks of, ...Of a voluntary and natural free composition, without being enslavd so much to the quantity of syllables. Nor were the *Greeks* before *Homer*, nor the *Romans* before *Livius Andronicus*, so curious in observing so punctually the length and shortnesse of syllables.

(p. 36)

The most eloquent and thoroughgoing exponent of the new ideas is Daniel, who in the course of his *Defence of Ryme* succeeds in denying nearly every principle on which the humanist attempt to match classical verse had been based. For Daniel, rhyme is 'a Harmonie farre happier than any proportion Antiquitie could ever shew us' (Smith, II, 360), and, having praised the long-maligned medieval Latin poets, he finds fault with classical verse:

We admire [the Greeks and Romans] not for their smooth-gliding words, nor their measures, but for their inventions...For to say truth, their Verse is many times but a confused deliverer of their excellent conceits, whose scattered limbs we are faine to looke out

and joyne together, to discerne the image of what they represent
unto us.   (Smith, II, 364)

Such a view of classical eloquence could scarcely be more
heretical for a Renaissance humanist – but then Daniel is plainly
not that. He refuses to accept an argument whose force had
been felt by nearly every writer on metre from Ascham onwards:
that the acceptance of quantitative verse would restrict poetry
to the skilled and diligent few (see Chapter 7 above). 'Idle wits
will write in that kinde, as do now in this', he remarks, 'And
this multitude of idle Writers can be no disgrace to the good'
(Smith, II, 363). What is more, he even denies that it is for the
learned that poetry is written: 'Nor will the Generall sorte for
whom we write (the wise being above books) taste these
laboured measures but as an orderly prose when wee have all
done' (Smith, II, 362).

The Elizabethan admiration for quantitative verse was part
of their admiration for intricately-worked artifice, and Daniel
makes it plain that his dissatisfaction extends to the wider
context: he refers in passing to the 'tyrannicall Rules of idle
Rhetorique' (Smith, II, 363), and after complaining about the
unnatural word-order of Latin verse, he confronts Elizabethan
attitudes to art directly:

Such affliction doth laboursome curiositie still lay upon our best
delights (which ever must be made strange and variable), as if Art
were ordained to afflict Nature, and that we could not goe but in
fetters. Every science, every profession, must be so wrapt up in
unnecessary intrications, as if it were not to fashion but to confound
the understanding: which makes me much to distrust man, and
feare that our presumption goes beyond our abilitie, and our
Curiositie is more then our Judgement.   (Smith, II, 365)

As he proceeds, Daniel widens the scope of his argument still
further, until it becomes clear that the attack on Campion's
quantitative experiments stems from a general dissatisfaction
with humanist ideals; he insists that 'all our understandings
are not to be built by the square of *Greece* and *Italie*' (Smith, II,
366), and devotes several pages to praise of the achievements
of the Middle Ages. The humanists are disparaged – '*Erasmus,
Rewcline,* and *More* brought no more wisdome into the world

233

with all their new revived wordes then we finde was before'
(Smith, II, 372) – and the Renaissance itself is seen as a
destructive force: 'This innovation, like a Viper, must ever
make way into the world's opinion, thorow the bowelles of her
owne breeding' (Smith, II, 373). Finally, we come to a consideration of Campion's specific proposals, and although we
must accept the justice of Daniel's remarks, it is easy to see that
many an Elizabethan might have felt that he was attacking
just those features of Campion's system which were most
impressive when he commented adversely on the 'many
intricate Lawes' or talked of 'all these unnecessary precepts'
(Smith, II, 376, 378). But Daniel is thinking about art in a
different way, and a final quotation will serve to sum up the
new attitude to 'artificiality' which the *Defence* illustrates:

See the power of Nature; it is not all the artificiall coverings of wit
that can hide their native and originall condition, which breakes
out thorow the strongest bandes of affectation, and will be it selfe,
doe Singularitie what it can.[1]   (Smith, II, 378)

Daniel's observations on the quantitative movement and on the
excesses of Renaissance humanism and Elizabethan taste cannot
but command our assent, and come as a cool breeze of common
sense after the hot-house atmosphere of the poetry and theorising we have been considering, but what is important to note is
that the rejection of the first implies the rejection of all the rest:
quantitative experiments, the humanist enterprise, and the
taste for 'artificiality' in art interconnect no less closely in
Daniel's *Defence* than they do in Stanyhurst's *Aeneis* or Webbe's
Discourse.

Daniel's views were not, of course, shared by all his contemporaries (Jonson told Drummond that on the subject of
versification he disagreed with both Campion and Daniel,

---

[1] Views approaching this had no doubt been held by many during Elizabeth's
reign, though they found little expression in the face of the orthodox humanist
attitudes. But there is perhaps a foreshadowing in Puttenham, for all his interest
in ornament: we have seen that he enjoyed medieval verse (p. 101 above), and he
believes that 'the naturall Poesie...being aided and amended by Art, and not
utterly altered or obscured, but some signe left of it (as the Greekes and Latines
have left none), is no lesse to be allowed and commended then theirs' (Smith,
II, 11).

'especially this Last'; *Works*, I, 132), but they can be seen clearly as part of the larger pattern of change by which the modes of thought characteristic of the sixteenth century gave way to others. It is not inappropriate that Bacon, one of the architects of this change, should have taken the trouble to condemn the quantitative experiments, first indirectly in *The Advancement of Learning* (1605; *Works*, III, 401–2) and then more explicitly in its rewritten Latin version, *De Augmentis Scientiarum* (1623), in which he states that the ancient poets suited their metre to their subject, and continues,

Neque haec prudentia recentioribus poëtis in linguis propriis defuit. Illud reprehendendum, quod quidam antiquitatis nimium studiosi linguas modernas ad mensuras antiquas (heroïcas, elegiacas, sapphicas, &c.) traducere conati sunt; quas ipsarum linguarum fabrica respuit, nec minus aures exhorrent. In huiusmodi rebus sensus iudicium artis praeceptis praeponendum; ut ait ille,

Coenae fercula nostrae
Mallem convivis quam placuisse cocis.

Neque vero ars est, sed artis abusus, cum illa naturam non perficiat sed pervertat.[1]   (*Works*, I, 656–7)

This does not mean, of course, that the conception of metre that we have been examining disappeared, at least as far as Latin is concerned: admiration for the classics remained intense, the pronunciation of Latin stayed as incorrect as ever, and Latin prosody continued to play an important part in school training. Even now, with pronunciation reformed and quantity once more related to the sound of the syllables, part of the appeal of Latin verse is still its high degree of organisation, and the end of Latin as a medium for spoken communication has meant that in some ways the poetry of Virgil and Horace is more, rather than less, 'artificial' than it was in the Renaissance. But probably at no other time have the attitudes towards metre engendered

---

[1] 'Nor have more modern poets, writing in their own languages, lacked the good sense to do this. What one must object to is that certain men, over-learned in matters of antiquity, have attempted to force modern languages into ancient metres (heroics, elegiacs, sapphics, etc.), which the structure of the languages itself rejects, no less than ears dislike it. In these things the judgement of the senses is to be preferred to the rules of art; as it has been said, "I would rather the dishes of our dinner pleased the guests than the cooks." And it is not art, but an abuse of art, since it does not perfect, but perverts, Nature.'

in English minds by a rigorous training in Latin prosody using an unclassical pronunciation fused so completely with the cultural and aesthetic ideals of the age as during the reign of Elizabeth; and however futile the quantitative movement may seem in retrospect, its achievements remain as impressive testimony to the power exerted by that synthesis.

Bibliography

Abercrombie, David. 'Forgotten Phoneticians', *Transactions of the Philological Society*, 1948, pp. 1–34.
'What is a "letter"?' *Lingua*, II (1949), 54–63.
'A Phonetician's View of Verse Structure', *Linguistics*, VI (1964), 5–13.
Aelfric. *Aelfrics Grammar und Glossar*, ed. Julius Zupitza. Erste Abteilung: Text und Varianten, Sammlung Englischer Denkmäler in Kritischen Ausgaben, I. Berlin, 1880.
Allen, W. Sidney. 'On Quantity and Quantitative Verse', in *In Honour of Daniel Jones*, ed. D. Abercrombie, *et al.* London, 1964, pp. 3–15.
Vox Latina: A Guide to the Pronunciation of Classical Latin. Cambridge, 1965.
'The Latin Accent: A Restatement', *Journal of Linguistics*, V (1969), 193–203.
Accent and Rhythm: Prosodic Features in Latin and Greek: A Study in Theory and Reconstruction. Cambridge, 1973.
Allot, Robert. *Englands Parnassus* (1600), ed. Charles Crawford. Oxford, 1913.
Alphabetum Graecum. See Beza (1554).
Alvarus, Emmanuel. *Prosodia, sive Institutionum Linguae Latinae*. Douai, 1617.
Animadversions upon Lillies Grammar, or Lilly Scanned. London, 1625.
Applegate, James. 'Sidney's Classical Metres', *Modern Language Notes*, LXX (1955), 254–5.
Arber, Edward. *See* Stanyhurst (1582).
Ascham, Roger. 'Imitatio' (from *The Scholemaster*, 1570, Book II). Smith, I, 1–45. *English Works*, ed. W. A. Wright. Cambridge, 1904.
Attridge, Derek. 'The Elizabethan Experiments in English Quantitative Verse.' Ph.D. diss., University of Cambridge, 1971.
Augé-Chiquet, Mathieu. *La Vie, les idées et l'oeuvre de Jean-Antoine de Baïf*. Paris and Toulouse, 1909.
B., H. *Certen observacons for Latyne and Englishe versyfyinge* [1589]. (Leaf A2 only; Bodleian Library, Douce fragment b.1. (79).)
B., R. *Greenes Funeralls* (1594). In B. R.–R. B., *Greenes Newes both from Heaven and Hell, 1593 and Greenes Funeralls, 1594*, ed. R. B. McKerrow. London, 1911.
Bacon, Francis. *Works*, ed. J. Spedding, R. L. Ellis and D. D. Heath. 14 vols. London, 1857–74.
Baïf, Jean-Antoine de. *Chansonettes*, ed. G. C. Bird. Vol. I, Texte Inédit. Vancouver, 1964.

Euvres en Rime, ed. C. Marty-Laveaux. 5 vols. [Paris, 1881–90]; reprinted, Geneva, [1965].

Baldwin, Thomas Whitfield. *William Shakspere's Small Latine & Lesse Greeke*. 2 vols. Urbana, 1944.

Barker, Thomas. *Barker's Delight: or, the Art of Angling*. 2nd edn. London, 1657.

Barnfield, Richard. *The Poems of Richard Barnfield*. Introd. Montague Summers. London, [1936].

Baroway, Israel. 'The Bible as Poetry in the English Renaissance: An Introduction', *Journal of English and Germanic Philology*, XXXII (1933), 447–80.

'The Hebrew Hexameter: A Study in Renaissance Sources and Interpretation', *ELH*, II (1935), 66–91.

'*The Lyre of David*: A Further Study in Renaissance Interpretation of Biblical Form', *ELH*, VIII (1941), 119–42.

'The Accentual Theory of Hebrew Prosody: A Further Study in Renaissance Interpretation of Biblical Form', *ELH*, XVII (1950), 115–35.

Baxter, Arthur H. *The Introduction of Classical Metres into Italian Poetry*. Baltimore, 1901.

Beare, William. *Latin Verse and European Song: A Study in Accent and Rhythm*. London, 1957.

Bennett, Walter. *German Verse in Classical Metres*. The Hague, 1963.

Bentley, Richard (ed.). *Publii Terentii Afri Comoediae*. Cambridge, 1726.

Berli, Hans. *Gabriel Harvey: der Dichterfreund und Kritiker*. Zürich, 1913.

Beza, Theodorus. 'Scholia in quibus disputatur de germana Graecae linguae pronunciatione', in *Alphabetum Graecum*, [Paris], 1554, sigs. C5*v*–E3*v*.

De Germana Pronuntiatione Graecae Linguae. In Stephanus (1587).

Bird, John. *Grounds of Grammer Penned and Published* (1639). Facsim. edn. Menston, 1971.

Blenerhasset, Thomas. *The Second Part of the Mirror for Magistrates* (1578), in *Parts Added to 'The Mirror for Magistrates'*, ed. L. B. Campbell. Cambridge, 1946.

A Revelation of the True Minerva (1582). Facsim. edn., introd. J. W. Bennett. New York, 1941.

Bradley, Henry. Preface to Sargeaunt (1920), pp. 3–5.

Brinsley, John. *Ludus Literarius; or, the Grammar Schoole* (1st edn. 1612), ed. E. T. Campagnac from 1627 edn. Liverpool and London, 1917.

Brittain, Frederick. *Latin in Church: The History of its Pronunciation*. Rev. edn. Alcuin Club Tracts, XXVIII. London, 1955.

Brown, J. Howard. *Elizabethan Schooldays*. Oxford, 1933.

Bukofzer, Manfred F. 'Speculative Thinking in Mediaeval Music', *Speculum*, XVII (1942), 165–80.

Bullokar, William. *Booke at large, for the Amendment of Orthographie for English speech* (1580), ed. Max Plessow. Palaestra, LII. Berlin, 1906.

Butler, Charles. *Rameae Rhetoricae Libri Duo*. Oxford, 1597.

Rhetoricae Libri Duo. Oxford, 1600. Further edns. Oxford, 1618; London, 1629.

The English Grammar (1634), ed. A. Eichler. Neudrucke Frühneuenglischer Grammatiken, IV, 1. Halle, 1910.

The Principles of Musik. London, 1636.

Butler, Christopher. *Number Symbolism*. London, 1970.

Buxton, John. *Elizabethan Taste*. London, 1963.
  Sir Philip Sidney and the English Renaissance. 2nd edn. London, 1964.
Byrd, William. *Psalmes, Sonets, & songs of sadnes and pietie. Superius*. London, 1588.
Caius, John. *De Pronunciatione Graecae et Latinae Linguae* (1574). Facsim. edn., introd. and tr. J. B. Gabel. Leeds, 1968.
Campion, Thomas. *Works*, ed. P. Vivian. Oxford, 1909.
  The Works of Thomas Campion, ed. W. R. Davis. London, 1969.
  Observations in the Art of English Poesie (1602). Smith, II, 327–55.
Carducci, Giosuè (ed.). *La Poesia Barbara nei Secoli XV e XVI*. Bologna, 1881.
Carew, Richard. *The Excellency of the English Tongue* (1595–6?). Smith, II, 285–94.
Cayley, C. B. 'Remarks and Experiments on English Hexameters', *Transactions of the Philological Society*, 1862–3, pp. 67–85.
Certaine grammar questions for the exercise of young Schollers. [London?, 1602?]
Chalmers, Alexander (ed.). *The Works of the English Poets, from Chaucer to Cowper*. 21 vols. London, 1810.
Chamberlain, Robert. *Nocturnall Lucubrations: or Meditations Divine and Morall*. London, 1638.
Cheke, Sir John. *De Pronuntiatione Graecae potissimum linguae disputationes*. Basle, 1555.
Chomsky, Noam and Morris Halle. *The Sound Pattern of English*. New York, Evanston, and London, 1968.
Church, Margaret. 'The First English Pattern Poems', *PMLA*, LXI (1946), 636–50.
Clajus, Johannes. *Prosodiae...libri tres*. Wittenberg, 1576.
Clark, Arthur Melville. 'Milton and the Renaissance Revolt against Rhyme', in *Studies in Literary Modes*. Edinburgh and London, 1946, pp. 105–41.
Colse, Peter. *Penelopes Complaint: Or, A Mirrour for wanton Minions* (1596), in *Occasional Issues of Unique or Very Rare Books*, ed. A. B. Grosart, XII, 159–83. Manchester, 1880.
Comenius, J. A. *See* Robotham (1640).
Cooper, Charles Gordon. *An Introduction to the Latin Hexameter*. Melbourne, 1952.
Coryate, Thomas. *Coryats Crudities* (1611). 2 vols. Glasgow, 1905.
Danes, John. *A Light to Lilie* (1637). Facsim. edn. Menston, 1968.
Daniel, Samuel. *A Defence of Ryme* (1603). Smith, II, 356–84.
Davis, W. R. 'A Note on Accent and Quantity in *A Booke of Ayres*', *Modern Language Quarterly*, XXII (1961), 32–6.
Davison, Francis. *A Poetical Rhapsody* (1602–21), ed. H. E. Rollins. 2 vols. Cambridge, Mass., 1931–2.
Dickenson, John. *Prose and Verse*, ed. A. B. Grosart. Blackburn, 1878.
Dobson, Eric John. 'Robert Robinson and his Phonetic Transcripts of Early Seventeenth-Century English Pronunciation', *Transactions of the Philological Society*, 1947, pp. 25–63.
  (ed.). *The Phonetic Writings of Robert Robinson*. Early English Text Society. London, 1957.
  English Pronunciation 1500–1700. 2nd edn. 2 vols. Oxford, 1968.
Donne, John. *The Sermons of John Donne*, ed. George R. Potter and Evelyn M. Simpson. 10 vols. Berkeley and Los Angeles, 1953–62.

239

Droz, E. 'Salomon Certon et ses amis: contribution à l'histoire du vers mesuré', *Humanisme et Renaissance*, VI (1939), 178–97.

Dunn, Catherine M. 'A Survey of the Experiments in Quantitative Verse in the English Renaissance.' Ph.D. diss., University of California, Los Angeles, 1967.

Edwards, T. W. C. *The Eton Latin Grammar*. London, 1826.

'Elizabethan Decoration: Patterns in Art and Passion', *TLS*, 3 July 1937, 485–6.

Ellis, Alexander J. *On Early English Pronunciation, with especial reference to Shakspere and Chaucer*. 5 vols. Early English Text Society. London, 1869–89.
Practical Hints on the Quantitative Pronunciation of Latin. London, 1874.

Elze, Karl. *Der Englische Hexameter*. Dessau, 1867.

Erasmus, Desiderius. *De Recta Latini Graecique sermonis pronuntiatione*. Basle, 1528.

Evans, R. O. 'Spenser's Role in the Controversy over Quantitative Verse', *Neuphilologische Mitteilungen*, LVII (1956), 246–56.

Fabricius, Georgius. *De Re Poetica Libri Septem*. Paris, 1575.
'Methodus Cognoscendarum Syllabarum', in Smetius (1614).

Fairclough, H. R. 'The Influence of Virgil upon the Forms of English Verse', *Classical Journal*, XXVI (1930–1), 74–94.

Farnaby, Thomas. *Systema Grammaticum* (1641). Facsim. edn. Menston, 1969.

Fenyo, Jane K. 'Grammar and Music in Campion's *Observations in the Art of English Poesie*', *Studies in the Renaissance*, XVII (1970), 46–72.

Fiedler, H. G. *A Contemporary of Shakespeare on Phonetics and on the Pronunciation of English and Latin*. London, 1936.

First Booke of the Preservation of King Henry the vii. See Preservation...

Fleming, Abraham. *The Bucoliks of Publius Virgilius Maro*. London, 1589.

Fletcher, J. B. 'Areopagus and Pleiade', *Journal of English and Germanic Philology*, II (1898–9), 429–53.

Flügel, Ewald. 'Kleine Mitteilungen zur Litteraturgeschichte des 16. Jahrhunderts', *Anglia*, XIII (1891), 455–67.

Foucault, Michel. *Les mots et les choses*. Paris, 1966. (Tr. as *The Order of Things*, London, 1970).

Fowler, Alastair. *Triumphal Forms: Structural Patterns in Elizabethan Poetry*. Cambridge, 1970.
See also Willes, *De Re Poetica*.

Fraunce, Abraham. *The Lamentations of Amyntas* (1587), ed. F. M. Dickey. (Pub. with Thomas Watson, *Amyntas*, ed. W. F. Staton.) Publications of the Renaissance Text Society, II. Chicago, 1967.
The Arcadian Rhetorike (1588), ed. Ethel Seaton. Oxford, 1950.
The Lawiers Logike (1588). Facsim. edn. Menston, 1969.
The Countesse of Pembrokes Yvychurch. London, 1591.
The Countesse of Pembrokes Emanuel...togeather with certaine Psalmes (1591), in *Miscellanies of the Fuller Worthies Library*, ed. A. B. Grosart, III, 45–146. Blackburn, 1871.
The Third part of the Countesse of Pembrokes Yvychurch: Entituled, Amintas Dale. London, 1592.

Fulton, Edward. 'Spenser, Sidney, and the Areopagus', *Modern Language Notes*, XXXI (1916), 372–4.

Fussell, Paul. *Theory of Prosody in Eighteenth-Century England*. New London, Connecticut, 1954.

G., L. See *Sorrowes Joy* (1603).

Gair, W. R. 'Literary Societies in England from Parker to Falkland (1572–c. 1640).' Ph.D. diss., University of Cambridge, 1969.

Gascoigne, George. *Certayne Notes of Instruction* (1575). Smith, I, 46–57.

Getty, R. J. 'Classical Latin Metre and Prosody 1935–1962', *Lustrum*, VIII (1963), 103–60.

Gil, Alexander. *Logonomia Anglica* (1st edn. 1619), ed. Otto L. Jiriczek from 1621 edn. Quellen und Forschungen, XC. Strasbourg, 1903. (Jiriczek gives the name as 'Gill'.)

Gilbert, A. H. 'Mock Accents in Renaissance and Modern Latin', *PMLA*, LIV (1939), 608–10.

Godshalk, W. L. 'Sidney's Revision of the *Arcadia*, Books III–V,' *Philological Quarterly*, XLIII (1964), 171–84.

Googe, Barnabe. *The Zodiake of Life written by...Marcellus Pallingenius stellatus*. London, 1565.

Grange, John. *The Golden Aphroditis* (1577). Facsim. edn. New York, [1937].

Granger, Thomas. *Syntagma Grammaticum, or an easie, and methodicall explanation of Lillies Grammar*. London, 1616.

Greene, Robert. *The Life and Complete Works in Prose and Verse of Robert Greene*, ed. A. B. Grosart. 15 vols. 1st pub. 1881–6; reprinted, New York, 1964.

Greville, Fulke. *Poems and Dramas of Fulke Greville*, ed. Geoffrey Bullough. 2 vols. Edinburgh and London, [1939].

Gualtherus, Rodolphus. *De Syllabarum et Carminum Ratione*. London, 1573.

Haine, William. *Lillies Rules construed*. London, 1638.

Hale, W. G. 'Syllabification in Roman Speech', *Harvard Studies in Classical Philology*, VII (1896), 249–71.

Hall, Joseph. *The Collected Poems of Joseph Hall*, ed. A. Davenport. Liverpool, 1949.

Hall, Vernon. *Renaissance Literary Criticism: A Study of Its Social Content*. New York, 1945.

Hamer, Enid. *The Metres of English Poetry*. London, 1930.

Hampton, Barnabas. *Prosodia Construed, and The meaning of the most difficult words therein contained* (1st edn. 1639). London, 1704.

Harrison, G. B. 'Books and Readers, 1591–4', *The Library*, 4th series, VIII (1927), 273–302.

Harrison, T. P. 'The Relations of Spenser and Sidney', *PMLA*, XLV (1930), 712–31.

Hart, John. *John Hart's Works on English Orthography and Pronunciation (1551, 1569, 1570)*, ed. Bror Danielsson. Part I: Introduction, Texts, and Index Verborum; Stockholm Studies in English, V, Stockholm, 1955. Part II: Phonology; Stockholm Studies in English, XI, Stockholm, 1963.

Harvey, Gabriel. *Ciceronianus* (1577), ed. H. S. Wilson, tr. C. A. Forbes. University of Nebraska Studies, Studies in the Humanities, IV. Lincoln, Nebraska, 1945.

From *Foure Letters* (1592). Smith, II, 229–38.

Foure Letters and certeine Sonnets (1592), ed. G. B. Harrison. Bodley Head Quartos, II. London, 1922.

Marginalia, ed. G. C. Moore Smith. Stratford-upon-Avon, 1913.

Letter Book of Gabriel Harvey, AD 1573–1580, ed. E. J. L. Scott. London, 1884.

Harvey, Gabriel and Edmund Spenser. *Three Proper and wittie familiar Letters; Two other very commendable Letters*, (1579–80). Smith, I, 87–122.

Hendrickson, G. L. 'Elizabethan Quantitative Hexameters', *Philological Quarterly*, XXVIII (1949), 237–60.

Herescu, N. I. *La Poésie latine: étude des structures phoniques*. Paris, 1960.

Hieatt, A. Kent. *Short Time's Endless Monument: The Symbolism of Numbers in Edmund Spenser's 'Epithalamion'*. New York, 1960.

'*Sir Gawain*: Pentangle, *Luf-lace*, Numerical Structure', in *Silent Poetry*, ed. Alastair Fowler, London, 1970, pp. 116–40.

Hobsbaum, Philip (ed.). *Ten Elizabethan Poets*. London and Harlow, 1969.

Hoenigswald, H. M. 'A Note on Latin Prosody: Initial *S* Impure after Short Vowel', *Transactions and Proceedings of the American Philological Association*, LXXX (1949), 271–80.

Hollander, John. *The Untuning of the Sky: Ideas of Music in English Poetry 1500–1700*. Princeton, 1961.

Hollowell, B. M. 'The Elizabethan Hexametrists', *Philological Quarterly*, III, (1924), 51–7.

Hoole, Charles. *The Latine Grammar Fitted for the Use of Schools* (1651). Facsim. edn. Menston, 1969.

A New Discovery of the old Art of Teaching Schoole (1660), ed. E. T. Campagnac. Liverpool and London, 1913.

Vocabularium Parvum Anglo-Latinum. London, 1666.

Howell, James. *A New English Grammar*. London, 1662.

Howell, Wilbur Samuel. *Logic and Rhetoric in England, 1500–1700*. Princeton, 1956.

Hughey, Ruth (ed.). *The Arundel Harington Manuscript of Tudor Poetry*. 2 vols. Columbus, Ohio, 1960.

Hume, Alexander. *Grammatica Nova* (1612). Facsim. edn. Menston, 1969.

Of the Orthographie and Congruitie of the Britan Tongue (written ca. 1617), ed. Henry B. Wheatley. Early English Text Society. London, 1865.

Hunter, G. K. 'The English Hexameter and the Elizabethan Madrigal', *Philological Quarterly*, XXXII (1953), 340–2.

Ing, Catherine. *Elizabethan Lyrics: A Study in the Development of English Metres and their Relation to Poetic Effect*. London, 1951.

Inge, W. R. 'Classical Metres in English Poetry', *Essays by Divers Hands* (*Transactions of the Royal Society of Literature*), ed. W. R. Inge, New series, II (1922), pp. 131–51.

Jakobson, Roman. 'Linguistics and Poetics', in *Style in Language*, ed. T. A. Sebeok, Cambridge, Mass., New York and London, 1960, pp. 350–77.

James VI. *Ane Schort Treatise conteining some Reulis and Cautelis* (1584). Smith, I, 208–25.

Jodelle, Estienne. *Les Oeuvres et Meslanges Poetiques*, ed. Ch. Marty-Laveaux. 2 vols. Paris, 1868–70.

Jones, Richard Foster. *The Triumph of the English Language*. London, 1953.

Jonson, Ben. *The Works of Ben Jonson*, ed. C. H. Herford, Percy and Evelyn Simpson. 11 vols. Oxford, 1925–52.

K., E. Epistle Dedicatory to *The Shepheardes Calender* (1579). Smith, I, 127–34.

Kabell, Aage. *Metrische Studien II: Antiker Form sich nähernd*. Uppsala Universitets Årsskrift 1960: 6. Uppsala, 1960.

Kastendieck, Miles M. *England's Musical Poet, Thomas Campion*. New York, 1938; reprinted 1963.

Knight, W. F. Jackson. *Accentual Symmetry in Vergil*. Oxford, 1939.

Koller, Kathrine. 'Abraham Fraunce and Edmund Spenser', *ELH*, VII (1940), 108–20.

Kollmann, E. D. 'Remarks on the Structure of the Latin Hexameter', *Glotta*, XLVI (1968), 293–316.

Kuryłowicz, Jerzy. 'Accent and Quantity as Elements of Rhythm', in *Poetics, Poetyka, ПОЗТИКА*, II, ed. R. Jakobson *et al*. The Hague, Paris, Warsaw, 1966, pp. 163–72.

Languet, Hubert. *Epistolae Politicae et Historicae ad Phillipum Sydnaeum*. Leyden, 1646.

Lathrop, Henry Burrowes. *Translations from the Classics into English from Caxton to Chapman 1477–1620*. University of Wisconsin Studies in Language and Literature, 35. Madison, Wisconsin, 1933.

Lehiste, Ilse. *Suprasegmentals*. Cambridge, Mass., and London, 1970.

Lewis, C. S. *English Literature in the Sixteenth Century, Excluding Drama*. Oxford, 1954.

Liddell, Mark H. 'Stress pronunciation in Latin', *Language*, II (1926), 108–18.

Lily, William. *A Shorte Introduction of Grammar*, and *Brevissima Institutio seu Ratio Grammatices cognoscendae* (1567). Facsim. edn., introd. V. J. Flynn. New York, 1945.

Lipsius, Justus. *De Recta Pronunciatione Latinae Linguae*. Leyden, 1586. (Also in Stephanus, 1587.)

Llorente, V. J. Herrero. 'La lectura de los versos latinos y la adaptación de los ritmos clásicos a las lenguas modernas', *Estudios clásicos*, XII (1968), 569–82.

Lloyd, Richard. *Artis Poeticae*. London, 1653.

Lodge, Thomas. *A Defence of Poetry* (1579). Smith, I, 61–86.

Long, Percy W. 'Spenser and Sidney', *Anglia*, XXXVIII (1914), 173–92.

Lowbury, Edward, Timothy Salter and Alison Young. *Thomas Campion: Poet, Composer, Physician*. London, 1970.

Lucie-Smith, Edward (ed.). *The Penguin Book of Elizabethan Verse*. Harmondsworth, 1965.

Luick, Karl. *Historische Grammatik der Englischen Sprache* (1914–40). 2 parts. Reprinted Oxford and Stuttgart, 1964.

MacDonagh, Thomas. *Thomas Campion and the Art of English Poetry*. Dublin, 1913.

McKerrow, R. B. 'The Use of So-called Classical Metres in Elizabethan Verse', *Modern Language Quarterly* (London), IV (1901), 172–80; V (1902), 6–13.

'A Note on So-called Classical Metres in Elizabethan Verse', *Modern Language Quarterly*, V (1902), 148–9.

Marouzeau, J. 'Qu'est-ce que l'allongement "par position"?' *Revue des Études Latines*, XXXII (1954), 100–2.

'L'Allongement dit "par position" dans la métrique latine', *Revue des Études Latines*, XXXIII (1955), 344–51.

Mar-Prelate, Martine. *An Epistle to the Terrible Priests of the Convocation House* (1588). Puritan Discipline Tracts. 2nd edn. London, 1843.

Maxwell, J. C. 'Gabriel Harvey: A Reply to Mr. G. M. Young', *Essays in Criticism*, I (1951), 185–8.

Maynadier, H. 'The Areopagus of Sidney and Spenser', *Modern Language Review*, IV (1909), 289–301.

Mayor, Joseph B. *Chapters on English Metre* (1st edn. 1886). 2nd edn. Cambridge, 1901.

Mekerchus, Adolphus. *De Veteri et Recta Pronuntiatione linguae Graecae commentarius.* Bruges, 1565. (Also in Stephanus, 1587.)

Mercer, Eric. *English Art 1553–1625.* Oxford, 1962.

Meres, Francis. From *Palladis Tamia* (1598). Smith, II, 308–24.

Monro, C. J. 'Latin Metres in English, after Sidney, Tennyson, and Mr. Ellis', *Journal of Philology*, IV (1872), 223–30.

Montgomery, Robert L. *Symmetry and Sense: The Poetry of Sir Philip Sidney.* Austin, Texas, 1961.

Moore Smith, G. C. 'The English Language and the "Restored" Pronunciation of Latin', in *A Grammatical Miscellany Offered to Otto Jespersen*, Copenhagen and London, 1930, pp. 167–78.
See also Harvey, *Marginalia*.

Morley, Thomas. *A Plaine and Easie Introduction to Practicall Musicke* (1597). Facsim. edn., introd. E. H. Fellowes. Shakespeare Association Facsimiles, XIV. London, 1937.

Morris, Harry. 'Richard Barnfield, "Amyntas", and the Sidney Circle', *PMLA*, LXXIV (1959), 318–24.
Richard Barnfield, Colin's Child. Florida State University Studies, XXXVIII. Florida, 1963.

Mulcaster, Richard. *The First Part of the Elementarie* (1582). Facsim. edn. Menston, 1970.

Nashe, Thomas. Preface to Greene's *Menaphon* (1589). Smith, I, 307–20.
From *Strange Newes* or *Four Letters Confuted* (1592). Smith, II, 239–44.

Needler, G. H. *The Lone Shieling: Origin and Authorship of the Blackwood 'Canadian Boat-Song'.* Toronto, 1941.

Newdigate, B. H. 'The English Pronunciation of Latin AD 1529', *Notes and Queries*, CLXXVII (1939), 245.

Nichols, John. See *Sorrowes Joy*.

Norberg, Dag. *Introduction à l'étude de la versification latine médiévale.* Acta Universitatis Stockholmiensis, Studia Latina Stockholmiensia, V. Stockholm, 1958.
'La récitation du vers latin', *Neuphilologische Mitteilungen*, LXVI (1965), 496–508.

Omond, T. S. *English Hexameter Verse.* Edinburgh, 1897.
A Study of Metre. London, 1903.
English Metrists. Oxford, 1921.

Ong, Walter J. *Ramus and Talon Inventory.* Cambridge, Mass., 1958.
Ramus, Method, and the Decay of Dialogue. Cambridge, Mass., 1958.
The Barbarian Within and other Fugitive Essays. New York, 1962.

Osborn, James M. *Young Philip Sidney, 1572–1577.* New Haven and London, 1972.

Pallavicino, Cosimo. See *Versi, et regole de la nuova poesia toscana*.

Palsgrave, John. *Lesclarcissement de la Langue francoyse* (1530). Facsim. edn. Menston, 1969.

Park, Ben A. 'The Quantitative Experiments of the Renaissance and After as a

Problem in Comparative Metrics.' Ph.D. diss., University of Oklahoma, 1968.

Pattison, Bruce. 'Sir Philip Sidney and Music', *Music and Letters*, xv (1934), 75–81.

Music and Poetry of the English Renaissance. London, 1948.

Peele, George. *The Life and Works of George Peele*. General ed. C. T. Prouty. 3 vols. New Haven and London, 1952–70.

Pembroke, Mary Herbert, Countess of. *The Psalms of David. See* Rathmell, 1963, 1964.

Pevsner, Nikolaus. 'The Counter-Reformation and Mannerism', in *Studies in Art, Architecture and Design*, I, London, 1968, pp. 10–33.

Phillips, James E. 'Daniel Rogers: A Neo-Latin Link Between the Pléiade and Sidney's "Areopagus"', in J. E. Phillips and D. C. Allen, *Neo-Latin Poetry of the Sixteenth and Seventeenth Centuries*. Los Angeles, 1965, pp. 5–28.

Phoenix Nest, The, ed. R. S. (1593). Ed. H. E. Rollins. Cambridge, Mass., 1931.

Piper, W. B. 'The Inception of the Closed Heroic Couplet', *Modern Philology*, LXVI (1969), 306–21.

Poirier, Michel. *Sir Philip Sidney: Le Chevalier poète élizabéthain*. Travaux et Mémoires de l'Université de Lille, Nouvelle Série – Droit et Lettres, XXVI. Lille, 1948.

Poole, Joshua. *The English Parnassus: or A Helpe to English Poesie*. London, 1657.

Pope, Emma F. 'The Critical Background of the Spenserian Stanza', *Modern Philology*, XXIV (1926), 31–53.

Pope, Mildred Katharine. *From Latin to Modern French*. Rev. edn. Manchester, 1952.

Preservation of King Henry the vii, The First Booke of the (1599). In *Illustrations of Old English Literature*, ed. J. Payne Collier, vol. II, no. 3. London, 1866; reprinted New York, 1966.

Puttenham, George. *The Arte of English Poesie* (1589). Smith, II, 1–193.

The Arte of English Poesie, ed. G. D. Willcock and A. Walker. Cambridge, 1936.

Pyles, Thomas. 'Tempest in a Teapot: Reform in Latin Pronunciation,' *ELH*, VI (1939), 138–64.

R., R. *An English Grammar: or, a plain Exposition of Lilie's Grammar*. London, 1641.

Ramus, Petrus. *Scholae Grammaticae*. Paris, 1559.

Grammaticae libri quatuor. 3rd edn. Paris, 1560.

Gramerę. Paris, 1562.

Libri Duo de Veris Sonis Literarum & syllabarum, é scholis Grammaticis. Paris, 1564.

Scholae in Liberales Artes. Basle, 1569.

Grammaire. Paris, 1572.

Grammatica. Leyden, 1584.

The Latine Grammar of P. Ramus Translated into English. Cambridge, 1585. (Another edn., London, 1585.)

Rathmell, J. C. A. (ed.). *The Psalms of Sir Philip Sidney and the Countess of Pembroke*. New York, 1963.

(ed.) 'The Psalms of Sir Philip Sidney and the Countess of Pembroke.' Ph.D. diss., University of Cambridge, 1964.

Raven, D. S. *Latin Metre: An Introduction*. London, 1965.

Rees, Joan. *Samuel Daniel: A Critical and Biographical Study*. Liverpool, 1964.

Reeve, Edmund. *The Rules of the Latin Grammar Construed*. London, 1657.

Reeves, James and Martin Seymour-Smith. *A New Canon of English Poetry.*
London, 1967.

Return from Parnassus, The Second Part of the. In *The Three Parnassus Plays (1598–1601)*, ed. J. B. Leishman. London, 1949.

Ringler, William A. 'Master Drant's Rules', *Philological Quarterly*, XXIX (1950), 70–4.

See also Sidney, *Poems.*

Robertson, Jean. 'Sir Philip Sidney and his Poetry', in *Elizabethan Poetry*, Stratford-upon-Avon Studies, II, London, 1960, pp. 111–29.

Robinson, Robert. *See* Dobson (1957).

Robotham, John. 'To the Reader', in J. A. Comenius, *Janua Linguarum Reserata*, 5th edn., tr. Thomas Horn, rev. John Robotham. London, 1640.

Røstvig, Maren-Sofie. 'Structure as Prophecy: The Influence of Biblical Exegesis upon Theories of Literary Structure', in *Silent Poetry*, ed. Alastair Fowler. London, 1970, pp. 32–72.

Rowland, Daniel B. *Mannerism – Style and Mood: An Anatomy of Four Works in Three Art Forms.* New Haven and London, 1964.

Rudenstine, Neil L. *Sidney's Poetic Development.* Cambridge, Mass., 1967.

Rudmose-Brown, T. B. 'Some Medieval Latin Metres, Their Ancestry and Progeny', *Hermathena*, LIII (1939), 29–58.

S., R. See *Phoenix Nest.*

Sabie, Francis. *Pan's Pipe* (1595), ed. J. W. Bright and W. P. Mustard. Chicago, 1910.

Flora's Fortune: the second part and finishing of the Fishermans Tale. London, 1595.

Saintsbury, George. *A History of English Prosody from the Twelfth Century to the Present Day.* 3 vols. London, 1906–10.

Salesbury, William. *A briefe and a playne introduction teachyng how to pronounce the letters in the British tong* (1550). Facsim. edn. Menston, 1969.

Sandford, James. *Houres of recreation.* Rev. edn. London, 1576.

Sargeaunt, John. *The Pronunciation of English Words Derived from the Latin.* S. P. E. Tract no. IV. Oxford, 1920.

Scaliger, Joseph Justus. *Animadversiones in Chronologica Eusebii.* In Eusebius Pamphili, *Thesaurus Temporum...Chronicorum Canonum omnimodae historiae libri duo.* Leyden, 1606.

Opuscula Varia Antehac non Edita. Paris, 1610.

Scaliger, Julius Caesar. *Poetices libri septem.* Geneva, 1561.

Schelling, Felix E. 'The Inventor of the English Hexameter', *Modern Language Notes*, V (1890), 212–14.

Second Part of the Return from Parnassus. See *Return from Parnassus...*

Serjeantson, Mary S. *A History of Foreign Words in English.* London, 1935.

Shawcross, John T. 'The Prosody of Milton's Translation of Horace's Fifth Ode', *Tennessee Studies in Literature*, XIII (1968), 81–9.

Shearman, John. *Mannerism.* Harmondsworth, 1967.

Short, R. W. 'The Metrical Theory and Practice of Thomas Campion', *PMLA*, LIX (1944), 1003–18.

Sidney, Sir Philip. *The Poems of Sir Philip Sidney*, ed. William A. Ringler. Oxford, 1962.

An Apologie for Poetrie (pub. 1595). Smith, I, 148–207.

The Countess of Pembroke's Arcadia (The Old Arcadia), ed. Jean Robertson. Oxford, 1973.

Sledd, James. 'Baret's *Alvearie*, an Elizabethan Reference Book', *Studies in Philology*, XLIII (1946), 147–63.

Smetius, Henricus. *Prosodia...Promtissima*. Lyons, 1614.

Smith, G. Gregory (ed.). *Elizabethan Critical Essays*. 2 vols. London, 1904.

Smith, Hallett. 'English Metrical Psalms in the Sixteenth Century and their Literary Significance', *Huntington Library Quarterly*, IX (1946), 249–71.

Smith, John Pye. *A Manual of Latin Grammar*. 2nd edn. London, 1816.

Smith, Sir Thomas. *De recta & emendata Linguae Graecae Pronuntiatione* and *De recta & emendata Linguae Anglicae Scriptione*. Paris, 1568.

Sonnenschein, E. A. 'The Latin Sapphic', *Classical Review*, XVII (1903), 252–6.

Sorrowes Joy (1603). In *The Progresses...of King James I*, ed. John Nichols, I, 1–24. London, 1828.

Spencer, Theodore. 'The Poetry of Sir Philip Sidney', *ELH*, XII (1945), 251–78.

Spenser, Edmund. *Spenser's Prose Works*, ed. Rudolf Gottfried. *The Works of Edmund Spenser: A Variorum Edition*, ed. E. Greenlaw, *et al.* Baltimore, 1949. *See also* Harvey and Spenser (1579–80).

Spingarn, Joel E. *A History of Literary Criticism in the Renaissance*. 2nd edn. New York, 1908.

Stanyhurst, Richard. *Thee First Foure Bookes of Virgil his Aeneis* (1582), ed. Edward Arber. London, 1880.

Aeneis (1582), ed. Dirk van der Haar. Amsterdam, 1933.

From the Dedication and Preface of *Aeneis*. Smith, I, 135–47.

Stephanus, Henricus (ed.). *De Vera Pronuntiatione Graecae et Latinae Linguae, Commentarii*. [Paris, Geneva?], 1587.

Sternfeld, Frederick W. 'Music in the Schools of the Reformation', *Musica Disciplina*, II (1948), 99–122.

Stetson, Raymond Herbert. *Bases of Phonology*. Oberlin, Ohio, 1945. *Motor Phonetics*. 2nd edn. Amsterdam, 1951.

Stone, William Johnson. *Classical Metres in English Verse* (1st edn. 1898). Reprinted with Robert Bridges, *Milton's Prosody*. Oxford, 1901.

Stowe, A. Monroe. *English Grammar Schools in the Reign of Queen Elizabeth*. New York, 1908.

Strype, John. *The Life of the Learned Sir Thomas Smith*. London, 1698. *The Life of the Learned Sir John Cheke*. London, 1705.

Sturm, Johann. *Nobilitas Literata* (1st pub. 1549). In [Schola Torunensis], *Institutionis Literatae*, I, 301–54. Thorn, 1586.

A ritch Storehouse or Treasurie for Nobilitye and Gentlemen, which in Latine is called Nobilitas literata. Tr. T. Browne. London, 1570.

Surrey, Henry Howard, Earl of. *Fourth Boke of Virgill* (1554?), ed. Herbert Hartman. New York, 1933.

Talaeus, Audomarus. *Rhetorica*. Paris, 1577.

Thomas, Thomas. *Dictionarium Linguae Latinae et Anglicanae*. Cambridge, 1587.

Thomasson, Lieutenant-Colonel de. 'La Poésie métrique française aux XVIe et XVIIIe siècles', *Le Français Moderne*, V (1937), 41–54.

Thompson, E. Seymer. 'The Latin Sapphic', *Classical Review*, XVII (1903), 456–8.

Thompson, John. *The Founding of English Metre*. London, 1961.

Trevelyan, R. C. 'Classical and English Verse-Structure', *Essays and Studies by Members of the English Association*, XVI (1930), 7–25.

Tuve, Rosemond. *Elizabethan and Metaphysical Imagery*. Chicago, 1947.

Underdown, Mary E. I. 'Sir Philip Sidney's "Arcadian" *Eclogues*: A Study of his Quantitative Verse.' Ph.D. diss., University of Yale, 1961.

Van Dorsten, J. A. *Poets, Patrons, and Professors: Sir Philip Sidney, Daniel Rogers, and the Leiden Humanists*. Leyden and London, 1962.

Verrall, A. W. 'The Latin Sapphic', *Classical Review*, XVII (1903), 339–43.

Versi, et regole de la nuova poesia toscana. Rome, 1539.

Vossius, Gerardus Joannes. *Grammatica Latina*. 5th edn., Leyden, 1644–5.

Vossius, Isaac. *De Poematum Cantu et Viribus Rythmi*. Oxford, 1673.

Vossler, Karl. *Einführung ins Vulgärlatein*, ed. Helmut Schmeck. Munich, 1954.

Walker, D. P. 'The Aims of Baïf's *Académie de Poésie et de Musique*', *Journal of Renaissance and Baroque Music*, I (1946), 91–100.

'Musical Humanism in the 16th and Early 17th Centuries', *The Music Review*, II (1941), 1–13, 111–21, 220–7, 228–308; III (1942), 55–71.

'The Influence of *Musique Mesurée à L'Antique*, Particularly on the *Airs de Cour* of the Early Seventeenth Century', *Musica Disciplina*, II (1948), 141–63.

Walker, D. P. and François Lesure. 'Claude Le Jeune and *Musique Mesurée*', *Musica Disciplina*, III (1949), 151–70.

Walker, John. *A Key to the Classical Pronunciation of Greek and Latin Proper Names*. London, 1798.

Waltz, R. ''ΡΥΘΜΟΣ et numerus', *Revue des Études Latines*, XXVI (1948), 109–20.

Watson, Foster. *English Writers on Education, 1480–1603: A Source Book* (1902–6). Facsim. edn., introd. K. D. Pepper. Gainesville, Florida, 1967.

The English Grammar Schools to 1660: their Curriculum and Practice. Cambridge, 1908.

Webbe, William. *A Discourse of English Poetrie* (1586). Smith, I, 226–302.

A Discourse of English Poetry, ed. Edward Arber. London, 1870.

Weismiller, Edward R. 'Studies of Verse Form in the Minor English Poems', in *A Variorum Commentary on the Poems of John Milton*, ed. Merrit Y. Hughes, vol. II, by A. S. P. Woodhouse and Douglas Bush, London, 1972, pp. 1007–87.

Westaway, Frederick William. *Quantity and Accent in the Pronunciation of Latin*. Cambridge, 1913.

Wilkinson, Lancelot Patrick. 'Accentual Rhythm in Horatian Sapphics', *Classical Review*, LIV (1940), 131–3.

Golden Latin Artistry. Cambridge, 1963.

Willcock, G. D. 'Passing Pitefull Hexameters: A Study of Quantity and Accent in English Renaissance Verse', *Modern Language Review*, XXIX (1934), 1–19.

Willes, Richard. *Poematum Liber*. London, 1573.

De Re Poetica (1573), ed. and tr. A. D. S. Fowler. Luttrell Reprints, XVII. Oxford, 1958. (Fowler gives the names as 'Wills'.)

Wilson, Harold S. 'Gabriel Harvey's Orations on Rhetoric', *ELH*, XII (1945), 167–82.

'The Humanism of Gabriel Harvey', in *Joseph Quincy Adams Memorial Studies*, ed. J. G. McManaway *et al.*, Washington, 1948, pp. 707–21.

Wilson, Mona. *Sir Philip Sidney*. London, 1931.

Wither, George. *A Preparation to the Psalter* (1619). [Manchester], 1884.

Wittkower, Rudolf. *Architectural Principles in the Age of Humanism.* 3rd edn. London, 1962.

Wölk, Konrad. *Geschichte und Kritik des Englischen Hexameters.* Normannia, III. Berlin, 1909.

Wyatt, William. *A new and easie Institution of Grammar.* London, 1647.

Yates, Frances A. *The French Academies of the Sixteenth Century.* London, 1947.

Young, George Malcolm. 'A Word for Gabriel Harvey', in *Last Essays.* London, 1950, pp. 243–7. (Reprinted from *Life and Letters,* 1930.)

Zarlino, Gioseffo. *Le Istitutioni Harmoniche.* Venice, 1558.

Zirin, Ronald A. *The Phonological Basis of Latin Prosody.* The Hague and Paris, 1970.

Žirmunskij, V. *Introduction to Metrics: The Theory of Verse,* tr. C. F. Brown; ed. E. Stankiewicz and W. N. Vickery. London, The Hague and Paris, 1966.

INDEX

Figures in bold type indicate main entries

Abercrombie, David, 39, 70n
'Académie de Poésie et de Musique',
    122, 126, 130n, 175, 214
'Accademia della Nuova Poesia', 123
accent, 7n, 13n
    in English, 7n; accounts of, 60, 91,
        149n, 220–2; position of, 11–12,
        48, 143; role in verse, 16, 91–2,
        96, 98, 108–11, 186, 212, 225, 228
    in Latin: acute, 51–2, 53, 54–61,
        221; circumflex, 51–2, 53, 54–5,
        57–61, 76, 145; differentiative,
        55–7, 59n, 76; grave, 53, 55–9,
        91, 221; no phonetic embodi-
        ment of, 54–7, 58, 59, 76;
        position of, 12, 48; teaching of,
        48, 51–2, **53–61**; vocal expression
        of, 7n, 13n, **57–61**, 79, 83
    see also accentual verse; oxytone
        words; paroxytone words;
        proparoxytone words; quantita-
        tive verse, in English (accentual
        patten of), in Latin (accentual
        pattern of); quantity, and accent,
        by penultimate rule
accentual verse
    compared with quantitative verse,
        see quantitative verse, compared
        with accentual verse
    in English: on classical models,
        129n, 137, 212, 216, 218;
        defences of, 90, 101, 229–30, 231,
        232–5; development of, 3–4, 113,
        166, 224; easy to write, 91–4,
        96–8, 102–5, 119, 233; lacking in
        art, **89–113**, 127–8, 129, 199, 230;
        rhythm of, 16, 38–9, 53, 77, 92,
        99, 108–9, 228, *see also* hexa-
        meters, English (accentual);
        theories of, 16, 91–2, 191, 219,
        224, 225; unrhymed, 95, 98–9,
        108–11, 129, 130n, 199
    a medieval phenomenon, 92, 93–4,
        100–2

Aelfric, 22
Agustín, Antonio, 126
Aiméric, 39
Alamanni, Luigi, 125
Alberti, Leon Battista, 116–17, 123,
    125
alcaics, 203–4
alexandrines, 111, 130n
Allen, W. Sidney, 9, 10, 12, 14, 18n,
    23n, 24n, 39, 54, 55n
Allot, Robert, 131
Alphabetum Graecum, 83
anacreontics, 185, 203
Arber, Edward, 170n
'Areopagus', 130n, 138
aristophanics, 131n, 187, 210
arsis and thesis, 34–5, 83, 84
art, Renaissance attitudes to, **114–19**,
    230–1
    see also 'artificiality'
'artificiality'
    attacks on, 233–4
    in modern times, 18n, 235
    value placed on, **105–8**; in accen-
        tual verse, 90, 106–7, 165; in
        'figure-poems', 90, 105–6; in
        quantitative verse, 18n, 76, 103–4,
        107–8, 113, 127–8, 133, 165, 171,
        225, 230
Ascham, Roger, 32
    on accentual verse, **93–100**, 101
    as an authority, 149
    influence of, 102, 109–10, 124
    quantitative verse by, 129, **196**,
        200, 208
    on quantitative verse, 97–8, 112,
        114, 120, 122–3, 127, 130, 136,
        161–2
asclepiads, 169, 186, 197, 203, 220
Atanagi, Dionigi, 125
Attridge, Derek, 136n
Aubigné, Agrippa d', 126
Auden, W. H., 129n
Augustine, St, 21–2, 115